Cleaning Windows® XP

FOR

DUMMIES®

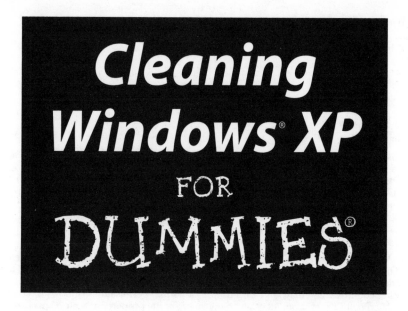

Cleaning Windows® XP

FOR DUMMIES®

by Allen Wyatt

Wiley Publishing, Inc.

Cleaning Windows® XP For Dummies®

Published by
Wiley Publishing, Inc.
111 River Street
Hoboken, NJ 07030-5774
www.wiley.com

WILEY

About the Author

Allen Wyatt, an internationally recognized expert in small computer systems, is president of Discovery Computing, Inc., a computer and publishing services company located in Mesa, Arizona. He has worked in the computer and publishing industries for almost two decades, writing more than 50 books and numerous magazine articles. Allen's popular lectures and seminars have reached audiences throughout the United States, as well as throughout Mexico and Costa Rica.

Besides writing books and technical materials, Allen helps further the computer book industry by providing consulting, production, and project management services. He publishes two free weekly newsletters, WordTips and ExcelTips (www.VitalNews.com).

Allen can be reached by e-mail at awyatt@dcomp.com.

Author's Acknowledgments

I would like to thank the good folks at Wiley for their invaluable assistance in bringing this book to fruition. The people I worked with — Greg Croy, Nicole Sholly, and Tonya Cupp — were all very professional and helpful in creating what you now hold in your hands. I also extend a special thanks to Jim Kelly for his technical expertise, liberally provided as a technical reviewer.

Publisher's Acknowledgments

We're proud of this book; please send us your comments through our online registration form located at www.dummies.com/register/.

Some of the people who helped bring this book to market include the following:

Acquisitions, Editorial, and Media Development

Project Editor: Nicole Sholly

Acquisitions Editor: Greg Croy

Copy Editor: Tonya Cupp

Technical Editor: Jim Kelly

Editorial Manager: Kevin Kirschner

Media Development Manager: Laura VanWinkle

Media Development Supervisor: Richard Graves

Editorial Assistant: Amanda Foxworth

Cartoons: Rich Tennant, www.the5thwave.com

Composition

Senior Project Coordinator: Nancee Reeves

Layout and Graphics: Andrea Dahl, Denny Hager, Joyce Haughey, Stephanie D. Jumper, Michael Kruzil, Lynsey Osborn, Heather Ryan

Proofreaders: Laura Albert, Brian H. Walls, TECHBOOKS Production Services

Indexer: TECHBOOKS Production Services

Publishing and Editorial for Technology Dummies

    Richard Swadley, Vice President and Executive Group Publisher

    Andy Cummings, Vice President and Publisher

    Mary Bednarek, Executive Acquisitions Director

    Mary C. Corder, Editorial Director

Publishing for Consumer Dummies

    Diane Graves Steele, Vice President and Publisher

    Joyce Pepple, Acquisitions Director

Composition Services

    Gerry Fahey, Vice President of Production Services

    Debbie Stailey, Director of Composition Services

Contents at a Glance

Table of Contents

Introduction

A computer is nothing but a tool. It's bigger than a hammer (well, most hammers), heavier than a screwdriver, and generally less noisy than a circular saw — but is nonetheless a tool. You can do more stuff with a computer than you can with a hammer and a screwdriver, but hammers and screwdrivers are simpler to use and easier to clean up. (Circular saws are another story; things can get messy really fast.)

Your computer *does* get messy; have no doubt about it. Programs load and unload, files pop into existence and then slither off to unknown parts of your hard drive, and spyware tries to adhere itself to your operating system. Every day your system changes, as information is added and new demands are placed on old programs.

All these things add to the unique clutter that comes to define and weigh down your system. You can redefine your system and free your system, all by identifying and removing the clutter. *Cleaning Windows XP For Dummies* shows you how.

How to Read This Book

I'm a firm believer that you should read this book out loud, while standing on the coffee table in your neighbor's living room. It surely will make an impression on the neighbors' kids and free up time you previously spent going to dinner parties.

Whether you decide to read this book out loud or not, you should read the first two chapters before reading any others. Dire consequences won't result if you decide not to, but those chapters lay a pretty good foundation for everything else you find in the book.

After that, read whatever strikes your fancy. You know your system better than I do. If your big problem is getting updates to Windows XP properly, skip to Chapter 15. If instead you want to focus on archiving your data, turn to Chapter 7.

You get the idea — this book can be as flexible as you are.

Assumptions About You

Being the amazingly gifted and highly skilled author that I am, I can report that I've achieved every author's ideal and made no assumptions about you in writing this book.

Well, I guess that's not entirely true. I do assume that you read English. And that you're using Windows XP. And that you know how to turn your computer on. And that you know how to navigate through your system using My Computer or Windows Explorer. And that you think your system might be cluttered. And that you want it to be less cluttered.

Nope; I make no assumptions at all other than those. Oh, and that you know how to use a Web browser. And an e-mail program. And that you aren't afraid to try new things once in a while. And that you want your system to run like it did when it was new. And that you're tired of menus longer than the want ads and file folders that go on forever.

That should be it. Except that I assume you're tired of being deluged with e-mail. And that you want to protect yourself from spyware and viruses. And that you aren't sure if cookies are a bad thing. And that you think you can do something to make your system cleaner.

Dang. I guess I do make some assumptions about you. But, being the somewhat gifted and nominally skilled author that I am, I know that these assumptions only identify you as a person who wants to use your computer better and recognizes that cleaning that computer can help toward that end.

Working together, we can make that happen. (That's why assumptions can be a good thing.)

A Word about Operating Systems and Service Pack 2

This book (as you can probably tell from the title) is about Windows XP. The examples in the book assume you have Windows XP and are comfortable — or at least conversant — with using it. If you and the operating system still don't get along at all times, don't worry — the examples in this book will help you show it who's really the boss.

If you don't have Windows XP, some of the concepts discussed in this book will still be of value to you. In fact, many of the ideas related to cleaning things up and making your system run better are easily applicable to any version of

Windows. You'll need to do your own "translations" of examples so they will
work on your system, and you may need to do some digging to find out how to
make the detailed steps work properly, but it shouldn't be a huge job.

While discussing operating systems, a word or two is in order about
Windows XP Service Pack 2 (SP2 for short). The computing world is all atwit-
ter about SP2. Many view it as much more than a run-of-the-mill service
update to Windows. In fact, Microsoft is pushing heavily for every computer
that has XP to upgrade to SP2. (Chapter 25 can help you determine whether
you want to upgrade.)

SP2 introduces a set of "security technologies" (Microsoft's wording) that
should improve the ability of Windows XP to withstand attacks from viruses
and worms. That's a good thing — if you think about it for a couple of nanosec-
onds. By installing SP2, you can help fortify XP so that it turns away the bad
guys.

Will SP2 help to unclutter your system? No, not really. It strengthens the security of your system, which can stop it from getting cluttered in the first place,
but if your system is already cluttered, SP2 won't magically make it uncluttered. You still need to go through the "deep cleaning" process required of all
cluttered computer owners. SP2 helps keep bad things (worms, viruses, and
so on) off your system, but if there are bad things on your system already,
you still need to take steps to get them off. This book can help you do that.

How This Book Is Organized

My editor tells me that organizing a book into parts is a good thing. It helps
keep the chapters from running into each other. (Apparently having unre-
lated chapters freely associating with each other is unhealthy.) To keep
with longstanding tradition and to keep my editor from yelling at me, I've
organized *Cleaning Windows XP For Dummies* into the following parts.

Part 1: The Basics of Cleaning Your System

Get off on the right foot by discovering why you even need to clean your
system (as if you didn't know). You find out what you should clean, when you
should clean it, what tools to use, and whether you should consider getting a
new system.

Part II: Programs and Data

Programs and data are the two great components of any computer system — including yours. Part II focuses on identifying what programs you have, how to make them run faster, and how to get rid of programs you no longer need.

You also find out how to identify all the data on your hard drive, as well as targeting and deleting the data you no longer need. I've dedicated a full chapter to concepts about organizing and archiving your important data.

Part III: E-Mail and the Internet

E-mail and the Internet are, for better or worse, a part of most people's daily lives. This part zeroes in on how you can manage the glut of e-mail you get daily. You discover how to deal with spam and organize the e-mail you keep.

You also find out the telltale signs of virus and spyware infections, as well as how to get rid of these troublesome pests. Finally, you discover how to deal with information (not related to e-mail) that you may receive when using the Internet.

Part IV: The Operating System

Windows XP is nothing if not flexible and configurable. Part IV discusses how to clean up the user interface so using Windows is easier than ever before. You discover how to streamline Windows so it runs faster, as well as how to speed up the file system.

Microsoft wants you to have the most up-to-date system possible, and Windows XP makes it easy to stay updated with automatic downloads. You'll understand how to use the update system and find out when it makes sense to get a new system rather than clean up the old one.

Part V: Advanced Cleaning for the Truly Brave

This part focuses on things you can do to implement deep-cleaning strategies. You determine whether you need more memory in your system or a larger hard drive. You discover ways to make your system more secure, and thereby minimize the chance of having others clutter your system. I also discuss the special needs of cleaning up in a networked environment.

An entire chapter covers the ins and outs of working with the Registry, your computer's central nervous system. You find out how to edit the Registry and use special software to keep it in tip-top shape.

The final chapter in this part explains different ways to fix a corrupted Windows XP installation. You even find out how to start all over by wiping out your computer system and installing Windows anew.

Part VI: The Part of Tens

Ahhh! The Part of Tens. Here's where you find small, bite-sized tidbits that can help get your system cleaned up and keep it that way. You find troubleshooting ideas, software tools for cleaning, and a multitude of online resources to help you tidy up.

Customs and Practices

I followed a few conventions that you might be interested in. Why? Because then you know why I chose to do something, and we can understand each other better.

First, if I talk about clicking the mouse, I mean clicking the left button. If I want you to click the right button, I specifically talk about right-clicking. (Quite a bit of right-clicking goes on in Windows.)

If a procedure takes more than a couple of discrete steps to complete, I try to detail those steps as much as I can. It's frustrating as heck to read "do this" in a book, and when you do it, the steps don't work for you. The steps should work if you're using Windows XP; I've tried them out, as have my editor and my technical editor. (Three heads are better than one.)

Finally, if you must make a series of choices with the mouse, I separate the choices with an arrow. For example, if you see "Choose Start⇨All Programs⇨ Accessories⇨Notepad," that means you should click the Start menu, then the All Programs option, then Accessories, and finally Notepad.

Icons Used in This Book

As part of agreeing to write this book, I insisted that Wiley break with tradition and include cute little icons that call your attention to things that I think need your attention. They tried to balk at my demand, but I held firm, with my only desire to put your needs, my reader, first. Finally, they got tired of my expert negotiating and gave in to my demand. (I hope the other *For Dummies* series authors appreciate all my hard work in this area.)

With that in mind, you see the following icons sprinkled liberally throughout this book. Pay attention to this; you'll have a test later!

If something is really short and really cool, I used this icon. Tips are bite-sized nuggets of information that can — hopefully — make your life easier and more fulfilling. (They should at least make you feel better about cleaning your Windows system.)

This icon alerts you to the gotchas of cleaning your Windows system. Ignore these tidbits at your own risk. (Ohh . . . that sounds ominous!) Warnings are given for a reason: primarily to help you avoid problems that can cause you grief and a whole lot of extra work.

This icon doesn't mean you can forget everything else in the book. Nope; I included it so that you can make special note of something you need later. Or it could be a piece of information designed to jog your memory about something you should have picked up earlier in the book. Remember — the remember icon can help you remember what you need to remember.

A few of these icons are thrown into the mix so that the geeks among us feel comfortable. If geekiness scares the bejeebers out of you, ignore anything with this icon. If you really want a moment of technical clarity, you might find anything with this icon very illuminating.

Where to Go from Here

I think the best place to go is to the next page, but it doesn't matter what I think. You can use or abuse this book in any way you see fit. If something on page 153 strikes your fancy, then go for it! You can always return to page 152 (or any other page) at a later time, when the need arises.

You see, that's the really cool thing about cleaning your system and *For Dummies* books — they don't have to be done or read in any particular order. And the sky is the limit in *Cleaning Windows XP For Dummies*. You can start reading anywhere you like, on any topic you like. When you tire of that topic, move to one that strikes your fancy.

As for me, I still think the best place to start is on the next page. . . .

Part I
The Basics of Cleaning Your System

The 5th Wave By Rich Tennant

"The funny thing is he's spent 9 hours organizing his computer desktop."

In this part . . .

Discover why you need to clean your system, what you should clean, when you should clean it, what tools to use, and whether you should consider getting a new system.

Chapter 1

First Things First: Why You Should Clean

My system isn't messed up, is it? (What? Me worry?)

Yes, you should worry. Or, you should at least be aware that you may need to worry. Computer systems easily and quickly become untidy and messed up. If you don't clean yours, you run the risk of big problems down the road.

Do I really need to point out the benefits of a clean computer system? (I do — a little later in this chapter.) Does someone need to come into your house and point out why you need to pick up your clothes, dust the furniture, wash the dishes, and tend to the dog? Probably not; you know that a clean house is healthful, inviting, and safe.

It's the same with computers. Over time, your computer can become cluttered with unused programs, unknown data, and unwanted visitors. With a little effort, you can clean your system so that it runs at top form, and you can breeze through your work faster and easier than you can in an unclean system. In addition, clean systems are more reliable, less prone to failure, and easier to protect from attack by malicious programs.

Before you can begin cleaning, however, you need to recognize the need to clean and why you should spend the time to do it.

Telltale Signs of an Unclean Computer

How can you know if your system needs cleaning? I've compiled a list of several sure-fire signs that you need help (envision Jeff Foxworthy standing in front of your computer):

You know you have a messed-up computer . . .

- ✔ If you have to leave a trail of breadcrumbs so you don't get lost finding your way through the options in your Start menu
- ✔ If every pop-up on your computer apologizes for bothering you and quietly closes on its own
- ✔ If you try to install a new program and the installation program reports your system to the Board of Health
- ✔ If you think *Defragment* is the name of a new rap song by Eminem (Yo!)
- ✔ If the only way to add more icons to your desktop is to get a larger desktop
- ✔ If you start the program to balance your checkbook, only to find that your son's illegal copy of Splinter Cell ate the last month's worth of transactions
- ✔ If someone mentions "backup" and chills run up and down your spine
- ✔ If virus software refuses to install itself on your system

Perhaps such observations aren't worthy of Jeff Foxworthy, but this list highlights those things that really are good indicators your computer needs cleaning. The next few sections detail some other obvious signs that you need help.

The view from the desktop isn't pretty

Does your desktop look like the one shown in Figure 1-1? If so, you have problems. Maybe you bought into the old adage that a clean desk is a sign of a sick mind, and in the process lost your ability to effectively use your system. Whatever got you to this point, you need your Windows cleaned. Badly.

Your computer desktop is supposed to be a clean, inviting place where you store only a *few* icons of your most commonly used programs. For too many people, they become "catch-alls," repositories of every stray icon that comes their way.

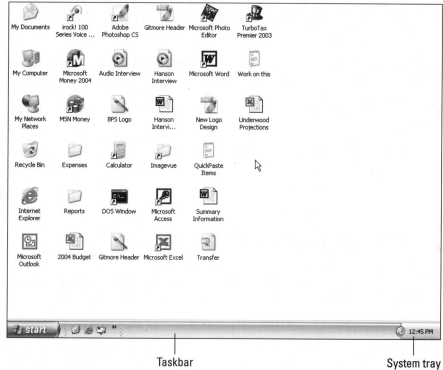

Taskbar   System tray

A cluttered desktop is a good sign that your entire PC is cluttered. The solution is to clean your system and rid yourself of all that mess.

If your desktop is as cluttered as the one shown in Figure 1-1 — and especially if it's even more cluttered — head to Chapter 12, where I give you some help regaining control.

Traversing the Start menu jungle is an adventure

Can you imagine running Windows without the Start menu? Neither can I. The Start menu is indispensable to quickly and easily finding the programs you want to run.

At least, that's the way it's supposed to be.

On many systems that I've seen, the Start menu gets unorganized and cluttered with lots of programs the user seldom, if ever, uses. Figure 1-2 shows one such Start menu, just itching to be cleaned.

The Start menu is supposed to provide a convenient path to all the programs installed on your system. Over time, some paths are used more than others, and some paths become completely unused. Removing unused items from the Start menu and organizing what is left can make your system easier to use.

As you remove unused programs from your computer (which I show you how to do in Chapter 5), your Start menu will look better and better. When you really need to give your Start menu a makeover, Chapter 12 (where I discuss taking back control of the user interface) will be invaluable.

Your PC is slower than molasses

I remember shortly after microwave ovens first came out (yes, I'm that old) watching my grandma use one to bake some potatoes. She would anxiously look through the oven's door and mumble "hurry up, hurry up."

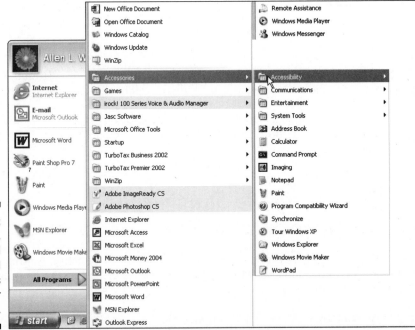

Figure 1-2:
Long,
deep, and
cluttered
Start menus
can hinder
your work.

I chuckled about it then, but years later I find myself doing the same thing with my computer. When I got the computer, it seemed really, really fast. Now, after using it for a year or so, it seems to be slower than I remember it. Yes, it is still faster than doing things "the old way" (sort of like baking potatoes in a conventional oven), but I find myself talking to the computer, begging it to "hurry up."

If your PC seems slower than it should — particularly if it seems slower than when you first got it — then your system is a prime candidate for cleaning. Over time, the detritus that's collected during everyday use can start to bog down your computer. If you don't periodically banish that junk, it can affect the work you do. The change is typically slow, ever so slow, until you notice one day that your computer just doesn't run like it used to.

If you want to make your programs run faster, you're in luck because I show you how to do that in Chapter 4. To make Windows itself hum right along, check out Chapters 13 and 14, which cover getting the cobwebs out of Windows and making your file system run faster, respectively.

You have files older than your dog

I've had my dog for just over eighteen months, which makes him ten or eleven years old in dog years, right? Does that mean he's been chewing up my son's shoes for eighteen months or eleven years? Hmmm. . . . Converting people years to dog years may be philosophically confusing, but there is nothing confusing about examining the age of the files on your computer. If you use My Computer or the Windows Explorer to look at the files on your computer, I'll bet you could find some that are three, five, or even ten years old.

I can hear you now: "Not on my system. I just got it a year ago, so I don't have anything as old as your dog." Wrong, bucko! Computer files tend to follow you around, over the years, without you even realizing it. For instance, computer files are commonly transferred from an old system to a new system. When transferred, the files retain their old file dates — they are old files.

You may also share files with other people in your office, family, or circle of friends. Place the files on your computer, and you may quickly forget about them. But they are there, aging like a not-so-fine wine, taking up space and adding to the general clutter of your system.

A large number of old, old files are a sure sign that you need to clean your system. You can archive your data or create backups that allow you to remove unneeded data from your hard drive, freeing up space for other data and tasks. Chapter 7 gives you the straight scoop on how to keep only the data you need.

Your system tray looks like a parking lot

The system tray is the area at the right side of your taskbar. Take a look at the bottom of your computer screen. Now, shift your eyes all the way to the right. You probably see the current time, and you may see a few icons. Even if you don't realize it, that's the system tray (refer to Figure 1-1).

In Windows XP, the system tray is a little deceiving because it hides some of the icons. Perhaps the folks in Redmond don't want you to be consciously aware of how cluttered this area can become. Don't let that stand in your way, however. If you click the small left-pointing arrow at the left side of the system tray, you see the entire contents of the system tray.

Each icon in the system tray represents a utility program that is currently running in your system. You may see icons for any number of programs. How many do you see? Five? Ten? More? Some programs that you install on your computer are a bit egotistical. They think they're so important that they deserve a place of honor in your system tray. When you install one of these egotistical programs, besides adding itself to your Start menu and your desktop, it stakes out prime ground in your system tray.

Clutter, clutter, clutter. If you have a bunch of icons in your system tray, your system is a prime candidate for cleaning. Get rid of a few of these babies, and you may find your system running leaner and faster than before.

 Don't try to delete any of the system tray icons yet. Some of the icons will go away as you remove old programs. You also find out how to reclaim this prime area of your system by controlling what programs are run when your computer starts; Chapter 13 provides this important information.

Cleaning Up: The Pros and Cons

If your system needs cleaning, you've come to the right place. *Cleaning Windows For Dummies* is a great resource that you can use to get your system back to near-new condition. If you're not convinced that your computer needs a good cleaning, then you're obviously a discerning person who needs to examine all the ins and outs of an issue before making a commitment. (That, or you're in denial and won't make a change until you're operating in crisis mode. Don't clean, and, I promise you, the crisis will come soon enough.)

If your mind works like mine — I know that is a scary thought for some — then you will want to examine the pros and cons of cleaning your system. Doing so can help provide the rationale for the cleaning work you do.

The pros

You've finally reached the big time — the pros! Oh, sorry, wrong homonym. . . . In this instance, "the pros" mean *benefits*. Specifically, the benefits of cleaning up your system, which I list here:

- ✔ **Speed:** A clean system runs faster than one that needs cleaning. Do you remember when you first got your PC? You probably thought it ran very fast. If your system stays clean, you shouldn't notice it running any slower over time. Unfortunately, most systems don't stay clean and require your attention. Give it that attention — that is, do the cleaning — and your system can run just as fast as it did the day you got it.

- ✔ **Efficiency:** If you're using a clean system, you can get through your work faster, and you are therefore more efficient. A clean system doesn't make you immensely more efficient — if it did, the self-help publishing market would shrink dramatically. You can still get sidetracked playing games or arguing religion and politics on various message boards, but with a clean system you can do even those things more efficiently.

- ✔ **Reliability:** A huge benefit of a clean system is that it is more reliable than one that isn't. If you fail to clean your system, over time it goes from clean to cluttered to messed-up to unstable. Unstable systems crash. Unstable systems have a tendency to lose data. Unstable systems are a real pain. Clean your system, and you should see stability jump dramatically. No pain, big gain.

- ✔ **Stress reduction:** Do you like to sleep at night? Do you prefer having no worry? Believe it or not, having a clean system can reduce anxiety and provide peace of mind. How so? Consider the worry you would have if a virus infected your system, or if you weren't sure that the financial data on it was safe, or if you didn't know what programs were running on the system, or . . . . You get the idea. Worry comes in all shapes and sizes. If you clean your computer, you have a better handle on what's on your computer and how it's being used.

- ✔ **Economics:** Cleaning your computer can save you money — sometimes lots of money. I suspect that hard-drive clutter has helped boost the bottom line of hard drive manufacturers significantly over the past decade. Running low on space? Get a new drive. Computer running slow? Get a new system. Chances are, some of those new drives and new systems would have been unnecessary had the users done just a little housecleaning.

The cons

Every coin has two sides, and unless you're a bunko victim, the two sides aren't the same. I'm no bunko artist, so I'm pleased to point out that doing a cleanup also has its negatives. You need to be aware of those negatives, right from the get-go:

- ✔ **Time-consumption:** Cleaning your computer takes time. You probably feel strapped for time right now, don't you? (Most people do.) Cleaning your computer can take anywhere from a trivial amount to a substantial amount of time. I've cleaned some systems — completely — in as little as two hours, while I've spent *days* cleaning other systems. How much time will your clean-up take? I can't answer that, but I can say be prepared for a time commitment and be patient — your time will pay off in the end when your computer is running more smoothly.

  Fortunately, you have some control over how and when to spend that time. You don't have to spend it all in a single block, although you could. You can spend the time over a period of days or weeks, as the time becomes available. Check out chapter 2, where I discuss setting up a cleaning schedule, which can help you manage your cleaning time.

- ✔ **The learning curve:** Part of the time required to do the cleanup is rooted in another drawback: the learning curve. Figuring out how to use some of the tools you use to clean takes time. If you're already comfortable with your computer and the cleaning tools, then your learning curve is lower than for those who are unfamiliar.

- ✔ **The bother:** I won't lie to you — cleaning up your computer can be a bother. If you approach the task as a chore, then it *will be* bothersome. But I encourage you to fight the urge to procrastinate cleaning; don't put it off as you might other bothersome tasks. To borrow a phrase, remember that it's not just a job — its an adventure. Try to overcome the "bother factor" by looking on it as a learning experience. If necessary, spread out the cleanup over several days so that you don't max out your stress level in a single session.

Balancing pros and cons

You may come up with other pros and cons than those I present in the preceding two sections. Some may be specific to your particular situation. (Is your job in jeopardy if you don't clean up your computer?) If you write the pros on the left side of a sheet of paper and the cons on the right side, you can easily see how they balance out — and then determine which side wins.

Paying the price

If you're short on time, you may be tempted to pay someone else to clean your system. After all, you pay someone to clean your car, clean your office, clean your house, and clean your yard. Why not have someone else do your cleaning for you?

Why not, indeed. You certainly can have someone else clean your computer, but chances are good that you won't like the price. Plan on paying anywhere from $50 per hour to $150 per hour for computer cleaning. Do the math — if it takes two, four, six, or more hours to clean your computer, how much will you pay? Ouch!

Also, you should understand that cleaning isn't just a one-time thing. But if you change your behavior, you won't have to clean as often or pay as much in the future. You can't pay someone else to change your computer behavior. Because you can learn so much while you're cleaning, it is well worth your while to do the cleaning yourself, at least for the first time.

In general, I think that the pros outweigh the cons by a significant amount (hence, this book). I'm guessing you think so, too; that's why you're reading this book. But you may need to work on timing, or you may need to work on attitude before you bring yourself to actually do it. Just keep in mind that having a clean computer is something that is beneficial in more ways than you can imagine.

Keeping Your House Tidy

Just like keeping your house tidy takes concerted effort on your part, keeping your computer system clean takes effort also. Some people mistakenly think that caring for their computer should be as mindless and easy as caring for their TVs and don't even think about cleaning their computers. But if you've read this whole chapter, you now know you need to clean your system — and that there are benefits to cleaning it. So you're ready to jump right in and tackle the job. (You are ready, right?)

I show you that you don't have to dread cleaning your system. Sure, this job takes some time, but it doesn't have to be an intimidating task. In fact, you can even clean your system over a period of weeks — a little here and a little there — and before you know it, it's done.

As you seek to clean up your system, the different areas you can focus on include

   ✔ **Your programs:** The entire purpose of your computer is to create an environment in which you can effectively use different programs. If your programs don't run well, the value of your computer decreases. If you focus on cleaning up your programs or making them run faster (the focus of Chapters 3, 4, and 5), you immediately increase the value of your system.

✔ **Your data:** Chances are good that your programs eat, sleep, and breathe data. Programs need data to run, to fulfill their purpose in life. If your data is messed up, then your programs may just refuse to work properly. Managing data can be a monumental task, but doing so effectively will free up space on your hard drive and allow your programs to run faster. Head to Chapters 6 and 7 to find out more.

✔ **Your e-mail:** We live in a well-connected world. If you use e-mail (and who doesn't), then you can clutter up your system without even realizing it. Spam and viruses routinely bombard your system through e-mail. If you better manage your e-mail (I show you how in Chapters 8 and 9), you lessen clutter and make your system more secure.

✔ **Your Internet use:** E-mail isn't the only use for your Internet connection. As you browse around the Web, your system is routinely filled up with files you don't even know about. Whether these files are benign or harmful, they all add to the clutter of your system. If you pay attention to what's stored on your system, you can reduce the clutter and improve overall performance. Chapters 10 and 11 can help you tackle the Internet beast.

✔ **The operating system:** Ah, Windows. What can be said about Windows? Actually, quite a lot can be said — and not all of it bad! Windows is a great operating system, and one of its biggest strengths is its configurability. In Part IV, I show you ways to tweak and prod Windows into running faster than it ever did before.

There are also some advanced things you can do, such as tweaking your hardware (or adding new hardware), improving your security profile, and [shudder] diving into the Registry. Such endeavors (which I cover in Part V) are usually relegated to the last, after you have worked through the other cleaning areas. I recommend that you proceed into these areas with extreme caution.

How will you know when your system is finally clean? You'll know you've succeeded when your system runs smoother, faster, and more reliably than before. You'll know when you are able to finish your work quicker, without getting bogged down.

Chapter 2

Determining What to Clean and When

In This Chapter

▶ Practicing safe cleaning so you don't get burned

▶ Locating just the right cleaning tools

▶ Scheduling your cleaning tasks

▶ Answering the cleaning conundrum with new hardware

*W*hen you think about cleaning your Windows system, do you feel the walls closing in? Do you find it hard to breathe? Does everything start spinning and go dark?

If so, you've been sitting at the computer too long. Or maybe someone has spiked your drink. Or you sat in one position so long that you've cut off oxygen to your brain. Stand up. Stretch a bit. Go outside for a breath of fresh air.

You see, cleaning your computer is neither rocket science nor something even harder (like assembling your kids' Christmas toys after one-too-many egg nogs on Christmas Eve), but it involves multiple steps: creating lists, taking precautionary measures, finding helpful tools, making a cleaning schedule, and asking yourself (and then answering) tough questions, such as "Should I just wipe out the system and start anew?" or "Do I need new hardware?" After the fresh air and helpful stretch, read on and discover how you can approach these steps to get your computer back to its pre-messed-up glory.

How to Eat an Elephant

I'm sure you've heard the old joke "How do you eat an elephant?" The answer, of course, is one bite at a time. Cleaning your computer system is the same thing. (I could try to stretch the analogy by talking about elephants/computers and memory, but will gladly spare you the pain.)

Face it — you can do quite a bit to clean the average Windows system. Files proliferate, programs fall out of favor, viruses reproduce, e-mail clusters, and pop-ups populate. Throw in a little systemic neglect and before you know it, you have a messed-up system that badly needs cleaning.

So how do you do it all? One bite at a time. Don't put off doing some cleaning today with the hope that you will have more time tomorrow. Truth be told, cleaning a Windows system is more about behavior than it is about one or two tasks. Granted, you need to do some remedial work to get your system back in peak condition, but once you do, keeping your system clean on an ongoing basis is much easier than doing the remedial work in the first place.

So which part of the elephant should you chew on first? At the end of Chapter 1 you find out the different areas of your computer system that you should clean. In general, you should work on the most accessible parts of the elephant first and then move on to the rest. Following is a list of items that I recommend you do even if you're really pressed for time. (I give you ideas about setting up cleaning routines in the later section, "Creating Cleaning Schedules.")

- ✔ **If you have only limited time available, get rid of unused and unneeded files.** Archive your old-but-still-valuable files to get them off your system. When you have more time, you can go back and deal with your programs and your system as a whole. (Generally you should get your programs under control before worrying about your data, but the key here is time restriction. Working on programs simply takes longer than does taming your data.)

- ✔ **If you have more time available, do a program inventory and remove the programs you no longer need.** (See Chapters 3 and 5, where I discuss creating an inventory and deleting unwanted programs.) You'd be amazed at how much clutter this can remove from your system. Then go back and clean up your data and archive your older information.

- ✔ **Get rid of spyware and spam and get your Internet environment under control.** If you do this, you find that using the Internet can again become productive, rather than frustrating. (Part III covers a ton of territory in this regard.)

- ✔ **Closely examine what your computer loads without your knowledge.** This is one of the key places many people overlook (even when suggesting ways to clean your computer), but Windows encounters instructions to automatically load different programs from a myriad of places (most on the Web). These programs can hog resources and slow down your system's overall performance.

  Of course, tracking down such unseen scoundrels can take a bit of time. When you have that time (and after you've done the other things in this list), jump in and try to figure out what's going on. Windows provides some utilities that can help, such as the System Configuration Utility (msconfig), which I tell you about in Chapter 13.

✔ **If you really have some time to kill — or you just fancy yourself a masochist — you can wade into the murky waters of the Windows Registry.** The *Registry* is the centralized database that controls virtually everything that happens in the operating system. It is mind-numbingly complex and staggeringly obtuse for normal humans to deal with. However, you can do things in the Registry that you cannot do in any other way. An entire chapter of this book (Chapter 20) deals with this very topic.

Working in the Registry is not for the faint-of-heart. Make sure you double-check every action *before* you take it. One wrong step and you can bring your system to its knees. (Don't be overly worried; Chapter 20 explains how to make backups of the Registry in case of problems.)

After you've tackled the elephant that is your Windows system, you will undoubtedly look back and be glad you went through the process. (You'll also be glad you're done, but that's another story.)

Precautions for Safety's Sake

It's a jungle out there. (It's too bad you ate your elephant; you could use it to help you get through the jungle.) In the jungle, bad things can happen to good people. Because you are good people, you may be interested in some things to help stave off or completely avoid the bad things.

Cleaning a Windows system necessarily involves moving things, adding things, deleting things, and sometimes renaming things. Any of these tasks, while necessary, can have unintended consequences. Heaven forbid you should delete a critical system file or wipe out the wrong data key in the Registry. (Refer to the previous bulleted list, where I define the Registry and explain its importance.)

These precautions help you avoid the bad things:

✔ **Don't delete files without knowing what you are deleting.** If you are in doubt, simply move the file to a different directory or rename it. Then, if you restart your system (or the program) and find out you made a mistake, you can always move the file back or restore its original name.

✔ **Make periodic backups of your system.** (You've heard this before, right?) If you're getting ready to do a huge cleaning session, you might want to make a backup right before you start. If you want to rely on an older backup, you might want to have it close by, in case you need it when you start your cleaning session.

✔ **Be careful how you delete programs.** In the wonderful days of DOS, in the misty past, programs usually consisted of a couple of files or all the files in a given directory. Not so in Windows. When you install a program, the installation program can move pieces and parts all over the place. When you run the program, it can move more of itself to still other places. Because of that, the best way to delete a program is to use either the uninstaller provided with the software or the Add/Remove Programs applet in the Control Panel. Don't just delete the main folder for the program — pieces and parts will remain scattered hither and yon. (Hither is easy to find; yon is more difficult.)

✔ **Know what you are doing with the Registry.** The Registry is a largely incomprehensible place. Be careful when you are changing or deleting things in the Registry. In fact, I recommend making a backup of the Registry before you do any big changes, or simply export a data key when you are getting ready to make more minor changes. (A *data key* is geekspeak for a branch in the Registry. Find out more about keys and how to back them up in Chapter 20.) Windows does not have a Recycle Bin for the Registry — if you delete something by mistake, you will be glad you made a copy ahead of time.

✔ **If a new icon shows up on your desktop one day, don't double-click it.** If you don't know why it's there, someone (or some program) has possibly deposited it there. If you don't know what it does, why double-click it and run it? A safer course of action is to right-click the icon, choose Properties, and then examine what programs the icon runs.

✔ **Keep your original program discs accessible.** If you change the a program's installation, you probably need the discs. If you delete a part of the program you shouldn't, you probably need the discs. If you want to reinstall the program, you probably need the discs. Just keep them close. And it wouldn't hurt to have any necessary *software keys* (those pesky ten-character — or longer — codes required to install or unlock your software) for the discs, either.

✔ **Use only programs from reputable sources.** This book talks about lots of programs you can use to help with your system cleaning. You can download most of these programs from the Internet. Rest assured that the programs I suggest have been tested and are reliable. You can't make that same assumption with all the software you find on the Internet. If you download and run a program from a disreputable source, you could possibly infect your system with a virus or do some other system-crashing function.

I didn't list these precautions in any particular order. They simply give you some guidance as you start on your worthy quest through the jungle. Rest assured, however, that you already possess the best safeguard you can have: common sense. Trust your common sense and it will help you through a large number of the problems you may face.

As you're cleaning your system, keep a notepad and pen nearby. Jot down each cleaning step you take, along with any oddities you observe. This could be helpful if you later need to track down a problem that crops up.

Finding the Right Tools

The Right Tools. Man, I loved that movie. Sam Shepard, Scott Glenn, Ed Harris, and Dennis Quaid were amazing. It had me on the edge of my seat, especially when . . . no, wait — that was *The Right Stuff.* (Dang it. *The Right Tools* would probably star Tim "the tool man" Taylor in a 1965 Ford Mustang convertible. Guess I'll have to wait for that one.)

You don't have to blast off into space to find the right cleaning tools. In fact, many of the proper tools are already on your system, provided with Windows. Others are third-party tools that you have to find on the Internet.

Finding Windows tools

You probably don't know about the tools already on your system because Microsoft just throws them in without any fanfare. In fact, on Windows XP these tools are downright hard to find.

Think I'm kidding? Follow these steps and you see what I mean:

1. **Right-click on any blank area of the taskbar and choose Properties from the Context menu that appears.**

   The Taskbar and Start Menu Properties dialog box appears.

2. **Select the Start Menu tab.**

   As shown in Figure 2-1, a nice, idyllic scene appears, reminiscent of when you first got Windows XP and you ran through the lush, green grass in your bare feet. (That whole scene reminds me of some bothersome anti-allergy pharmaceutical commercial.)

3. **Select the Start Menu option and click Customize.**

   The Customize Start Menu dialog box appears.

4. **Click the Advanced tab.**

   Windows displays a plethora of options, as shown in Figure 2-2.

5. **Scroll to the bottom of the Start Menu Items list.**

   You're looking for a section of the list titled System Administrative Tools. Notice, when you find it, that the Don't Display This Item option is selected. (Told you Microsoft made this hard.)

6. **Choose the Display on the All Programs Menu and the Start Menu options.**

Figure 2-1:
This is the
dialog box
where you
slice and
dice your
Start menu.

7. Close all the dialog boxes.

All you need to do is click OK a few times. This saves your change.

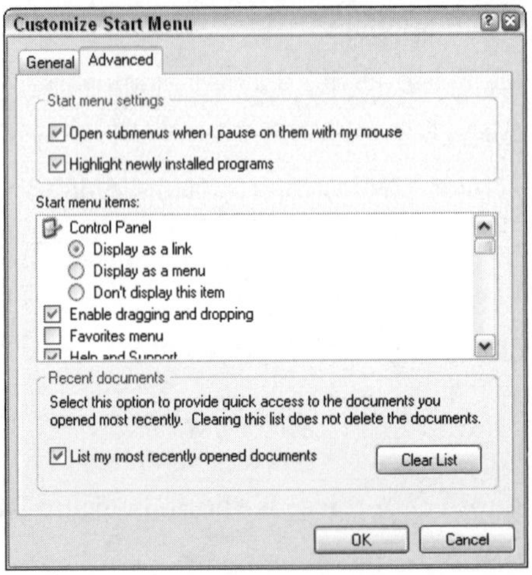

Figure 2-2:
Ah ha!
The long-
hidden
utility
features of
Windows
XP.

Now when you click your Start menu button, you should notice that a new
Administrative Tools option appears, right below the Control Panel option.
This option — which Microsoft hides because someone in Redmond feels you
aren't ready for the responsibility — can help you clean up your system and
access many helpful-yet-geeky tools. Some of these tools are explained later in
this book, in various chapters. Other tools accessible through Administrative

Tools are designed for heavy-duty system administration, and aren't terribly useful when cleaning your system. Feel free to explore the tools to see whether they're beneficial to you.

Many other Windows tools are accessible only from the Run menu; I detail those at the appropriate places throughout this book. (I wouldn't want you to get too much power right away, without a proper explanation. There could be cosmic consequences.)

Finding third-party tools

Third-party tools are those provided by people or companies other than Microsoft. (You're the first party, Microsoft is the second party, and everyone else is third-party.) Many, many tools are available in your local computer store or on the Internet, each one promising to help you run your system faster, safer, smoother, and with less chaffing than ever before. Some work well; some don't. You need to be careful that you don't fall for all the advertising glitz, however. The old adage that "if something sounds too good to be true, it probably is" readily applies here.

With that caveat in mind, you can go searching for tools in several places, if you're so inclined. I recommend trying these:

- ✔ **Tucows.** Once just a straight download site, Tucows has become much more. For that reason, I generally jump right to the Windows-specific section at www.tucows.com/windows.html. For most folks, this site is the gold mine of downloadable software.

- ✔ **CNET.** One of those megasites (www.cnet.com), it includes not only downloads, but also all sorts of reviews of products they want you to buy.

- ✔ **Shareware.com.** This site, at www.shareware.com, is actually run by the folks at CNET. You get many of the same results here that you do at CNET.

- ✔ **Major Geeks.** An interesting site with a military motif, www.majorgeeks.com is a site for, well, people who are geeks in a major way. Lots of different downloads help you do everything from *benchmarking* (testing your system's speed and performance) to multimedia.

- ✔ **SysInternals.** Top-notch freeware utilities for Windows systems can be found at www.sysinternals.com. The utilities here are hard-core and totally geeky by definition. Real good stuff, though.

I show you how to use a good number of third-party tools in the different chapters of this book. For instance, in Chapter 6 you discover System Mechanic, an award-winning tool from Iolo Technologies. In Chapter 8 you get a quick overview of different spam-combating programs. And in Chapter 20 you find out about different software solutions for cleaning the Registry.

These examples are just a portion of what's in store for you when it comes to third-party software. The point is, lots of good third-party software is out there and new stuff is rising to the top of the heap all the time. With a little looking around and checking it out, you can find different tools that will help you clean your Windows system and keep it clean.

For a more detailed list of my favorite tools, check out Chapter 23. For a really cool bunch of online resources you can use, refer to Chapter 24.

Creating a Cleaning Schedule

I've said it before and I'll say it again: Cleaning your Windows system doesn't need to be intimidating. Sure, cleaning can take some time to accomplish, but you don't need to do the cleaning all at once. You can break up the big job of cleaning into smaller, more manageable tasks, doing a little here and a little there until you're done cleaning completely.

Or are you?

In reality, cleaning is never done *completely* — it should be an ongoing endeavor. If you set up a schedule for your cleaning, your system can remain clean and you lessen the chance of having a messed-up computer. Plus, your life will be happier, your kids smarter, and the sun shine brighter on your home. (I threw that in for the movie version of this book. It doesn't hurt to think ahead.)

So what type of schedule should you set up for cleaning? Well, the next few sections detail things you can do now (as in today), things you can do once a week, once a month, and every year. I'm sure you will find enough info here to create your own schedule.

Now. Do it now — right now.

Got some spare time on your hands today? The following list explains just five things that you can do in as little as 10 or 20 minutes to help make your system cleaner:

✔ **Take out the trash:** If the trash in your kitchen overflows, you either take it out or the dog treats it as a toy box. Your computer probably has trash everywhere and you don't even realize it — it doesn't overflow and the dog doesn't care. To empty your computer trash, right-click your Recycle Bin (on the Desktop) and choose Empty.

✔ **Eliminate unneeded e-mail messages:** Skip over to your e-mail program and empty the e-mails from three areas: Sent Items, Deleted Items, and Junk E-mail. (These names are typical in Outlook; the folder names may be different in your e-mail program.) For a detailed look at how to get a handle on your e-mail, refer to Chapters 8 and 9.

✔ **Delete unused programs:** Choose Start⇨Control Panel⇨Add/Remove Programs to open the Add/Remove Programs applet. Examine the programs listed there and see if you can delete any. (**Hint:** If you don't use it any more, you should delete it.) Find out more about identifying your programs in Chapter 3 and how to get rid of them in Chapter 5.

✔ **Clean out the Web cache:** The *Web cache* is your system's repository of temporary files downloaded from the Internet. You go through your Web browser to access the cache and delete anything you don't need. Exactly how you do this depends on the type of browser you have, but in Internet Explorer you choose Tools⇨Internet Options to display the Internet Options dialog box. Select the General tab and click Delete Files. Chapter 11 contains details on how to tame the cache files.

✔ **Delete cookies:** *Cookies* are small data files stored on your system to customize your browsing experience on some Web sites. If desired, you can clean out the cookies stored by your browser. Some people like to do this, but doing so generally doesn't save a whole lot of disk space. Deleting cookies carries a downside, so make sure you read through Chapter 11 before you clean them out.

There. That didn't take too long, did it? And, truth be told, you probably freed up several megabytes of space on your hard drive. Cool.

Once a week should do it

All across America, in offices large and small, people start watching the clock at about 2:00 pm on Fridays. Time seems to slow down and drag on forever as quitting time approaches and the weekend beckons.

Don't let your zeal for the weekend, however, stop you from doing a few cleanup tasks every week. Friday afternoons are a great time to do these things, but you can actually do them any time during the week — it doesn't really matter.

✔ **Delete temporary files:** Temporary files tend to proliferate, for a variety of reasons, and do nothing but occupy space. Locate them, delete them, and then empty the Recycle Bin. Chapter 6 helps you with this process.

✔ **Make backups:** If you don't already do it daily, make backups of your data. Folks, this is cheap insurance. It isn't a matter of *whether* you need your backups, but *when* you need them because you *will* need them — so make backups! (Wow. Was that forceful enough?) After you make the backups, store them somewhere safe. Chapter 7 includes information about making and storing backups.

✔ **Clean out the root directory:** The *root directory* is a special place on each hard drive; it represents prime real estate in the file-storage world. Unfortunately, root directories also have a tendency to become cluttered easily. If you take a look at them once a week and clean them out as necessary it helps keep your operating system happier. You probably don't want to delete files willy nilly; Chapter 7 contains the details on how to keep root directories in tip-top shape.

After you get good at completing these weekly tasks, they won't take you long at all. Plus, your system will be cleaner and your data more secure. Don't you feel better now? Is it quitting time yet?

It's the end of the month already!

The months click by, and the older you get, the faster they click by. You do different things every month, like clockwork. You turn a page on the calendar. You reconcile your checkbook with the bank statement. You pay your mortgage or rent. You rake the gravel in your front yard. (Okay, so I'm weird. It comes naturally; my sun-baked brain lives in Arizona.)

Add a few tasks to your monthly routine and your computer system will remain clean and tidy:

✔ **Clean up your desktop:** The dreaded "icon creep" can result in more icons on your desktop today than there was a month ago. Identify the ones you don't need and delete them. Chapter 12 has all the grungy details.

✔ **Archive project data:** If you're a project-oriented type of person, you probably finished up a few projects this past month. Why not archive the data associated with those projects so that it no longer clutters your hard drive? I discuss archiving data details in Chapter 7.

✔ **Eliminate spyware:** *Spyware* is a growing plague on many computer systems. Spyware started as a way for unethical marketers to track what you do with your computer. Not cool. Now it has grown to include all sorts of pop-ups that sprout like crabgrass on your monitor. Very uncool. Your pop-up blocker may suppress the symptoms, but the underlying problem — spyware — is still there. Read Chapter 10 and eradicate spyware at least once a month.

✔ **Examine your startup files:** Every time your computer starts, it automatically starts some programs. You may not know about this. If something changes the programs that run at startup, you may not know about the change, either. Unless, of course, you check to see what's running automatically. Review the information in Chapters 3 and 13 to find out how to identify and control these types of programs. Then, on a monthly basis, check out your startup files to make sure no surprises are lurking there.

✔ **Defragment your hard drive:** One thing you really benefit from every month is defragmenting your hard drive. As you add, change, rearrange, and delete files, information stored on the hard drive can become discombobulated. (Yes, that is a valid technical term — trust me, I know these things.) Information is stored in bits and pieces here and there so that Windows has to grab data from all over your hard drive when you open a file. That slows down the system. You can knock things back into whack by defragmenting your hard drive, which essentially puts pieces of individual files back together. When done, Windows can more easily and quickly access your files. Want to find out more about defragmenting? (Nod your head. Good.) Turn to Chapter 14 for all the nitty-gritty defragmenting details.

Defragment your hard drive at the end of the day. You can leave the program running while you run home to decompress from the day.

Now that your system is cleaner and tidier and your bank account is reconciled, aren't you glad that the month is over? Now you get to start all over again. . . .

Time for the annual clean-a-fest

Should old acquaintance be forgot, and never brought to mind, we'll fill the hard drive with our drafts and sing of auld lang syne.

With appropriate apologies to Robert Burns, over the course of a year many computer acquaintances can be forgotten. Or dropped. Or misplaced. Or whatever. Creating an annual checklist to keep your Windows system lean, mean, and clean is a good idea:

✔ **Review all data files on your computer and archive as necessary:** Perhaps the biggest annual task is doing a comprehensive review of the data files on your computer. If you have been doing monthly archives, you can now add other files to the annual pile and shuffle them off to archive media. Chapter 7 tells how to do everything you ever wanted to do with archives. (Well, almost everything.)

✔ **Review your Web browser's favorites list and delete items you don't use anymore:** You should also plan on firing up your Web browser and reviewing the items in your favorites list. Chances are good that what you considered your favorites a year ago no longer qualify as such. Keeping your favorites list pared down helps you find what you need faster, and that can be a huge benefit. Chapter 11 discusses, among other things, how to best deal with your Web favorites.

✔ **Visit manufacturers' Web sites to check for updates:** Take some time to visit the Web sites for the manufacturers of you system hardware. Check for new drivers for printers, scanners, cameras, and so on, that have been released during the previous 12 months. Updating your drivers can improve speed and reliability. Chapter 13 discusses how to update (or remove) drivers.

✔ **Review your security precautions and update them as necessary:** It's a cruel, cruel world out there, and some of the perpetrators of cruelty are not content to remain "out there." Some of them want to get up close and personal with your computer. Your job is to stop them. Believe me — you don't want to encourage such relationships. You should, at least on an annual basis, make sure that you review your security precautions. Make sure you do your review with an eye toward major security changes in the past year and how you can be prepared for the coming year. Chapter 18 can help get you started.

✔ **Update your program inventory:** I recommend doing this on an annual basis. Work habits change; tools come and go. You need to make sure that your Windows system always reflects the way you currently use your computer. Chapter 3 walks you through the process of developing your program inventory and the benefits it offers.

Time for an Overhaul?

I know one technician whose standard answer to cleaning a Windows system is to reformat the hard drive and start all over again with a clean slate. While that's one way to tackle the problem, it isn't necessarily the best way. It's akin to using a bazooka to swat a mosquito: effective but overkill.

Is a complete system overhaul advisable? Sure; there are times when it's a good idea. But doing so should be your *last* resort and then only after you've thought through all the ramifications.

For instance, after you've cleaned systems for a while you get a feel for how long it takes to do the cleaning. You know what it takes to look through folder after folder, weeding out the files you no longer need. You know how long it takes to identify and remove programs, update drivers, and track down errant files. When you add up all those hours, you have a good idea of what it takes — time-wise — to clean your system.

Now, start adding up how long it takes to reformat your hard drive, reinstall Windows, locate and install your hardware drivers, dig out and reinstall your software, and back up and restore your data. Add up all those hours and you have a good idea of the time required to overhaul.

Compare the two time estimates. If the cleaning is within 10 percent of the estimate for an overhaul, go for the overhaul. Even if it takes a bit longer, you *do* end up with a "fresher" machine. You get the complete skinny on overhauling your system in Chapter 21.

The kicker is that overhauling your system (or cleaning it thoroughly) does no good if you don't change the behavior that resulted in the messed-up system in the first place. Make sure that in the future you make cleaning an integral part of your everyday computing.

Is New Hardware the Answer?

You've got that gleam in your eye. I can see it; yep, that's it. You want a new computer, don't you? I can see you thinking that getting a new computer would sure make the job of cleaning up much easier — after all, the new system starts clean.

That's the problem, though — it only *starts* clean. If you don't change how you use your computer, then your new system will be a sullied twin of your current system in short order. You need to know that it's behavior that messes up computers. (Have you heard this before?) If you keep the same behavior, you keep the same consequences of that behavior.

The same is true of adding individual hardware components to your system. Running out of hard drive space? If you add a hard drive without changing how you use the hard drive, you will fill the new one up as well.

You might be thinking that I am saying that new hardware is not the answer; I'm not. I'm just saying it isn't the easy answer you may assume it is. In fact, in Chapter 16 I describe how to justify, select, and implement a brand new system. Take a look at that information before deciding that getting a new system is the cure for your ills.

If you're thinking of upgrading to Windows XP SP2 and you're also thinking of getting a new system, why not combine the two? SP2 on a new system will help you start with a good, stable environment. (That's good.) You should still read Chapter 16 before getting a new system, though.

Part II
Programs and Data

In this part . . .

Part II focuses on identifying what programs you have, how to make them run faster, and how to get rid of unnecessary programs. You also find out how to identify all the data on your hard drive, as well as deleting or archiving data you don't need.

Chapter 3

Identifying What You Have

. . . .

In This Chapter

▶ Determining what programs you really need

▶ Discovering what is really installed

▶ Figuring out when programs are running automatically

▶ Uncovering what programs are running right now

▶ Using the information you uncover

. . . .

Do you know what programs are on your computer? Do you *really* know? Most people don't. Instead, they make assumptions. The problem with assumptions, of course, is that they can get you into trouble.

The first step toward cleaning your Windows system is to figure out what programs should be on your computer, compare that to what is actually on your computer, and determine what to do with the discrepancies.

This chapter helps you through this process. By the end of this chapter you will be well on your way to regaining control over a computer system that is probably more out of control than you know.

Creating a Program Inventory

If you run a warehouse, you need to know what you have in stock; you need an inventory. When you have an inventory, you are better able to manage everything within the warehouse walls. Without the inventory, every day is a bigger chore than it needs to be and probably full of unwelcome surprises. (Running an uninventoried warehouse isn't just a job — it's an adventure! And if you do it on roller skates, it's a zippy adventure.)

Although a computer is much smaller than a warehouse, managing a computer is not much different from a conceptual standpoint. When you take inventory in a warehouse, you are making a list of what is really there. When you take inventory of your computer, you start by figuring out what should be there. This list of what should be installed on your system is your computer inventory.

When figuring out your program inventory, you are probably tempted to click the Start menu and see what you have installed on your system. Don't! That comes later, after you figure out what the heck you do with your computer. (If you start by looking through the Start menu, what you find will improperly color your inventory. Trust me; you get better results by ignoring the Start menu for the time being.)

You can take either of two approaches to putting your inventory together: the think-tank approach and the laid-back approach. Read through the following sections and figure out which one you want to use. There is no right answer; just pick the one that appeals to you the most, and then do it.

The think-tank approach

The best way to put together a program inventory is to think through how you use the computer. I call this the *think-tank approach* because you are putting your list together in one fell swoop, using sheer brain power to hammer out an inventory that reflects the way you use your computer. (Plus, you can impress the heck out of your know-nothing friends by telling them you belong to a think-tank. If you tell them in a snobby voice, it sounds very impressive, indeed.)

To create an inventory using the think-tank approach, follow these steps:

1. **Turn off your computer, unplug the phone, grab a cold drink, and clear a place on your desk.**

   You can't think effectively if you are interrupted. (Despite what the personal productivity gurus try to sell us, multitasking is for computers, not for people.) Now you are ready; this is think-tanking at its best.

2. **On a fresh sheet of paper, start listing all the programs you need on your computer in order to do your work.**

   Think through the tasks you do on a regular basis and write down the names of the software you use to do those tasks. Do you do a lot of writing? Chances are good your inventory should include a word processor, such as Word or WordPerfect. Do you crunch numbers for a living? Then your inventory probably includes a spreadsheet program. Do you design Web pages? You probably have a page design program in your inventory. Write them all down.

3. **Include tasks that are easy to overlook, such as balancing your checkbook or entertaining your mind.**

   There are probably more than a couple of utility programs you use on a regular basis, such as WinZip or Adobe Reader. These should be on the list, as well.

4. **Check your bookshelves and write down what you find, but only if what you find is what you really use.**

   Chances are good that you have software manuals or installation disks stored somewhere. (Of course, they may be buried under a half-inch of dust, but rediscovering these old, dust-buried friends can be exciting.)

If you find items on your bookshelves that you no longer use, gently toss them into a corner. You can always donate them or maybe even sell them at eBay. Plus, you free up valuable space on your bookshelves.

Creating your inventory should take you about an hour only. If you find yourself taking more time than that, you are probably allowing yourself to become distracted. If you take much less time, then you are not successfully navigating the think tank and are probably missing some items.

The laid-back approach

If you like a more leisurely approach to life and your Windows system is not so bollixed up that you can't use it effectively, you can put together your program inventory another way: Keep a journal.

Yep, you read right — keep a journal. A program diary. The steps for creating an inventory the laid-back way are, well, laid back:

1. **Put a small notebook next to your computer.**

2. **Over the course of a typical week, write down every program you use.**

   If you start the program, write it down. You don't have to write times and dates for using the programs, just the program name.

3. **At the end of the week, admire what should be a nice long list of programs.**

4. **If you find duplicates on the list, remove them.**

   For instance, you may have written a program name down on Friday, forgetting that you already wrote it down on Tuesday. When you are done, your inventory should contain nothing but a unique list of programs you use in your work.

If you decide to take this laid-back approach, you've got some time on your hands. After all, you shouldn't move forward with the rest of your cleaning tasks until you have your inventory done. If your inventory takes a week to put together, what will you do with your free time?

I suggest going for a walk. Or, if you tend toward being a couch potato, catch a few reruns of *Law and Order*. Of course, you could read through the rest of this chapter, but don't do any of it yet — you really do need that inventory.

Instead, bookmark this page so that you can come back in a week, after a few leisurely walks or a better understanding of Detective Lenny Briscoe's acerbic wit. You should be ready to move along then.

Finding Out What Programs Are Installed

When you are done with your inventory, congratulate yourself and get another cold drink. Put the inventory away for a while, but don't forget where you put it. (You will need it shortly.)

Grab another sheet of paper and start writing down what programs are actually installed on your computer. You can look in lots of places to put this list together. All of them involve your computer, so make sure you are comfortably seated in front of it as you work through the following sections. To find out what is installed on your system, look in these four main places: the desktop, the Start menu, the Control Panel, and your program folders.

You are doing nothing right now except exploring your system and documenting what you find. Resist the temptation to start removing programs, regardless of how strong that temptation is. You have plenty of time to remove programs later; Chapter 5 covers that task very nicely.

Inspecting your desktop

Does your desktop look like the public bulletin board at your neighborhood Piggly Wiggly? Do you have icons crowded together so tightly that it's hard to see the wallpaper in the background? If so, you have problems. Don't worry, though — help is coming!

Every program you installed on your system probably asked (in a very helpful manner) if you wanted a program icon placed on your desktop. If you said yes, it is no wonder your desktop is a mess. Even though it is a mess, it is also a good indicator of what is installed on your system. This is good.

Take a quick look at each area of your desktop; it contains important clues to the programs installed on your system. Pay particular attention to the following areas:

> ✔ **Icons:** Look at each icon on your desktop, figure out what program it belongs to, and write the program name on your piece of paper. Unless your desktop is a disaster area, you should be able to breeze through this task in just a few minutes. Ignore non-program items (such as folders or data files) unless they help you remember a program installed on your system.

✔ **Taskbar:** Taskbars are typically full of all sorts of icons, each associated with some installed program. Pay particular attention to the Quick Launch area, just to the right of the Start menu icon. See Figure 3-1 for the taskbar. If there is an expansion icon to the right of the Quick Launch area, click it to see other icons in the area. Jot down the names of the programs responsible for these icons.

✔ **System tray:** The system tray, sometimes called the *notification area,* is to the right of the taskbar (refer to Figure 3-1). Again, each icon here is related in some way to a program on your system. Write them down. If you don't know what program they belong to, hover the mouse pointer over the icon until you see a helpful reminder. If you see a left-pointing arrow at the left side of the system tray, click it to see all the icons stored therein.

You find out more about cleaning up your desktop in Chapter 12.

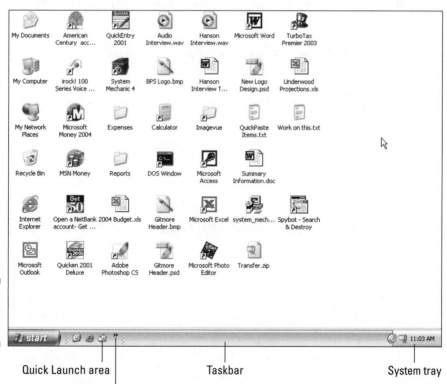

Figure 3-1:
Examining
the desktop.

Quick Launch area   Taskbar   System tray

Click to see more icons in the Quick Launch area

Scrutinizing the Start menu

The Start menu is the gateway to your system. Unless your system is a Gateway, and then the Start menu is the gateway to your Gateway. (Sorry; I wax philosophic sometimes.) Displaying the Start menu can tell you quite a bit about what is installed on your system. Spend some time clicking the various options in the Start menu to find out what is installed.

As you look through your Start menu, don't worry about visiting the Control Panel just yet. (I cover that in the next section.) Instead, focus on what you see when you click All Programs. This option presents a whole new world of menus, possibly several levels deep. (See Figure 3-2.) Look through them all and write down the names of the programs you find.

If you find the options available in your Start menu overwhelming, don't despair. Part of the reason you clean Windows is to reduce those feelings and help you get back in control of your system. You'll make it; hang in there!

Checking the Control Panel

Have you ever spent time in the Control Panel on your system? It's analogous to the cockpit of an airplane, giving you access to all the controls that make your computer work.

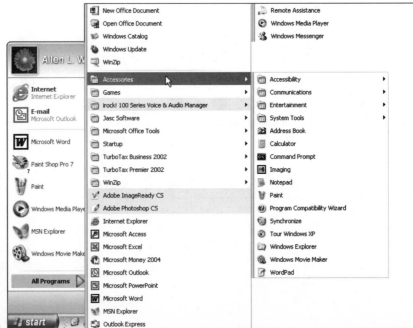

Figure 3-2:
Program menus accessible through the Start menu can extend several layers deep.

One area of the Control Panel specifically designed to help you figure out what's installed is the Add/Remove Programs applet. (*Applet* is geekspeak for a small program. The term is traditionally used to describe the various programs available through the Control Panel.)

1. **Open the Control Panel.**

2. **Click (or double-click, depending on how you are viewing the Control Panel) the Add or Remove Programs option.**

   Shortly you see a list of the programs that Windows XP thinks is installed on your system, as shown in Figure 3-3.

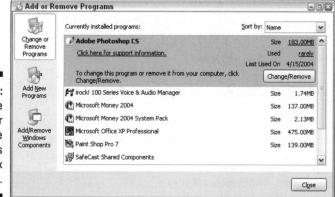

Figure 3-3:
This is the
Add or
Remove
Programs
dialog box
at work.

3. **Scroll through the list of programs and write them all down.**

   Chances are good that there are quite a few programs listed here, but you should not be fooled into thinking that the list represents every program installed on your system. It doesn't; that is why you are looking in places besides the Control Panel for installed programs.

4. **Close the Add or Remove Programs dialog box and the Control Panel.**

Peering in program folders

You should look in one final place to see what programs are installed on your system — the program folders. When you install a program on your system, the common convention is to install it in a folder called Program Files. This folder can contain dozens or hundreds of other folders, each of which is related in some way to a program installed on your system.

1. **Using My Computer, navigate to the Program Files folder and take a look at it.**

   On most systems, the Program Files folder is in the root directory of the C: drive. Figure 3-4 shows an example of a typical Program Files folder.

2. **Examine the name of each folder you see.**

   Most folders represent either the name of the program that uses the folder, or the name of the publisher of a program you installed. For example, folders named ATI Technologies, Intel, and Intuit contain additional folders for programs from those companies. Folders named Microsoft Office, Microsoft Works, and Microsoft FrontPage all refer to individual programs. (Microsoft is really good at spreading its programs through lots of folders in the Program Files folder.)

3. **Look through the folders in the Program Files folder, writing down the names of any programs not already on your list.**

4. **Close all the folder windows.**

   When you are through looking around and taking notes, tidy up your screen by closing all the open folder windows.

Over time, the Program Files folder can start to look like an old garbage dump, strewn about with folders that are no longer used. This happens because even though you delete old programs, the folders used by those programs could remain in the Program Files folder. Chapter 3 explains how to identify and remove these pesky left-behind folders.

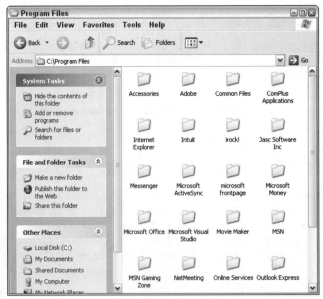

Figure 3-4:
The Program Files folder contains folders for many of the programs installed on your system.

Discovering What Programs Run When

Were you surprised by anything you found as you were putting together your program inventory? You find out shortly what to do with these lists, but first figure out what programs run at various times on your computer.

Most programs that you use are started whenever you choose to start them, such as through the Start menu or a desktop icon. A large number of programs run automatically when you start Windows. Sometimes, you may not even be aware that they are starting, since they may run behind the scenes.

Programs that run automatically on your computer — especially those that don't make themselves known to you — are some of the biggest speed thieves in any system. Every program uses *resources* (memory and drive space). The more programs loaded at the same time, the more resources are used for those programs.

You can configure programs to start automatically in Windows a couple of ways. Some of those ways are pretty technical; I cover them a bit later in this book (in Chapter 11). For right now, I examine a typical way that programs run: through the Startup folders on your system.

Starting up for all users

When Windows is first installed, one of the things it does is create a special Startup folder applicable to all the users on the computer. Anything placed in this folder is run and/or opened when you first start Windows. Sometimes real programs are stored in the Startup folder and sometimes it is just a shortcut to a program elsewhere on your system.

To open the Startup folder for all users, follow these steps:

1. **Right-click the Start button (at the left side of the taskbar).**

2. **Choose Open All Users from the context menu that appears.**

   Word opens a folder window called Start Menu. Each item in the folder represents an entry in the Start menu. This folder is nothing more than a directory on your hard drive, the same as any other folder.

3. **Double-click the Programs folder and then double-click the Startup folder.**

   The Startup folder (see Figure 3-5) shows you what sort of things are there (normally small "helper" programs used by other programs). For instance, my system has a program called QuickBooks Update Agent that is not a part of QuickBooks, but is used by QuickBooks to help determine whether new program updates are available.

Of menus and folders

The items in your two Startup folders appear in your Start menu — just choose Start⇨All Programs⇨Startup.

You may be wondering why you weren't just directed to the Startup menu in the first place, rather than opening the individual folders. The primary reason is because as you get ready to clean your system, you need to understand when your programs are running. Because the Startup menu displays a combination of things from both the all-user and single-user Startup folders, you cannot get the real facts on when a program is run just by looking at the menu. Instead, you must display the two individual folders.

As you examine the items in the Startup folder, check them against your installed program list. You may discover additional programs that you didn't know you had. If so, add them to your list. If they are already on your list, mark down on the list that the program is part of the Startup folder.

Starting up for just you

Windows creates another folder — a Startup folder — just for your user account. Anything in this folder is started whenever you log in to your Windows XP account.

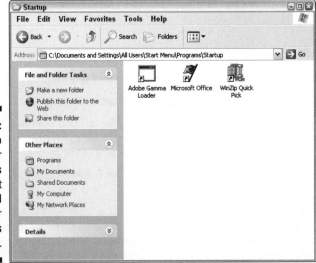

Figure 3-5:
The Startup folder contains items that are loaded whenever Windows begins.

On a single-user system, the Startup folder for all users and the Startup folder for your account are basically the same. Windows still maintains two separate Startup folders, and the contents of both are loaded and run whenever you start Windows and log in.

You can explore the contents of your Startup folder by following these steps:

1. **Right-click the Start button (at the left side of the Task bar).**

2. **Choose Open from the context menu.**

   Open should be the very first option on the Context menu. Word opens a dialog box called Start Menu. Each item in the folder represents an entry in the Start menu. This folder is nothing more than a directory on your hard drive, the same as any other folder.

3. **Double-click the Programs folder and then double-click the Startup folder.**

These steps look very much like the steps required to open the Startup folder for all users, which I describe in the previous section. The key difference, however, is that you choose a different option from the context menu. This opens a different Start Menu folder — one just for your user account — from the Start Menu folder opened in the previous section.

Check what you find against your installed program list. If you discover new programs, add them to your list.

Figuring Out What Is Running Right Now

Ready for another surprise? Your computer is running programs right now. Yep; programs are running even though you probably didn't know it. (How dare they!)

The Windows Task Manager is a great tool for figuring out what is running on your system.

1. **Exit all your programs, so that you have no buttons on your task bar.**

   This is so that you have the clearest idea of what is going on.

2. **Right-click a blank area of the task bar to display a context menu.**

3. **Choose Task Manager.**

   You see the Task Manager dialog box; the Applications tab should be selected. Look at Figure 3-6. The Applications tab lists all the application programs that are currently running on your system. Because you exited all your programs before starting the Task Manager, the list of programs is likely empty. This is great, but it doesn't tell the whole story — programs are still running.

4. Click the Processes tab (see Figure 3-7).

This tab shows any and all programs running right now. A bunch of information is available in the Processes tab, but right now you are only interested in the Image Name column. Here you find a bunch of cryptic names of what's running. These names are not terribly helpful, in and of themselves. You should still go through the list to figure out what the various processes are doing.

Figure 3-6: The Applications tab lists any programs running on your system.

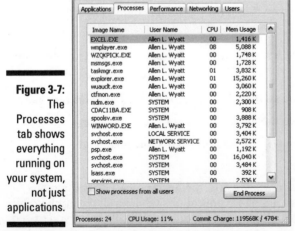

Figure 3-7: The Processes tab shows everything running on your system, not just applications.

If the Task Manager is the heart monitor for your system (and it is), then the Processes tab is the most important element of that monitor. If you want to keep your system in tip-top shape, you should become intimately familiar with the Processes tab. Nothing sneaks by it. Period.

The names used on the Processes tab are not terribly helpful (they remind me of the old DOS filenames), so don't feel bad if you need some help figuring out what each of them does. When I need help on a process, all I do is copy the name and search on it in Google.

For instance, one of the processes running on my system is WISPTIS.EXE. This name doesn't look familiar, so I fired up Google (`www.google.com`) and searched on that name. I was amazed that there were over 700 matches to what I consider an obscure term (see Figure 3-8).

Looking at just the first couple of matches, I was able to determine that WISPTIS.EXE is a safe program installed by Windows itself. Thus, it is okay to leave the program running in memory.

While searching through Google for process names, if you see any that are identified in a Google search as spyware or a virus, make special note of that process name. These programs are invalid and can seriously degrade the efficiency and reliability of your system. You find out how to handle invalid programs in Chapter 8.

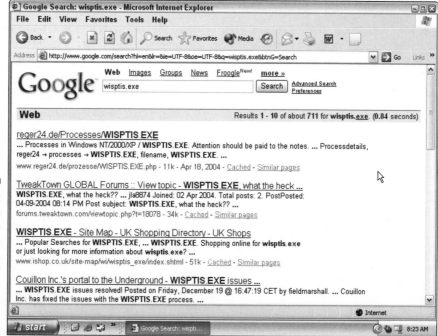

Figure 3-8: You can use Google to search for the names of processes running on your system.

If one of the running processes you search for is not a part of the Windows operating system, but is instead used by a Windows application, add that application name to your installed program list. (If the program is running on your system, that's a pretty good indicator that it is installed on your system.)

Making a Game Plan

Now that you are done looking through your system, grab the lists that you made and set them side by side. Your next task is to compare the program inventory (what you need) against the program list (what you have). Hopefully, everything on your inventory is also listed on your installed program list. If not, you may want to figure out how the program ended up on your inventory. (Perhaps you thought you had something installed but confused your system with a different system in your office.)

In comparing lists, you may discover some programs that you forgot you need. In that case, add those programs to your inventory. The more likely scenario, however, is that your installed program list is much longer than your program inventory.

Unused programs, or those you no longer need, are a prime source of clutter on any computer system. These programs are prime candidates for removal from your system; keep this in mind.

Hold on to the lists you created; they serve you well as you focus on cleaning your Windows system. The remaining chapters in Part II, in fact, rely heavily on these two documents — you may want to keep them close by.

Chapter 4

Making Your Programs Run Faster

Don't you feel special? You're finally taking control of your computing life, grabbing it by the proverbial horns. You have your *program inventory* — a list of what you want on your system — and you have your *installed program list* — what you have on your system already. (If terms like program inventory and installed program list leave you scratching your head, you need to make a quick detour to Chapter 3.)

In all likelihood your program inventory is a subset of your installed program list. Now's the time to focus on the program inventory, as you want to run those programs — and run them well.

This chapter introduces you to different ways to make your installed programs — the ones you care about — run faster than ever before. Your overall computer speed improves as you clean your Windows system, but you can also speed up individual programs.

Common Sense for Programs

An *oxymoron* is two or more words that together form a phrase but otherwise seem to contradict each other. Classic examples include military intelligence, jumbo shrimp, amicable divorce, and Microsoft Works. (Thousands of such examples abound in the wild, grazing peacefully, almost gleefully, on the English language.)

Add to the list *common sense.* Common sense is, more often than not, quite uncommon. With that in mind, I've put together a few common-sense concepts you can follow when trying to speed up your programs under Windows XP. Applying these ideas continues to benefit you as you further scrub your Windows system clean.

Turn off whiz-bang features

People like whiz-bang. They have the same reaction to whizzes and bangs as they do to fireworks on the Fourth of July: "Ohhh! Ahhh!" It makes them feel good about their computer systems.

You're not that way, right? You're more interested in uncluttering your life, cleaning your Windows system, and making things run as smoothly and quickly as possible. You're a pragmatist — keeping your focus razor sharp, ready for a no-nonsense approach to computing.

Right.

We all fall victim to the lure of whiz-bangs once in a while. We like to see our icons displayed in millions of colors, twirl around while waiting for us to click them, and have a cute animated pet see how we move the mouse pointer. These niceties come at a price, however.

The short of it? If you want your programs to run faster, turn off any whiz-bang features you have, unless you absolutely need them. Such features can tax your system and therefore slow it down.

Watch out for networking "gotchas"

If your computer is connected to a network, then you can share information and resources easily with other people. If everything is configured properly, you can easily access information on their machines, and they can access it on yours.

Therein, of course, lies the rub. If your network is set up so that your machine is providing information or resources to others on the network, your system can slow down dramatically during times of peak network usage. The following highlights just a few scenarios where your computer gets sluggish:

- ✔ While your coworkers access files on your system, less CPU time is available for your tasks because your computer is busy servicing the requests of your coworkers.

- ✔ If your system is doing double-duty as the network print server, then you can — and will — see drastic slowdowns as the print jobs are serviced.

✔ On networks, people can deposit information on your system that you have no control over. I'm not talking about viruses (although that could be a concern), but about actually storing files on your system. The trouble with this scenario is twofold:

- All that extra information clutters up your computer, causing it to run slower.

- If the people dropping off stuff aren't terribly tidy information managers, your system can get cluttered in a real hurry. Trying to track down what's safely deleted and what isn't can become a nightmare.

For more information about how to unclutter your network life, see Chapter 19.

Never upgrade unless you have to

"Really? Never upgrade? Wow. But I thought I always needed the latest and greatest version of my software."

No, you don't. My firm conviction is that software vendors (not just Microsoft) want you to always have the latest version of their software. If I were working for a software vendor, I would want you to have our latest software, as well. If you ask vendors why they want you to upgrade, they won't say "So we can enhance our bottom line." Instead, they focus on new features, increased productivity, or fewer problems.

Weren't these the same reasons they gave you for upgrading to the version you currently have? Yep. It's all part of the game — the game to get you to keep upgrading. The problem with upgrades is that they usually include features that you got along just fine without for years, and probably won't use now even though they're included. These add to the software's *bloat*, making it fatter, slower, and more resource-hungry than ever.

When you upgrade software, you run the risk of cluttering up your system with pieces and parts of programs left behind in the upgrade process. Upgrading only when you need to helps minimize this process and make cleaning Windows easier. (I'm not ranting against software companies; they have a right to sell their wares and attempt to convince you that your life is happier, safer, and more fulfilling once you get the latest version of Widget Whacker Deluxe. You just need to look at software differently than how the software companies want you to.)

So when do you *need* to upgrade? You should upgrade at these times:

✔ If you're developing your own products that rely on the newest versions of the software

✔ If you must remain compatible with people or companies using the newer versions

You don't *always* need to upgrade

Case in point: Microsoft Word. (I'm not picking on Word; I'm just using it as an example in thinking about upgrades.) The latest version is Word 2003 and it's sold as part of the Office 2003 suite. I still know people who are using Word 97 with absolutely no decrease in happiness, safety, or prosperity. They skipped the upgrades to Word 2000, Word 2002, and now Word 2003, and in the process saved well over a thousand dollars. The fact of the matter is, they were able to do everything they wanted using the older version of Word: so why upgrade?

But never, never, never, (did I say never?) upgrade unless you have to. Make sure you have a solidly thought-out reason for upgrading before you plunk down your hard-earned cash.

Speeding up specific software

Entire books could be written about how to speed up individual software programs. Don't let the plethora of available information stop you from reading through the next few sections, particularly if you have some of this software installed on your system.

Software travels in packs, never alone. When you install software on your system, additional "helpful" programs are often installed along with the primary application. These additional programs can affect the speed at which your computer works, and they can clutter up your system. Be alert to what is really installed on your system!

Microsoft Office

If you have Office 97 installed on your system, chances are good that a utility program called Find Fast is also installed on your system. This program allows Office applications to find files a bit faster, but it does this by performing background indexing of the files on your hard drive. The downside is that at times the background work done by Find Fast can bring your system to its knees.

The only solution is to remove Find Fast completely. (Most people never need the program anyway.) To remove it from your system, perform the following general tasks:

1. **Delete the Find Fast shortcut from the Startup folder.**

   Locating the Startup folders is discussed in Chapter 3.

2. **Double-click the Find Fast icon in the Control Panel and delete any indexes listed there.**

3. **Restart your computer and search for a file named findfast.cpl.**

   Only one of these should be on your hard drive; the file is the Control Panel applet for the program. Feel free to delete it, but only after you complete Step 2.

Just three short tasks and you're on your way to a leaner, meaner machine. You should notice an immediate improvement in your system's responsiveness.

All recent versions of Office (Office 97, 2000, 2002, and 2003) add another icon called Windows Office to your Start folders. No, this program doesn't start Office itself, but it spends a bit of time initializing different parts of your system so they work quicker with Office. The shortcut runs a program technically called the Office Startup Assistant. The program takes up some resources, but isn't the resource hog that Find Fast is. If you use Office only sparingly (once a day or less often), then feel free to remove the shortcut from your Startup folders.

Another tip is to check how you have your Office applications configured:

- ✔ **Make sure that the Fast Save feature in Word is not turned on.** With this feature on, your individual documents save slower in the long run and you risk corrupting the documents. In Word, choose Tools⇨Options and clear the Allow Fast Saves check box on the Save tab.

- ✔ **Make sure to minimize the number of external links in an Excel workbook or a Word document.** *External links* (links to resources outside of the workbook or document) are refreshed whenever you open the workbook or document, slowing down how quickly you can start using the data.

- ✔ **Don't save your data on floppies.** Their limited space makes them poor candidates for storing files and they're much slower and less reliable than hard drives.

- ✔ **Turn off the graphics display in your document or workbook.** You probably won't want to do this in PowerPoint, as the graphics are typically integral to your presentation. In Word, you choose Tools⇨Options and select the Picture Placeholders check box on the View tab. In Excel, you choose Tools⇨Options and select the Show Placeholders check box on the View tab.

Microsoft Outlook

I know, I know . . . Outlook is technically part of Microsoft Office, so you were expecting it in the previous section. Ha! Fooled you.

Outlook has become a staple on many people's computers, running everything from appointment calendars to task lists, all while also handling e-mail. Because it does so much, Outlook is a real resource hog. One feature of Outlook that is especially piggy deserves some close scrutiny: Journaling.

For the VBA macro writer . . .

Macros are used to perform repetitive tasks quickly so that you don't have to do them manually. As the macro completes each of its tasks, the program (such as Word or Excel) updates the screen to reflect the changes made by the macro. Because the macro is working so quickly, this updating often makes the screen look like it's gone haywire. You can speed up the macros by turning off screen updating. Just add the following line at the beginning of the macro:

```
Application.ScreenUpdating =
    False
```

After your macro is complete, set the ScreenUpdating property to True.

When the Journal feature is turned on, an Outlook journal entry is written every time you make changes to files in other Office applications, such as Word and Excel. Unless you really, really need this feature, turn it off. For most people, it does nothing except slow down how they use the system, bogs down applications, and sucks up hard drive space.

In Office 97, journaling is turned on by default. In later versions of Outlook, journaling is turned off by default, but the feature could inadvertently get turned on (by other users, macros, gremlins, and so on). To make sure that journaling is disabled, follow these steps:

1. **Within Outlook, choose Tools⇨Options.**

   Outlook displays the Options dialog box.

2. **If you're using Outlook 97, display the Journal tab. If you're using a later version of Outlook, display the Preferences tab and click the Journal Options button.**

   The Journal Options dialog box appears.

3. **Clear the check boxes in the Also Record Files From area of the dialog box.**

4. **Close all the open dialog boxes.**

Quicken

All the versions of Quicken that I've seen have a feature called Billminder. This feature is installed automatically when you install Quicken. It runs every time you start your computer, whether you plan to work with Quicken or not.

Billminder reminds you of upcoming bills and obligations, with an eye toward helping you remember the ways in which you have spent your money. Do you need it? You can make up your own mind, but most people I know of don't use Billminder, which means it uses resources that are best freed up for other purposes.

Try this to make sure that Billminder doesn't run every time you start Windows:

1. **Choose Start➪All Programs➪Quicken.**

   You should see a submenu that lists Quicken-related programs.

2. **Choose Billminder.**

   The Billminder program starts up, which you can see in Figure 4-1.

3. **In Billminder, click Options to display the Billminder Options dialog box.**

4. **Clear the Enable Billminder on Windows Startup check box and click OK.**

5. **Exit Billminder.**

In some versions of Billminder, these steps may not work as noted. In that case, you can simply open the Startup folders on your system and delete the Billminder icon.

The biggest thing you can do to increase Quicken's speed is to decrease the size of the Quicken data file. If you're a long-time Quicken user, your files probably still contain a bunch of old data. This info is great for those times you want to get misty-eyed over the good old days, but it really is an anchor when trying to slice and dice the current data.

Figure 4-1:
Not many
people need
Billminder,
but by
default
it runs
whenever
Windows
starts.

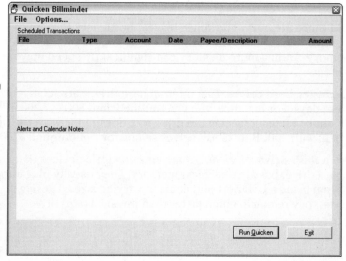

Use Quicken's Copy File feature to move part of your data file into a separate data file. The feature allows you to specify a date range for items you want moved. More information on the Copy File feature is available in the online Help system for Quicken.

Speeding Up Access to Large Data Files

Have you ever worked with word processing documents that are 1,600 or more pages? How about spreadsheets with 10,000 rows of formulas? Or databases with 35MB of data?

Computers have made it possible to amass huge quantities of data, and sometimes even process it! (Just finding what I want in an avalanche of data is my biggest stumbling block in processing.) If you're running programs that process huge data files, you'll find the next few sections helpful. They outline some specific things you can do to make your system run faster.

Change your hardware

I get a bit tired of people who tell me that the answer to life, the universe, and everything is to get new hardware. (In reality, the answer is 42.) After some investigation I typically find that those people either (a) have no concept of money or (b) have a vested interest in selling the hardware. Drives me crazy.

Buying new hardware is *not* the answer to every problem, but it can help alleviate some problems, such as dealing with large amounts of data. I further discuss new hardware in Chapter 17.

- ✔ **Add more memory.** The single biggest bottleneck in many Windows systems — especially those that process large amounts of data — is memory. Adding more memory can significantly speed up your overall system.

- ✔ **Use faster hard drives.** Fast internal hard drives are relatively cheap these days. For instance, you can routinely find 80GB, 7,200 RPM drives for under $100. Increasing the drive size doesn't increase the price that much, with 200GB to 250GB drives selling for right around $200.

- ✔ **Use a flash drive.** *Flash drives* are amazing little devices that act like a hard drive, but are really fast memory. They usually plug into your system using a USB port and come in varying sizes. Lacking mechanical parts, they're much, much faster than physical hard drives.

One sure sign that more memory or a larger hard drive would be helpful is when your system spends a lot of time accessing your hard drive. Most systems have a disk-access LED on the front of the computer case. Watch it sometime, particularly as you switch from one program to another. If you notice a response lag and the LED flashes for extended periods of time, it means that Windows is swapping memory out to the hard drive to make room for the program you're switching to. Adding memory reduces the need for swapping, and a faster hard drive makes any necessary swapping faster.

Reconfigure your data

If adding memory or changing your hard drives is not a viable solution, you may want to rethink how you use the data within your programs:

- ✔ If your e-mail client is keeping track of thousands of old messages, archiving a few of them (thereby reducing the work that the client has to do) may be worth your time.

- ✔ If you're using a database program for your customer management tasks, you may want to export your old customer data into a separate database file. That way, as you're working with newer data, your system won't be slowed down because of the older, unused data.

Your ability to reconfigure your data depends, of course, on your needs and your software's capabilities. You should evaluate your needs to determine whether reconfiguration is viable, and you should check your software to see whether exporting or archiving is available.

Reconfigure your program

When companies write programs, they do so with a target audience in mind. The company has to make certain assumptions about the software user, such as the type of machine being used, the condition of data, the way the user works, and so on.

One assumption concerns the size of data files you're using with the software. Most software is written with the expectation of using small- to medium-sized files. If you start using larger data files and notice that the software becomes sluggish, you need to examine different configuration settings for your software. (I'm talking configuration within the software itself, not within Windows.)

As an example, some software has an automatic backup or autosave feature. This is a great safety feature to have, depending on the value of the data you're using. The feature may be set up so that every five minutes or so your data is automatically saved. The problem creeps in if you're using such a feature with large files. If saving a file takes 30 seconds or longer, then frequent saving can disrupt your workflow. You may want to reconfigure the software so that it forces a save less frequently or (if you're well-disciplined) not at all.

Programs commonly save temporary files to your hard drive while you're working within them. If the temporary files are related to the size of your main data file, then your system may fill up with temporary files and cause problems — particularly if the software doesn't properly delete the files. (See Chapter 6 for more information on identifying and getting rid of temporary files.) If possible, you may want to configure your software so that it saves its temporary files in a set location. This makes getting rid of the temporary files a breeze.

Are We Compatible?

Do you have a program on your program inventory that doesn't appear on your installed program list? Is the program on your wish list but not installed because it won't run under Windows XP? Well, Bucko, fasten your seat belt because I'm gonna tell you how you can make that program run just fine under XP! (Wow. This is exciting.)

In the past, every new version of Windows meant more and more programs had to be put out to pasture — they just wouldn't work with the new versions of Windows. As a partial solution to that problem, XP introduced something euphemistically called the Windows Application Compatibility mode. Despite the totally geeky name, the feature is really very cool.

Suppose that you try to install a program under XP, or you did an upgrade to XP and a previously installed program stopped working correctly. Chances are good that the program worked fine under a previous version of Windows, but under XP it simply goes on a permanent vacation. (Perhaps it doesn't really go on vacation, but simply acts stupid all of a sudden.)

To try to correct this situation, here's what you need to do:

1. **Right-click the program icon that you want to fix and choose Properties from the Context menu.**

   Make sure you right-click the actual program icon, not a shortcut to the program. To find the program icon, you may have to browse through your hard drive. If you're trying to run an installation program for an application, locate and right-click the icon for the setup or install program.

   Windows displays the program's Properties dialog box. You should make sure the Compatibility tab is displayed, as shown in Figure 4-2.

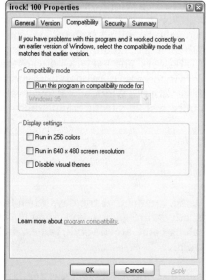

Figure 4-2:
The Compatibility tab
is something
that's easy
to miss,
unless you
know where
to find it.

2. **Select the Run This Program in Compatibility Mode For check box.**

   When you click the check box, the drop-down list under the check box becomes active.

3. **Using the drop-down list, select a version of Windows with which you know the program works.**

   You can choose from Windows 95, Windows 98/Windows Me, Windows NT 4, and Windows 2000. If you don't know which one to choose, pick the version of Windows that you had before you upgraded to XP or refer to the system requirements on the program's software package.

4. **If desired, make other selections in the dialog box.**

   You can choose to limit the display settings or modify the input settings. These changes are typically only necessary for very old programs or for some games.

5. **Click OK.**

6. **Double-click the program icon to run the program.**

   Windows XP sets up a virtual environment that closely matches the version of Windows you specified in Step 3. Your program should work fine, and it'll probably run even faster than it used to in the old version of Windows.

Not all programs are appropriate to use in a Windows XP environment, even in a Windows Application Compatibility mode. Some programs — particularly system tools — are designed for specific operating systems and can cause problems for you even if you run them in a compatibility mode. Programs such as anti-virus software, firewalls, CD burners, and backup software that are not designed specifically to work with Windows XP may operate at such a low level that they're essentially incompatible with the Windows XP low-level routines. Programs such as these should not be installed using compatibility mode.

Playing Games

At the risk of seriously dating myself, I remember the days when the ruling games on PCs were Scott Adams' adventure games. You could fit the whole thing on a single diskette. Then along came arcade-style games, including the one that changed everything: Doom.

Now, computer game publishers hire scriptwriters, songwriters, orchestras, and actors. It isn't unusual for a computer game to require 10 CDs or to ship on a DVD.

Games also push computer systems to the limits. Realistic scenery, 3D images, great music, and lots of special effects all tax a system. If you walk into a computer store, you find computer systems optimized for computer games. (The price is also optimized — all that horsepower doesn't come cheap.)

Eliminate most clutter immediately

Kids and computers seem to be drawn to each other. (Perhaps they're mutually magnetic.) One thing that kids are prone to do is to install games on a computer. If this drives you nuts, you can do one of several things:

✔ **Set rules for installing software.** If you paid for the computer, you own it. Be authoritarian and set rules about what can be installed and how that should happen.

✔ **Limit computer use.** The chances of your children installing rogue programs increases exponentially relative to your proximity to the computer. If you set guidelines for when the computer can be used, you help safeguard your programs and your data.

✔ **Lock your computer.** If you're away from your computer for a time and you want to lock it, press the Windows key+L. (Pretty cool, huh?)

✔ **Get a computer for the kids.** That way if they want to muck up their computer, it won't affect yours in the least.

Setting ground rules and taking sensible precautions can help you manage what's on your machine, thereby reducing clutter and the chance of your system getting messed up.

What does that have to do with clutter? Game players tend to gravitate around a limited number of games, and the games tend to suck up lots of time. The game publishers know this, so some of them assume their particular game is the only one running on your system. When a game (or any program, for that matter) thinks it has complete run of a system, the upshot is that installing the game can cause problems when running other software.

If you have multiple game players in the house and everyone is sharing the same system, games also can cause conflicts with each other. Plus, you may have one gamer who likes to install every new game that comes along, play for a couple of days, and then install the next new game. Immediate clutter and a potential mess.

These tips help your games run faster and with fewer problems:

- ✔ **Install only the games you actually play.** Don't use your system as a repository of every game ever published, thinking you'll get to them someday.

- ✔ **Make sure you have a fast CD-ROM drive.** Many games don't install everything they need on your hard drive; they reference the CD-ROM quite often. Make sure you have a fast one, with a large buffer, so you can get the performance you need.

- ✔ **Make sure you have a DVD drive.** Some games — particularly the larger and more elaborate ones — are being distributed on DVD. Make sure you have one installed. (Besides, you can watch movies if you get tired of games.)

- ✔ **Install your game on a fast hard drive.** One designed for multimedia use should work just fine. Also, install the game on a different drive than the one on which you installed Windows. That way, operating system requests that require hard drive access won't interrupt what the game hard drive is doing.

- ✔ **Get a video card optimized for games.** Some games require specific capabilities in your video card, so make sure you check that out as well.

- ✔ **Install the proper video drivers for your video card and for Windows XP.** Some games require specific technologies, such as OpenGL. These technologies are typically implemented through the video driver, not through Windows. Installing the proper video driver for your needs solves lots of potential game problems.

That should do it. You can try out lots of other things, but these most often affect the speed at which your games operate.

Pushing the Envelope: Multimedia Editing Programs

As Olivia Newton John might have said (had her singing career not tanked prior to the digital revolution), "I wanna get digital, let's get into digital." Everything these days is digital — digital video cameras, digital still-shot cameras, digital audio recorders, digital mixers, and so on.

All that digital equipment stores tons of information and can plug into your computer. Everyone wants to store, edit, play, and share all that digital information. New software is appearing all the time, promising the ability to slice and dice multimedia information 12 ways to Sunday.

The problem with having all that digital information on your computer, of course, is that it is huge, huge, huge! I'm not talking about popularity, but about the size of the files created for digital multimedia. Many things can affect the size of multimedia files, including quality, resolution, and audio or video speed. CD-quality audio can take 50KB of disk space per second. Video throws the storage needs through the roof: every second of video can require 6MB of file space. That is huge!

Say that you shoot two hours of digital video of your parents' 50th anniversary. You get everything — the grand entrance, the arrival of the siblings, the arrival of your aunts and uncles, the arguments, the food fight. Hmmm... Let's see; that's 7,200 seconds, or anywhere from 36 to 44GB of data. Ack! Just for a single event!

As you can imagine, programs that allow you to fold, spindle, mutilate, and otherwise process such huge files can place quite the burden on your computer system. Top-notch programs push the envelope, trying to squeeze all the performance out of your system that they can.

The following points are the best two ways to speed up those programs:

- **Make sure you have lots and lots and lots of RAM in your computer.** The more memory you can install, the better. If your motherboard can handle it, install 1GB or more of RAM. Windows XP can handle the added memory just fine, and the addition helps with editing Mom and Dad's anniversary party, so it doesn't show when Uncle Joe showed up with his walker and his surprise twentysomething bride.

- **Make sure you're using the fastest video card you can, along with a fast hard drive designed for multimedia use.** Yes, they do make hard drives just for multimedia use. If you have one of these babies, you won't be sorry when it comes to doing gymnastics with gigabytes of data.

Chapter 5

Getting Rid of Old Programs

● ●

● ●

Creating your *program inventory* — those programs that you need to have on your system — is the focus of Chapter 3. In Chapter 4, I show you how to make your programs run faster. In this chapter, you focus on the programs you want to get *off* your system. Unneeded and unwanted programs should be removed and tossed into the dustbin of personal computing history, and you're about to discover several ways you can do that.

Identifying Candidates for Removal

"Off with their heads!" Wouldn't it be cool if you could get rid of unwanted programs with as much ease as the Queen of Hearts got rid of unruly subjects in *Alice's Adventures in Wonderland?* You could swagger around, giving orders all day long with the assurance that your every whim would be carried out at your very decree. (And you could attend some very interesting croquet matches.)

It's not that easy in the Windows world. Before you can behead a program, you have to track it down, figure out the best way to axe it, and then make it happen. Unlike the decree-wielding Queen of Hearts, you serve as investigator, judge, jury, and executioner — you don't just give the orders: You have to do all the work yourself, too.

So, put down your scepter for a moment and grab your investigator's notebook. You're going for a trek that leads you to all the places you can identify different programs that need to be removed.

Windows security at its best

Depending on how you have your Windows XP system set up, you may run into what I call the *mother-hen security feature* when you try to display the Program Files folder. Like a busybody mother hen, Windows refuses to show you the contents of your C: drive and then of your Programs Folder. Instead, you see this ominous message:

```
These files are hidden. This
   folder contains files that
   keep your system working
   properly. You should not
   modify its contents.
```

Ignore the clucking mother hen. Click the Show the Contents of this Folder link and the warning goes away, never to return for that particular drive or folder. Instead, you're greeted with the contents you wanted to see in the first place.

Unused programs you installed

The first thing to check are programs that you once installed, but no longer need. In Chapter 3 you put together your program inventory and your installed program list. If you compare the two, you may see some programs on the installed program list that don't appear on the program inventory. Highlight these differences; these programs are prime candidates for removal.

If you didn't put together an installed program list and a program inventory, then you have a bit more work to do. You need to go through all the programs on your system — the ones you previously installed — and figure out which ones you no longer need. Jot down the program names on a piece of paper so that you know what to delete.

Preinstalled software

One of the things (among many) that drives me crazy is *preloaded software*. You buy a computer from Dell, Gateway, or any number of other retailers, and they throw in a boatload of software, already installed on the computer. The problem is that most of the software is of very little value. Sometimes all of the software is of no value. It's easy to fill up a computer with no-value software and tout what a great deal I'm getting. Hogwash!

Did your computer come with lots of software preinstalled? If so, I'll bet you don't use most of it. Take a look at what was installed when you got your system and add the unused software to your list of removal targets. Don't worry; removing preinstalled software won't make your computer stop working, void your warranty, or subject you to criminal prosecution. (Unlike that stupid little tag on mattresses that I'm still scared to remove.)

Stuff you find in the Program Files folder

Most mild-mannered programs (not to be confused with those arrogant programs that think they own your computer) are polite enough to install themselves in your Program Files folder. That's pretty cool, really — that means you can poke around in the folder and discover information about programs installed on your system.

On most systems, the Program Files folder is accessible from the C: drive. Just open the C: drive and double-click the Program Files folder. Voilá! You have found the secret clubhouse of all your programs. (The mild-mannered ones, at least.) Figure 5-1 shows an example of a typical Program Files folder.

Most of the folders in the Program Files folder are named after either the program that created the folder (such as Microsoft Money) or the software company that publishes the software that created the folder (such as Intuit or Adobe).

Take some time to browse through the different folders. See if you can figure out which software program installed each folder. If you find software you want to remove, write the program name on your list of deletion targets.

Don't delete anything in the Program Files folder quite yet. Deleting items can sometimes cause unintended problems and should only be a last resort. A little later in this chapter you find out when it's okay to delete things in the Program Files folder.

Figure 5-1:
Program
Files
contains
folders
for many
programs
on your
system.

Four Ways to Remove Unwanted Programs

An old saying states "all roads lead to Rome." This was first uttered by an Italian peasant who didn't have a clue concerning geographic realities. Since that fateful day when the peasant misled an unsuspecting traveler, others have translated this saying to mean that you can reach the same goal multiple ways.

So it is with removing programs: You can get them off your system several ways. The methods follow in order of preference:

1. Use the application's uninstall command.

2. Use the Windows Control Panel.

3. Use third-party removal software.

4. Use brute force to wrench it from your system.

I recommend that you try each method, beginning with the first and moving toward the last. The best method to use for removing programs is the one that is successful for you, with the least amount of work necessary. With that in mind, consider the following sections where I discuss each of these removal methods.

An application's uninstall command

Most well-behaved programs provide a way to get themselves off your computer with almost as much ease as you put them on. You normally won't find the uninstall command in any of the application's menus, but as a separate program, installed at the same time that you installed the application.

To remove a program by using its uninstall command, follow these steps:

1. **Choose Start⇨All Programs and navigate through the menu until you locate your program's menu option.**

   When you open the submenu that actually contains the options for the program, you often see other choices as well. See Figure 5-2.

2. **Examine the choices available; one of them should clearly be marked as an uninstall program.**

3. **Run the uninstall program and follow the presented instructions.**

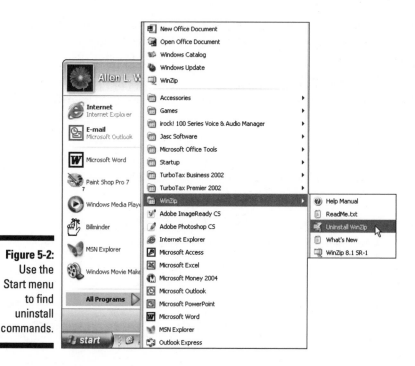

Figure 5-2:
Use the
Start menu
to find
uninstall
commands.

Even if your program has an uninstall command, it might not have been added to the Start menu. If you can locate the program folder for the application (quite possibly in the Program Files folder), then you may find an uninstall program in it. Do a little bit of snooping in Program Files, using the techniques described in the previous section, to find out if this is the case. You can then run the uninstall program from wherever you find it.

Some programs aren't as accommodating in getting themselves booted from your system. For instance, the program may require you to visit a Web site or jump through some other hoop in order to remove the program. The program's Help file is a good place to check for a nonstandard removal method. A section there may talk about how to remove the program. A Readme file may have been installed on your system when you first installed the program. Refer to Figure 5-2 to see a Readme file called ReadMe.txt in the WinZip menu folder. If you open the Readme file, you may discover instructions on how to remove the program.

The Add or Remove Programs applet in the Control Panel

The Control Panel is the nerve center of Windows XP and so it allows you to change all sorts of configuration settings. The Control Panel also includes an applet that allows you to add or remove programs from your system. This applet, appropriately enough, is called Add or Remove Programs. (I've often wondered how Microsoft comes up with such catchy program names.)

If you open the Control Panel and double-click the Add or Remove Programs applet, a unique dialog box lists the installed programs. See Figure 5-3.

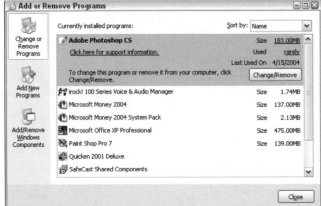

Figure 5-3:
Windows
keeps track
of the
programs
installed on
your system.

You should be aware that the Add or Remove Programs dialog box doesn't necessarily list all the programs installed on your system, and it may include programs that you already removed from your system. This occurs because the dialog box lists only programs registered in a specific area of the Registry. If during installation a program doesn't properly inform the Registry of its existence, then it won't show up in the list. Likewise, if an uninstall program doesn't clean up the Registry, or you remove a program manually without editing the Registry, then the program may still show up in the list. I further discuss the Registry a little later in this chapter and also in Chapter 20.

To remove a program, scroll through the list of those available until you find the program you want removed. When you click the program name, its entry expands to show some additional information, as well as a few buttons whose appearance depends on the program itself:

✔ **Change:** Click this button to make changes to the program, such as adding or removing specific features.

✔ **Remove:** Click this button to uninstall the program.

✔ **Change/Remove:** Some programs combine changing and removing into the same program, and this button accesses that program.

Programs have a tendency to travel in packs. When you remove one, make sure you look for others that may be related to that program. If you find ancillary programs in the list, delete them right after you delete the main program.

Third-party software

Ah, the sweet smell of capitalism at work! Isn't it wonderful that you can find a piece of software to fulfill almost every perceived need? You can find software for everything from keeping track of your rubber-band collection to modifying desktop icons to hacking into NSA supercomputers.

With all that variety to choose from, you might be wondering if anyone has developed software that removes unruly software from your system. The answer is a resounding "Yes!" Several different software packages on the market were created for this very purpose. Two that seem to work especially well are Spring Cleaning and Your Uninstaller!:

- ✔ **Spring Cleaning:** This is a general system cleaning utility, published by Aladdin Systems (www.aladdinsys.com/win/springcleaning/). One of the program's functions is to remove programs from your system. It can also back them up or move them to another computer, if you desire.

  All you need to do is start the software and choose the UninstallApps option. You can then select the application you want to remove, and make it go away. One of the really nice things about Spring Cleaning is that when it is through, it provides an activity report of what it did. This is helpful if you later have problems and want to track down the files deleted from your system.

- ✔ **Your Uninstaller!:** Extremely easy to use, this software specifically focuses on removing programs from your system. Published by URSoft, Inc. (www.ursoftware.com), the program uses a familiar interface that allows you to drag and drop a program to remove it (sort of like dragging a file to the Recycle Bin).

  Your Uninstaller! does a great job of cleaning programs out of the Registry. (Some uninstallers aren't too good about taking care of this detail.) The result is less clutter and a svelte system.

The brute-force method

In the old days of computing, things were different. (Let me hobble over to my rocking chair for a moment. Hand me that shawl, will you, son?) When you installed a program under the DOS system it went into a single folder, and life was wonderful. If you needed to delete the program, you just deleted the directory. Everything related to the program was deleted from your system in one swoop.

Not so any more. Today, only rarely are programs installed in a single place on your hard drive. Instead, installation programs act like that little spreader device on the back of salt trucks — the salt comes down the chute, hits the rotating blade, and is spread everywhere. Modern installation programs often place program pieces not only in the program directory, but also in your system folder, your profile folder, a drivers folder, and various other places. In addition, programs add things to the Registry, that central repository of all things most important to Windowsdom.

Thus, to delete a modern program from a Windows system involves two very important steps:

1. **Locate the files that make it work.**

2. **Clean up the Registry.**

The brute-force removal method should be the last way that you try to remove programs. Often programs install pieces of themselves in multiple places on your hard drive. Just because you delete the main program file and remove it from the Registry does not mean that all the far-flung pieces and parts have been removed. The orphan pieces likely won't interfere with the operation of your other programs, but they do — over time — clutter up your hard drive and occupy disk space. Therefore, brute-force removal involves a third step: doing away with the bits and pieces.

Locating and removing the program

Earlier in the chapter I show you around the Program Files folder. This folder is the traditional place where programs are installed on a Windows system. In this section I send you exploring again — this time looking for any folders that obviously belong to the program you want to delete.

To locate an unwanted program and then remove it by brute force, follow these steps:

1. **Right-click shortcuts or menu items and choose Properties.**

   Figure 5-4 shows an example of the Properties dialog box that is displayed. You should be able to see where the shortcuts point.

   Pay particular attention to the Target field. This field normally shows the complete path and program name executed by the shortcut or menu item.

2. **Write down the full path so that you have it after closing the dialog box.**

   Don't waste trees unless you have to. Open a Notepad window and copy the contents of the Target field to the Notepad window. That way you don't have to worry about transcription errors.

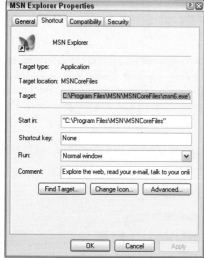

Figure 5-4:
The
Properties
dialog box
can give
clues about
where a
program is
stored.

3. **When you're satisfied that you located the folder containing the program files, open that folder.**

4. **Note in your Notepad window all the program names in that folder.**

   You need those filenames when you clean up the Registry.

5. **Delete the items in the folder that are related to the program you want to remove.**

   If the entire folder is used for the program, delete the entire folder.

   If in doubt concerning what you're about to delete, don't delete it. Instead, move it to a different place on your hard drive or rename it. Doing so allows you to see whether your change makes any difference to Windows. If you run into problems, you can always move back the file or folder or give it its original name.

You've completed the first part of brute-force removal. Continue the process with the steps in the next section.

Cleaning up the Registry

You must clean up the Registry after deleting program files; see the preceding section. The idea is to get rid of all Registry references to the deleted program. You do this by using the Registry Editor to search through the Registry.

Editing the Registry is, by nature, pretty technical. You've no way around it, though. If you're going to remove a program manually (that is, by brute force) from Windows, you must go through the Registry and remove it there, as well. This section talks about how to search for and edit information in the

Registry, but detailed information about cleaning the Registry is in Chapter 20. (Also pay attention to the safety tips about working with the Registry, in Chapters 2 and 20.)

Manually cleaning the Registry in this way is a perilous adventure, but one you can easily complete if you're very careful. Make sure you delete only those things that you're sure should be deleted and (as stated elsewhere in this book) make sure you have a backup of the Registry in case a problem crops up.

Grab the list of programs that you created in the previous section and follow the steps given here:

1. **Choose Run from the Start menu.**

   Windows displays the Run dialog box.

2. **Enter** regedit **in the Open field and click OK.**

   The Registry Editor starts, opening a window like what is shown in Figure 5-5.

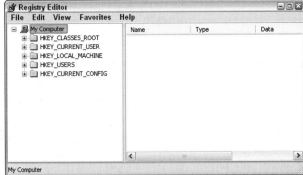

Figure 5-5:
The Registry Editor is a power tool in Windows.

3. **In the left window, collapse the Registry tree by clicking any My Computer subfolder minus signs.**

   The tree may already be collapsed, in which case you're done with this step. When collapsed, the tree should look like what's shown in Figure 5-5.

4. **Select My Computer at the left side of the screen and press Ctrl+F.**

   The Find dialog box is displayed, as shown in Figure 5-6.

5. **In the Find What field, enter the program name you want to search for.**

   Enter the program name from the list you compiled in the previous section. Enter just the program name along with any filename extension, such as .exe, .dll, or the like. Don't enter the full path name for the program. You should also leave the Keys, Values, and Data checkboxes selected in the Find dialog box.

6. **Click Find Next.**

   If the Registry Editor finds a match, it expands the tree in the left window to show where it found the match. It displays the matching data in the right window.

7. **Delete the information located, if appropriate.**

   Before deleting, examine the information, as well as other information in the key where the match was found. You can delete the item by pressing the Delete key.

8. **Press F3 to find the next occurrence of the program name.**

   If the Registry Editor finds a match, it expands the tree in the left window and displays the matching data in the right window.

9. **Repeat Steps 7 and 8 until you find no more program references to delete.**

10. **Repeat Steps 3 through 8 for each program that you listed in the previous section.**

11. **Close the Registry Editor.**

Congratulations! You deserve a break. Take a deep breath and get another cup of coffee before proceeding to the next section, where I describe the final part of brute-force removal. (Relax, it's the easy part.)

Sweeping away loose ends

A good cleaning job is never done. Work, work, work — it never ends! In order to finish up, you have a couple of other things to "sweep up." Specifically, you need to delete any shortcuts — desktop or menu — that point to the programs you just deleted.

> ✔ **To delete a desktop shortcut:** Click the shortcut once (to highlight it) and press Delete. Alternatively, right-click it and choose Delete.
>
> ✔ **To delete a menu item:** Right-click the menu item and choose Delete.

 Deleting a shortcut from the desktop, or removing an option from a menu, does *not* delete the whole program. You've only removed a way of accessing the program, not the program itself.

Eliminating Remnants of Failed Programs

A *failed program* is my name for a program that never did get installed correctly or work properly. Perhaps the failed program is one where you got halfway through the download and the dog yanked your Internet connection from the wall. Or it could be one where you got most of the way through the installation program and it unexpectedly exited. The reasons for failure could be myriad, and all such failures lead to a cluttered system.

If you want to reinstall your failed program, you should have no problem — just start the install process again. (Some install programs are even smart enough to figure out that you completed a partial installation before and overwrite the partial install.)

If you decide that you want to get rid of the failed program, put on your detective's cap and start looking around for what the program added to your system. You can do this in a couple of ways: either look for a log file or, if you can't find the log, manually search for files.

Many installation programs create log files that tell what was done during the installation process. If you can find the log file, you can read it to discover what was done, and then manually undo what was done. (Log files can typically be opened with Notepad or some other text editor.)

Installation log files can be in any number of places. If you downloaded a program to your hard drive prior to installation, the log file could be in the same folder where you placed the downloaded file. If the installation program already created a folder for the program, the log file could also be there. Or, the log file could be in a temporary folder that the install program used. Check the various Temp folders on your hard drive to see if anything is there.

If you cannot locate the log file, do a search for the files by following these steps:

1. **Choose Search from the Start menu.**

   Windows displays the Search Results dialog box.

2. **On the left side of the dialog box, click All Files and Folders.**

   The options on the left side of the dialog box change to reflect your choice. The dialog box should look similar to what is shown in Figure 5-7.

3. **In the All or Part of the File Name field, enter *.*.**

   The asterisk-dot-asterisk notation dates back to the early days of DOS. It is geek shorthand for "find all files."

4. **Click the down-arrow next to When Was It Modified?**

   The options in the left side of the dialog box expand.

5. **Choose the Specify Dates radio button.**

   The controls right under the radio button become active.

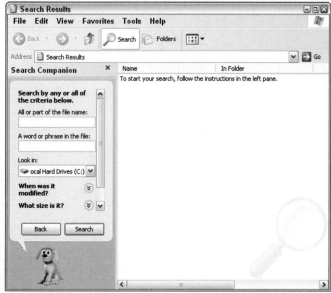

Figure 5-7:
Use the
Search
Results
dialog box
to find files
and folders.

6. Change the From and To dates to today's date.

This step assumes that you tried to install the failed program today. If not, wrack your brain to figure out when the failed installation took place and enter that date for the From and To dates.

7. Click Search.

Windows goes to work, feverishly trying to locate any files that were modified whatever day you specified in Step 6. When the search is completed, take a look at what it located. The results may lead you to the pieces of the failed program that were installed.

After you find the pieces, figure out whether it's okay to delete those pieces. If in doubt, rename or move the pieces to a different folder and restart Windows. If you experience no repercussions from making the change, you can easily delete the files for good.

Chapter 6

Data, Data Everywhere

● ●

In This Chapter

▶ Giving temporary files the boot

▶ Hunting for orphan data

▶ Using the Windows XP Disk Cleanup tool

▶ Dealing with multimedia files

▶ Discarding Recycle Bin contents

● ●

*W*hen I was a kid we lived in the last house on a dead-end street. There was a chain-link fence at the end of the street, and just past the fence was a huge three-story house. All the kids in the neighborhood knew there was a little old hermit lady who lived in the house, along with her cats.

When the lady died, her grown kids came by and started cleaning out the house. I remember watching as they placed a huge refuse container in the yard — the big type that had to be brought in with a semi. I can still envision people standing at the second-story windows, shoveling years of collected debris out the windows and into the refuse container. Magazines, newspapers, cat food cans, and who-knows-what, all shoveled out for days on end.

Those childhood years are gone, but I firmly believe that I have a little old hermit lady living in my computer. She, along with her dozens of cats, collect things and clutter up my hard drive with heavens knows what. My little old lady is a packrat, keeping things for years and years.

Truth be told, you probably have a little old hermit lady living in your computer, as well. How does all that data get on your system? Some say it breeds, on its own, during quiet times on the computer. That's doubtful, although it may seem that way.

Instead, data files collect all on their own. How many programs are on your program inventory? (See Chapter 1.) Each of those programs has its attendant data files, and each of those programs creates additional data files. In addition, you probably download data files and you might have coworkers that send you data files to review or use.

Over time, the collected mass of data can be staggering. It's probably time to open the second-story windows, back up the dumpster, and start shoveling things out. The purpose of this chapter is to help you identify data, determine whether you need it, and then get rid of what you no longer need. Chapter 7 helps you organize and manage the data that's left after your winnowing process.

Finding Temporary Files

Have I told you that programs create data? In case I haven't, let me tell you: Programs create data. Even when you don't think they're creating data, they often are. Large application software is the biggest culprit in file creation. Not only does the software create a document, a workbook, a spreadsheet, or a graphic, it also often creates temporary files.

Temporary files are intended to be just that — temporary. They're intended by their creators to store data for a short time and then be deleted. Sometimes they overstay their welcome, however. They become permanent residents of a hard drive, sitting quietly, not bothering anyone, and occupying space. Sometimes lots of space.

Hard drives they are a-growin'

Hard drives continue to get bigger and bigger. My first hard drive (for my original IBM PC computer) was a 10MB drive. It was the size of a large shoebox, and sat on the desk next to the computer. I thought I was in heaven.

Last week I stopped by my local computer store, and went browsing through the hard drive section. The smallest drive they had was 60GB (6,000 times larger than my first hard drive), and there were 300GB drives available.

Our hard drives continue to collect more data than I could ever have imagined when I was bursting with joy at my original 10MB hard drive. Left unchecked, it's easy to sink like a stone in a sea of data. But getting a bigger hard drive isn't the whole solution to dealing with this sea of data. First you should consider ridding your hard drive — no matter how big it is — of any data you just don't need anymore. That's what this chapter is for. Head to Chapter 17 if you determine that you really do need a bigger hard drive.

Temporary files collect on your system when the program that created them never gets around to deleting them. Perhaps the program was ended abnormally, before it could delete the files. Perhaps the program has a glitch that precluded the deletion. Who knows? The only thing you can be sure of is that the unneeded temporary files are cluttering up your system.

The best approach is to track down temporary files and make sure they're under control. You should search for both folders and specific types of temporary files. Once you find the files, you can determine whether you want to delete the files.

Locating and deleting files from temporary folders

Temporary files cluster together in temporary folders. The folders are temporary; they're just used as repositories for temporary files by individual programs or by the operating system itself. If you locate the temporary folders on your system, you can find a bunch of temporary files for possible deletion.

To locate the most likely candidates for temporary folders and then to delete their contents, shut down any programs you have running and follow these steps:

1. **Choose Search from the Start menu.**

   Windows displays the Search Results dialog box.

2. **At the left side of the dialog box, click All Files and Folders.**

   The options at the left side of the screen change to reflect your choice.

3. **In the All or Part of the File Name box, enter** temp.

   Folders using the letters *temp* in them are the most common repositories of temporary files. You may discover other likely candidates for folder names, depending on the software installed on your system. Don't be afraid to try searching for other folder names, as well (such as those containing the letters *tmp*).

4. **Click the More Advanced Options down arrow.**

5. **Use the Type of File drop-down list to select Folder.**

   This action tells Windows that you only want to find folders. If you don't do this, you get zillions of files returned by the search.

6. **Make sure the first three check boxes under the advanced options area are selected.**

   The three options are Search System Folders, Search Hidden Files, and Folders, and Search Subfolders. If these options are not selected, you may miss quite a few temporary folders on your system.

7. Click Search.

After a short time you should see a number of different folder names start popping up in the search results. You could have only a few results, or you could have many. I had 124 matches on my main system. Figure 6-1 shows the results of a search on a different system. Fewer matches were found on this system (22), but that is still quite a few potential temporary file folders.

Some of the matches aren't applicable, as you get folder names such as Templates or systemprofile. (Both contain the letters *temp*.) Others are clearly designed to hold temporary files, with names such as InstallTemp, WUTemp, or Temporary Internet Files. The bottom line is that each of these folders may contain old files that you can get rid of.

8. Open each potential folder, examine its contents, and decide whether you need to keep the files.

If you decide to delete them, delete only the files inside the folder, not the folder itself. Instead, rename the folder, such as keep temp or keepInstallTemp. Then, when you later restart Windows and use it for a while, you can see whether your system generates any errors. If not, then you know you can fully delete the folder.

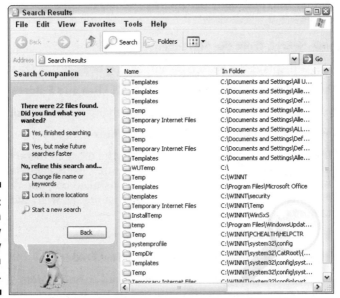

Figure 6-1:
There can be many temporary folders on a system.

Down, boy

Some people love cartoon animation; others think it has no place on a computer desktop. I tend to fall into the latter camp. I think animation is cool, but I hate to have animations foisted on me for the sake of cuteness.

Thus, the cute little dog that appears at the bottom-left side of the Search Results dialog box tends to drive me nuts. I don't want some animated dog sucking up CPU cycles that should be used to find my files as fast as possible.

If Rover drives you crazy, get rid of him. Click Change Preferences, and then choose Without an Animated Screen Character. The dog trots off the screen and you can get down to real work, sans the cuteness.

If you don't like all the extraneous information that shows up in the Search Results dialog box, try doing your search from the command line. Open a command line window (Start⇨All Programs⇨Accessories⇨Command Prompt) and then issue the following two commands, each on its own line:

```
cd\
dir temp.* /ad /s /b
```

The result is a short list of all the directories named Temp on the current drive.

Finding and eliminating specific files

The first step in looking for temporary files is to quit all of the programs you're running. Get out of them all; no exceptions! You never know whether those programs are creating temporary files. If so, you won't be able to delete the files. If you exit the programs, they should get rid of the temporary files with which they were working. The result are fewer "false positives" when doing your search.

Also make sure that no network users are using anything on your system. If files on your system are accessible through the network, those files' users could be creating some of your temporary files. For instance, if a Word document is on your system and someone opens it from a remote system, their Word program creates a number of temporary files on your system while working with the document.

The key to locating temporary files is to recognize that they often have characteristics in common. Use the Windows Search feature to locate the different files on your system that have these characteristics:

- ✔ **.tmp extension:** By far, the most common indicator of a temporary file is one that ends in the .tmp extension. If you see a file called MyDoc.tmp, you are pretty well assured that's a temporary file, ripe for deletion.

- ✔ **Tilde (~) as first character:** Not content with conforming to the .tmp extension standard, some programs create temporary files that begin with a tilde. For instance, you may see a file named ~DF3E05.tmp or ~$Report.doc.

- ✔ **Zero file length:** Sometimes a program may create temporary files and put nothing in them. Since these files have no characters, they have no size. They do nothing but take up space in the folder's directory; feel free to delete them.

- ✔ **.bak extension:** Technically, these files are not temporary. Instead, they're backup files, often created by software. If the file is old, chances are good that the file is no longer needed and you can safely delete.

- ✔ **.old extension:** When programs update some files, they rename the original file with the .old extension. If you see files like setup.old or channel.old, delete them.

After you search for and find files with these characteristics, feel free to delete the files — after determining that it's safe to do so — to free up space on your drive.

Tracking Down Orphan Data

When someone mentions orphans, do you have visions of Annie pop into your head, or perhaps Oliver Twist? Orphan data is hardly musical or literary. Instead, *orphan data* is information stranded on your computer when the program that created it was deleted from your system.

In Chapter 5, you find out how to rid your system of old programs. Perhaps some of those programs left data on your system — data you no longer need. That's what you need to track down and remove.

You track down orphan data using a number of techniques. These techniques aren't magical, but they do take time and they do require that you put on your detective's hat and do a bit of digging.

- ✔ **Look for folders.** Some programs create their own folders for storing data. When you remove programs, the data folders are often left behind, chock full of files. Use Windows Explorer to snoop through your hard drive's folders, with an eye toward locating possible folders you no longer need.

✓ **Look for extensions.** Different programs work with different types of files. These file types are most often identified by the filename extension used for the file. If a program you removed used files with the .xyz extension, then you can easily search for such files. If the program used a more common filename extension (such as .doc, .jpg, .txt, and so on), then you need to not only locate the files, but also determine whether other programs on your system need them.

✓ **Process of elimination.** Account for what you need. Whatever is left is a candidate for removal. Get a printout of the filenames for the data on your drive. Look through the filenames and cross off those with which you're familiar. By process of elimination you can target files.

If you have orphan data and think you may someday need it again, copy it to a long-term storage medium, such as a Zip disk or a CD-ROM. That way you can get it off your system but still access it. Chapter 7 provides guidance for how to archive data you no longer need.

Doing a Disk Cleanup

Windows XP includes a tool that has the express task of helping you clean your hard drive. Bearing the moniker *Disk Cleanup tool,* you might think that it can be helpful in taming your data.

In reality, the Disk Cleanup tool just barely scratches the surface in helping clean up your data. Don't take that as a negative statement of the program — it's not. The tool is a great place to reclaim some easily reclaimable hard-drive space. The most common areas checked by the program follow:

✓ **Temporary Windows files:** As Windows goes about its regular business, it periodically creates temporary files. If all goes well, those files are deleted when no longer needed. If (for some strange reason) they aren't, the Disk Cleanup tool identifies them as targets for deletion.

✓ **Temporary Internet files:** While browsing the Internet, lots of temporary files are automatically downloaded to your system. Getting rid of these can free up disk space, but it can also make accessing your favorite Web sites just a bit slower until the temporary files are again downloaded. (I recommend that you still delete them, however, because the temporary files include many from sites you may never visit again.)

✓ **Temporary program files:** Many programs create temporary files and place them (appropriately enough) in a system folder for temporary files. Disk Cleanup tool targets temporary files in this folder for deletion, but only if they haven't been modified in the past week.

✔ **Downloaded program files:** This doesn't mean the latest shareware you downloaded. It refers to controls and applets that are downloaded as part of the Web pages you visit.

✔ **Recycle Bin:** Delete a file? Bam! It ends up in the Recycle Bin faster than Emeril can chop an onion. If you're the type who forgets to empty the Recycle Bin, the Disk Cleanup tool is pleased to point out your character flaw.

✔ **Setup log files:** While installing various Windows pieces and parts, the system keeps track of what it does through log files. After a time, these files can be safely deleted.

To run Disk Cleanup, follow these steps:

1. **Choose Start⇨All Programs⇨Accessories⇨System Tools⇨Disk Cleanup.**

   • If you have multiple hard drives on your system, you're asked to choose which hard drive to analyze. The Select Drive dialog box appears (shown in Figure 6-2). Go to Step 2.

   • If you have only one hard drive, Disk Cleanup begins running. Eventually the dialog box shown in Figure 6-3 appears. Go to Step 3.

Figure 6-2: Disk Cleanup allows you to choose which drive to analyze.

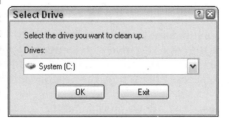

2. **Pick a hard drive and click OK.**

   The Disk Cleanup tool starts looking through the contents of the hard drive you selected, calculating how much space it can reclaim. After a time — the exact amount of time depends on how much data is on your hard drive — you see a dialog box from which you can pick what you want to clean. See Figure 6-3.

3. **Scroll through the Files to Delete list, highlighting items to find out more about them (cursory explanations appear in the Description area) and selecting the check box of each item you want to delete.**

   Pay attention to the disk space at the right side of the dialog box (under the Files to Delete list) — it tells you how much of your disk drive each item occupies.

Figure 6-3:
Choose
what you
want Disk
Cleanup to
work on.

4. **When you're satisfied with your choices, click OK.**

5. **Disk Cleanup asks if you want to proceed; you must click Yes to continue.**

   When you do, the deletions commence. Depending on what you asked Disk Cleanup to do, the actual cleanup can take a few minutes to complete.

TECHNICAL STUFF

Help! Send disk space — quick!

If your insatiable desire for data outstrips your capacity to store that data, you could run out of hard-drive space. When you start running low on disk space, Windows XP gets nervous and warns you about the situation:

✔ When you have only about 200MB of free disk space, a message lets you know. This message appears once during each Windows session.

✔ When you have only about 80MB of free disk space, a similar message is displayed, appearing once every four hours — up to two times per Windows session.

✔ When you have only about 50MB of free disk space, a message appears every five minutes.

✔ When you have only about 10MB of free disk space, Windows automatically calls up your local computer store and orders a new hard drive. The drive is installed by elves while you're asleep.

The last item would be pretty cool, but Windows hasn't quite gotten there — yet. (Microsoft has started hiring elves in preparation for the next version of Windows.) If you see a low disk space message, start getting rid of some files! If you click the message, the Disk Cleanup tool runs automatically.

When you tell Disk Cleanup to delete files, those files are deleted for good. They aren't moved to the Recycle Bin, as typically happens when you delete other files. Make sure you really want to delete the files that Disk Cleanup is proposing to delete.

If you want to use Disk Cleanup a lot and you don't want to traverse so many menu choices, just choose Start⇨Run and run the cleanmgr program.

Finding and Eliminating Duplicate Data

Duplicate duplicate data data can can be be a a problem problem on on any any system system. One of the problems with data is that, over time, you can end up with multiple copies of the same file on your system. It's easy to do:

> ✔ You copy a file, instead of moving it, from one drive to another.
>
> ✔ You create a copy with intentions of later deleting it, but forget to do so.
>
> ✔ You download a file, give it one name, and then download it later under a different name (same file; different name).

On my system (and I suspect on yours), it's particularly easy to end up with multiple copies of graphics files, audio files, and database files. Unfortunately, the tools that come with Windows don't provide an easy way to find duplicate files. You can compare file sizes of graphics or audio files, but this is a very tedious task.

Instead, I recommend that you turn to a third-party software program to help track down duplicate files. Finding duplicate files normally isn't a task relegated to a standalone program. Instead, the task is most often a feature in a larger utility application.

Anytime you start deleting a bunch of files (as is the case when you search for and remove duplicates), you should have a current backup of your system stored on removable media (such as discs). If you mistakenly delete a file you should not have deleted, you can use the backup to restore it. To minimize the chances of needing the backup, carefully examine any file you're about to delete to ensure it is something that really should be deleted.

A number of programs on the market include the capability to find and flag possible duplicate files. One such program that works exceptionally well is System Mechanic. This program is available as a download from Iolo Industries, at `www.iolo.com`. (You can download an evaluation version that is good for 30 days, after which time you need to register the copy and pay a nominal fee to continue using it. Trust me — you want to register your copy.)

To find duplicate files with System Mechanic, follow these steps:

1. **Start System Mechanic by choosing Start⇨All Programs⇨System Mechanic 4⇨Start System Mechanic 4.**

   The main screen appears (see Figure 6-4).

2. **Click Eliminate Duplicate Files.**

   System Mechanic allows you to search through the files on any drive. By default, System Mechanic looks for same-size files that were created on the same date and time. Depending on the number of files on the chosen drive, System Mechanic can take quite a while to figure out potential duplicates. If you have a cluttered drive, you may want to run the program over your lunch hour or while you're in a meeting.

   When the program is done searching, you see a list of potential duplicate files like that shown in Figure 6-5.

   It's not unusual for System Mechanic to find hundreds, if not thousands, of potential duplicate files.

3. **Go through the files presented and determine whether they should be deleted.**

4. **If you identify a file you want to delete, select the file and click Remove.**

   System Mechanic asks you to make sure you really want to delete the file.

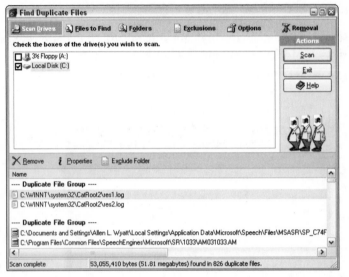

Figure 6-5:
Potential
duplicate
files are
listed at the
bottom of
the window.

 Remember that two files with the same size and creation date are not necessarily duplicates. The files could contain different information. Carefully examine potential duplicate files before actually deleting any of them.

A good duplicate-finding utility (such as System Mechanic) allows you to add files to an exclusion list. This allows you to tailor the program to your needs so that in the future it doesn't display the excluded files again. This can make future sessions faster and easier to work through.

What to Do with Multimedia Files

As I discuss in Chapter 4, multimedia files can be huge. Because of their size, multimedia files present a special problem when it comes to storage needs.

If you're working with multimedia files, consider these ideas for handling the amount of data you're faced with:

✔ **Get a new hard drive.** You can easily add a new hard drive to your system. Better, you can get a huge-capacity hard drive designed for multimedia use. Place your files on that drive so they're accessible as quickly as possible.

✔ **Archive often.** When you're done with an audio or video file, get it off your hard drive and onto a longer-term storage medium, such as a CD-ROM or DVD. (Chapter 7 focuses on how to archive information.)

✔ **Be selective about what you keep.** Keep your original and final files (the ones you slaved on for weeks), but you should consider getting rid of anything in between. Different versions of the same file are prime candidates for removal.

✔ **Get illegal files off your system.** Audio and video file swapping still enjoy a thriving underground. Some of this content is illegal. If you have any question about the files, get them off your system completely. Some swapping software makes your multimedia files automatically available to others, which means that the attorneys for the RIAA can locate the files and press charges. Trust me — you don't want the pain of a lawsuit.

Empty the Recycle Bin Often

When you use the Disk Cleanup tool described earlier in this chapter, it proposes to delete the files in your Recycle Bin. Many people forget they have data there. When you delete files and other objects from Windows, those things are normally stored in the Recycle Bin.

To see what's in your Recycle Bin and then to delete files from it, follow these steps:

1. **Double-click the Recycle Bin icon on your desktop.**

   A standard folder window opens and you can see the last gazillion files you deleted. Remember that everything in your Recycle Bin is still occupying space on your hard drive. It's a good idea to regularly empty the Recycle Bin.

2. **Select one file and press the Delete key to delete files individually.**

   Choose File⇨Empty Recycle Bin to delete all the files in the bin. I prefer to periodically right-click the Recycle Bin icon and choose Empty Recycle Bin because it's quick and easy.

After you empty the Recycle Bin (or delete an item from it), it's gone for good. If you have any question about actually deleting a file from the Recycle Bin, restore the file and move it to a different place on your hard drive for a short time. If everything works out and you actually want to delete it, you can then do so.

Some third-party system software programs, such as anti-virus software, may set up their own Recycle Bin, in addition to the Windows Recycle Bin. You should check the documentation that came with your software to see if this is the case. If so, make sure you periodically check that Recycle Bin and empty it, as well as the primary one.

Resizing the Recycle Bin

The Recycle Bin is a flexible place, willing to enlarge itself, as necessary, to accept your recently deleted files. By default, the space allocated by Windows for the Recycle Bin is up to ten percent of your hard-drive space. If you think about it, that's a ton of space.

Say you have an 80GB drive (not uncommon in today's computing environments). That means that the Recycle Bin can possibly occupy up to 8GB of your drive. That could be a huge number of files and is probably more than you would ever need.

The Recycle Bin is constructed so that it keeps whatever ends up there until you manually delete it (or until the allocated disk space fills up). If the disk space fills up, then the oldest files in the Recycle Bin are deleted to make way for the newer items. If you have 8GB (or more) set aside for the Recycle Bin, the sheer size of the allocated area means you're wasting a lot of disk space.

The solution is to change the amount of disk space allocated to the Recycle Bin:

1. **Right-click the Recycle Bin icon and choose Properties.**

Windows displays the Properties dialog box for the Recycle Bin. The dialog box contains a tab named Global and one tab for each system drive.

2. **On the Global tab, select the Use One Setting for All Drives option.**

You can configure your drives independently, but most people have no need to.

3. **Use the slider to specify a smaller percentage of your hard drive for Recycle Bin space.**

If you have a large drive or several large drives, consider setting the slider as low as one percent. (Remember that one percent of 80GB is 800MB. That's still a large block of disk space for the Recycle Bin.)

4. **Click OK.**

How does resizing the Recycle Bin help unclutter your system? Simple: When Windows doesn't need to track as many deleted files, the operating system is more responsive.

Chapter 7

Organizing and Archiving Data

- -

In This Chapter

▶ Figuring out an organization scheme

▶ Keeping your root directory clear

▶ Using default folders

▶ Archiving older data

- -

*W*ith so much data on your system, you need some way to organize it. I'm not talking about organizing with files and folders; that's a no brainer. Files and folders are the building blocks of any system. I'm referring to how you use files and folders to organize your data so that you can more easily access it.

Fortunately, you can take complete control of how your data is stored on your system. This chapter presents ideas for making sure your data is stored on your hard drive in an orderly fashion. If your data is stored willy-nilly, then your system needs help. (Willy-nilly is Swahili for "cluttered.") By imposing an organizational plan on your system, you reduce clutter and increase your system's efficiency.

In addition, this chapter focuses on the importance of archiving and backing up your data. Archives and backups are two important parts of any data-management scheme. If you archive regularly, your hard drive is cleaner and backups are easier. If you backup regularly, you decrease your chances of losing data due to unforeseen problems.

Organizing Your Data

Organized data — the term brings to mind visions of a small union hall, where twice a week your data meets to make sure its collective voice is heard. If they don't get what they think is fair, they go on strike, picketing for better storage conditions for data everywhere. Your applications stop working because they refuse to cross the picket lines.

Okay, I know that data cannot actually organize and go on strike. But if you fail to organize your data, your hard drive *will* become cluttered, you *will* lose track of your data, and it *will* seem like your data has indeed organized against you. You create a better scenario when you organize your data (without the union hall and pickets) so that your system can run as smoothly and efficiently as possible.

Organizing your data is more art than science. You need to think through how you want your data organized, figuring out the scheme that is best for your needs. You probably don't want me coming and organizing your kitchen — not because I can't organize a kitchen, but because the kitchen would then reflect *my* personality, not yours. Likewise, I can't organize your data for you. I can, however, provide pointers and insights that help as you wade through the process. The next sections examine organizational issues you should keep in mind.

Adding and partitioning hard drives

Multiple hard drives on a system are a really good idea because having multiple drives enables you to more easily organize different types of data. Consider the drive setup shown in Figure 7-1. It shows that the system has two hard drives, C: and D:. This arrangement allows one drive (C:) for Windows and any programs you want to install on the system and the other drive (D:) for your data. The benefit of such an organization scheme is simple: With your data all on one drive, backing up is a snap. You can effectively ignore drive C: backups because you can reinstall programs from the original CD-ROMs. On a single drive, your data is easy to access, back up, and restore.

You could actually install more than one physical hard drive, or you could partition a single physical hard drive so Windows treats it like multiple hard drives.

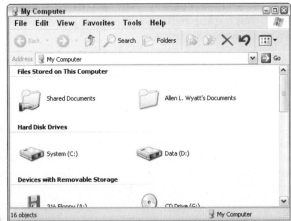

Figure 7-1:
This system has two hard drives available.

A *partition* is a logical division of a physical hard drive. Each physical hard drive can have multiple partitions, each of which is treated as a separate drive by Windows. A hard drive is partitioned when first installed and seldom changed from then on. If you want to change the partitions on a drive that already has data on it, use a third-party utility such as Partition Magic, from PowerQuest, a division of Symantec (`www.powerquest.com`).

I find the optimal system one that includes three drives. The first drive is for the operating system, the second for programs you install, and the third for data. Most of my systems have drives C:, D:, and E:, organized for this very purpose.

If you have only a single drive on your system, don't fret. You can still organize your data efficiently. The next few sections give you pointers on how to do so.

Creating a folder structure

In the Windows XP world of data management, folders really should demand your attention because they are the primary organizing tool. Ponder these points as you prepare to create a folder structure:

- ✔ **Determine how to use your folders (you have an unlimited supply) in the most effective way possible.** Some people, for instance, organize their data by project, with a separate folder for each project. Some people organize by application, with a separate folder for data created by each program they use. Still others organize by topic or date.

- ✔ **You can't do this the wrong way unless the method resembles the junk drawer in my kitchen.** If your hard drive is becoming a catchall for everything you throw there, then you don't really have an organization scheme. Other than that, there isn't a right or wrong way to organize.

- ✔ **Your hard drive's organization should reflect the way you think and the way you use the computer.** If your thinking leans towards projects, then organize by project. If your thinking reflects a different model, then organize around that way of thinking.

With those points in mind, follow these steps to put your data into a logical folder structure:

1. **Determine what major divisions you want to use and make a folder for each.**

   One of my major divisions is Web Sites, indicating the Web sites that I work on and manage. Another major division is Books and another is Newsletters. As you can tell, these are projects categories and I've named them intuitively. You can create folders for similar categories on your system, but they should reflect the work *you* do and the way *you* do that work.

2. **With major divisions in mind, create a folder in the root directory for each division: Right-click a blank space in the folder window and choose New⟹Folder.**

   For more about the root directory, see "Clearing Out Your Root Directory" later in this chapter.

3. **Type a new name for the folder and press Enter.**

4. **Place files in the newly created folders and subfolders within the new folders as necessary.**

   This is an ongoing step. These additional folders should further refine the content you plan to place within those folders.

Watching your depth

Scuba divers use a critical piece of equipment known as a depth gauge. This device allows the diver to see how far she has descended below the surface. This is important because the diver's depth can affect the use of other equipment (such as air tanks) and can indicate her susceptibility to conditions such as decompression sickness. Without a properly functioning depth gauge, a diver is at a significant disadvantage and could die.

As you organize the data on your hard drive, be careful not to run into a depth problem. You place one folder in another, and before you know it you have traversed many, many levels into your hard drive. Windows XP doesn't come with a depth gauge, but you can look at the path that leads to a file to determine how many levels deep it is (each level in your hierarchy is separated by a backslash):

```
C:\projects\acme\research\rr\finished\text\chap01.doc
```

Counting the root directory, the file chap01.doc is seven levels deep in organization. Windows XP can certainly handle several folder levels, but humans have more problems with it. More levels make it easier to forget where files are located and clutters your drive with misplaced and forgotten files.

If you find yourself creating folders deeper than four levels, consider a different organization. Think through how you use the files and look for ways to decrease the levels without sacrificing usability.

Moving, renaming, and deleting folders

As you organize your data, you generally do some tasks over and over again:

✔ Create new folders

✔ Rename existing folders

✔ Delete folders or files

✔ Move folders or files from place to place

If you've been using Windows for a while, you probably know how to do these tasks. If you right-click a file or a folder, you can choose to do all sorts of things, including renaming and deleting.

The task list

Windows XP provides many ways to move folders and files. Depending on how you configured your system, you can use the task list at the left side of a folder window to select common tasks, as shown in Figure 7-2.

To make the task list visible, choose Tools➪Folder Options. On the General tab, select the Show Common Tasks in Folders option and click OK. For instance, click a file and then use the task list to rename, move, or copy it elsewhere.

Figure 7-2: Windows XP can display a task list at the left side of any folder window.

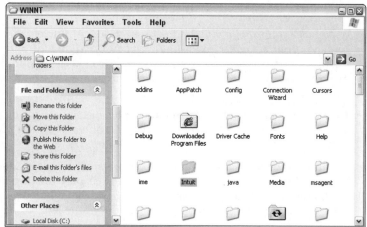

Windows Explorer

A huge drawback to using the task list is that you lose a sense of overall organization. The list is simplistic, designed to work on the items displayed in the folder window. You can get a better sense of your organization by using Windows Explorer, which is shown in Figure 7-3.

To open Windows Explorer, choose Start➪All Programs➪Accessories➪Windows Explorer. An easier way is to display the Start menu, right-click My Computer, and choose Explore. You can also invoke Windows Explorer by right-clicking any folder and choosing Explore from the resulting context menu.

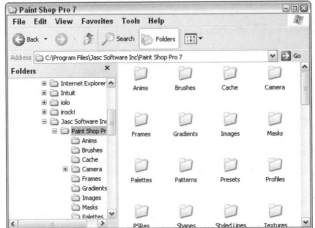

Figure 7-3:
Windows
Explorer
provides
a great
overview of
your data's
organization.

Using Windows Explorer is a quick, clean way to see what's going on with your data organization.

- ✔ Windows Explorer is divided into two sections. At the left side of the screen is your system's folder hierarchy. At the right side of the screen are the contents of whatever you have selected in the folder hierarchy. As you select different folders in the hierarchy tree, the contents of the right side of the window change.

- ✔ Many folders in the hierarchy tree have plus or minus signs next to them. If you click a plus sign, the detail within that object is shown. If you click a minus sign, the detail is rolled up and hidden.

- ✔ To move files and folders around on your system, display the objects to be moved in the right side of the screen and display the target folder in the hierarchy tree. Drag the file or folder from the right side of the screen and drop it on top of the target folder at the left.

Clearing Out Your Root Directory

The other day I was sitting in my root cellar, drinking root beer, and thinking about my root directory. (Things are often quiet — and weird — around the Wyatt household.) Why would I be thinking about my root directory? Because it's such a special and magical place. So special, in fact, that you should think about it, as well. Pull up a dusty trunk, grab yourself a mug of root beer, and let's talk.

Every disk drive has a *root directory,* the place at the top of the drive's file hierarchy. For instance, the root directory for the C: drive is C:\. All paths for other files and folders start with the root directory.

What makes the root directory special is that it's prime real estate. You can clutter up your root directory, sticking lots of files and folders there, but doing so can really slow down your system and make it much less organized. Periodically clearing out your root directory helps prevent this slowdown and disorganization. Take a look at the files and folders stored there. If possible, move the files elsewhere or delete them. The only folders that should be in the root directory are those that represent major data divisions. Move folders of lesser importance further down in the hierarchy. (See the earlier section, "Creating a folder structure," where I discuss exactly that.)

Windows XP supports FAT 16, FAT 32, and NTFS file systems. Of these three, FAT 16 is the oldest. If you upgraded to Windows XP from an older version of Windows, you may be using the FAT 16 file system without even knowing it. The root directory of a FAT 16 system can hold up to 512 files or folders. If you reach this limit, the drive shows as full, even if part of the drive is still empty. To overcome this problem, clean out your root directory and convert to the NTFS file system, which I discuss in Chapter 14.

What About the Default Folders?

When Windows XP is installed, it creates a number of *default folders* with catchy names such as My Documents, My Music, My Pictures, and so on. (I love the one named My Data Sources.) The My Documents folder is, by default, created as a folder in your user account path. For instance, if your account name is Jennifer Simpson, then My Documents is created here:

```
C:\Documents and Settings\Jennifer Simpson\My Documents
```

The other default folders (Music, Pictures, and so on) are created within your My Documents folder. When you install Microsoft applications (such as Word or Excel), they assume you want to store your files in the My Documents folder. Many other applications from other publishers make the same assumption.

I suspect that Microsoft came up with these default folders after handling one too many support calls, like I did. I remember one caller who was concerned because his computer was acting sluggish. I talked him through a few things to check before deciding that I needed to see his machine. After traipsing over to his office and looking at the root directory on the C: drive, I discovered that this guy had installed everything — and I mean everything — into the root directory, which contained literally thousands of files. Cluttering up the root directory in this manner can cause problems. Microsoft's solution? "Default" folders that move the majority of the clutter out of the root directory and place it into a set of well-hidden folders.

For this reason, I'm not a big fan of the default folders. Instead of helping users organize their hard drives, the default folders merely move the clutter someplace else. The only way to permanently solve the problem is to determine how your data should be organized and implement a structure that works for you. That structure does *not* have to include the default folders.

You, being the organized person you are, don't need to use those default folders at all. My advice is to just ignore the default folders. Don't place items there; put them in the structure that *you* set up (which I show you how to do in the earlier section "Creating a folder structure"). The default folders can remain where they are, so that Microsoft's "solution" will keep the rest of its software ignorant and happy.

After creating your own structure, you can force Windows to recognize the top of your data structure as the My Documents destination. You can do this because the My Documents option on the Start menu or desktop is nothing but a shortcut to a folder on your drive. If you change the folder that the shortcut points to, then you get to where you store your data every time you choose My Documents. For instance, suppose your data is stored on drive D:. If you want My Documents to open the D: drive, follow these steps:

1. **Click Start, right-click My Documents, and choose Properties.**

   Windows displays the My Documents Properties dialog box, shown in Figure 7-4.

2. **On the Target tab, click the Move button.**

   Windows displays the Select a Destination dialog box, shown in Figure 7-5.

3. **Select the D: drive and click OK.**

   Use the controls in the dialog box to locate and select the D: drive. (If you want to use some other folder or drive as the target, you can select it instead.)

Figure 7-4:
Windows allows you to modify the properties of the My Documents shortcut.

The D:\ drive (or the path to the folder or drive you selected) shows up as the target in the My Documents Properties dialog box.

4. Click OK to exit the My Document Properties dialog box.

Now when you choose My Documents from the Start menu, you're taken to the drive or folder you specified in Step 3. You've just made Windows match the way you want to work, rather than conforming to what Microsoft expects of you.

Figure 7-5:
You can pick any drive or folder as a target for My Documents.

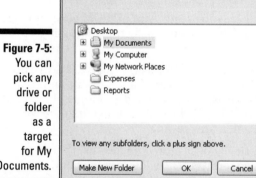

Archiving and Backing Up Data

Archives and backups are two essential parts of any data-management plan. Regular archiving translates to a cleaner hard drive and can make backups easier. Routine backups — an absolute must for people who rely on computer data for their jobs — decrease the chance of losing data because of unforeseen problems like power outages or tornados. (See the "Backups save lives . . . er, I mean, your data" sidebar to see what I mean about tornados.)

Archiving what you don't need

Some people simply delete files they think they won't need anymore. Other people — in far worse shape — don't delete anything, afraid that deleting it will be a mistake. The result is that their hard drive fills up with old data that does nothing for them. They also greatly increase the complexity of managing their data.

If you use your computer for any type of work, archive your old data. You never know when you might need your financial records from last year or your project files from last month. The answer isn't to leave the data on your system. If you archive the data, you can store it in a place that you can refer to later. Plus, you can leave all that data for posterity so they, too, can understand what a geek you are.

Archiving data simply means that you copy it to some sort of long-term storage media and delete it from your computer. (If you leave the data on your computer, the copy is not an archive but a backup. I discuss backups in the next section.) The general way to store archives these days is on CD-ROM, although other storage media are also appropriate:

- ✔ **CD-ROM:** CDs are cheap and easy to create, with CD-ROM burners being very inexpensive. CDs are also durable and easily transportable to other systems.

- ✔ **DVD:** If you have lots of data to archive, DVDs make sense. They're not as inexpensive as CDs (yet), but they're every bit as durable and transportable. Some confusion still exists as to which data format should be used to store information on DVDs, so do a bit of studying to see which way the winds of standardization are blowing.

- ✔ **Tape:** Lots of data has historically been stored on tape using any number of tape and recording formats. The wide variety of options means that tape archives are not as transportable as other media options. If you settle on one you like, make sure you keep your drivers and archive software up to date so you can always access the data.

- ✔ **Zip disk:** For small archiving needs, Zip disks provide a convenient alternative. Many computer systems come with Zip drives, and storage on this media is quite reliable.

Archiving — not just for geeks

I went on a behind-the-scenes tour at the rare books archive at a major university. The archivist showing me around was very matter-of-fact about the work they do. As he showed me through vault after underground vault, I was agog and agape at the materials archived. (These weren't small vaults, either. They were probably 5,000+ square feet each, with 16-foot ceilings.) It was so cool!

I immediately went home and told my wife that I wanted to build a few archive vaults in the back yard. She, in a jaded voice honed from years of being married to a geek, said, "Whatever you want, dear."

Since that time, I've thought better of digging up the back yard. Despite that, I am still impressed with the experience and more determined than ever to archive the materials on my computer — when they're ready for archiving. I urge you to do the same.

Pick the archive medium that is right for you and start moving old data off your system. It's a good idea to make data archiving part of your routine system-maintenance tasks, doing it either monthly or annually.

Periodically check your archive media to make sure you can still read it, particularly as newer hardware and storage methods become available. New storage methods replace old ones, and older archives therefore become inaccessible as the hardware to read those archives becomes unavailable. (Ask anyone who still has very old archives stored on 5.25-inch floppy disks.)

Backing up what you still need

Humor me for a moment while I tell you what you have probably heard a thousand times before: You need to make backups. Backups are cheap insurance. They protect you from glitches and catastrophes that do happen as you're using computers. If you don't make backups, then you run the risk of losing data that is difficult (if not impossible) to replace. If you thoughtfully organize your data, as I discuss earlier in this chapter, then your backup tasks should be easier than ever before. If your data is in a single place (perhaps one drive on your system) or in a limited number of folders, you can easily identify what needs to be backed up and then do it.

In order to create backups, use the same media that you use to create archives. (See the previous section.) The difference between backups and archives, of course, is that *backups* are snapshots of your data, as it exists today. If you're archiving your old data to get it off your system, then making backups is a relatively quick and easy task.

As you develop your backup routine, consider the following:

- ✔ **Choose your backup medium: CD-ROM, DVD, tape, or Zip disk.** If you decide to use CDs for your backup media, you can use a CD-RW drive. With this type of drive, you can both write data to and erase data from the CD. This makes it quite useful for backup purposes.

- ✔ **Decide how often to make backups.** This is, essentially, a business decision. (Even if you don't consider your computer a business computer, the decision is still a business decision.) Remember that backups are insurance against catastrophe. If you want your "insurance" to protect you so that you have to merely re-enter a week's worth of data, then you should make your backups weekly. If you want to lose only a day's worth of data, then you need to make them daily.

- ✔ **Get enough media that you can cycle through your backup disks.** For instance, if you decide to use Zip disks and want to make backups daily, get a week's worth of disks. That way, you have backups for each day of the week. If you run into a problem with today's backup, you'll always have yesterday's backup. (Redundancy is a good thing, at times.)

✔ **Consider any number of specialized software programs for backing up your data.** If you like one of them, use one of them — but note there's nothing magical about such software. In fact, you don't need to use a special program to make backups. If your backup medium has enough capacity, you can simply copy files to it. The important thing isn't *how* you make the backup; the important thing is that you *do* make the backup.

Storing backups and archives

You need to be concerned with only two words when it comes to storage: *off site*. You need to get your backups out of your office or home and stored somewhere else. The reason is quite simple: The catastrophe that befalls your computer could be related to physical damage. If your backups or archives are off site, then you won't lose them in the damage.

You can put your backups and archives in many good off-site storage places. Some people place them in safety deposit boxes. Others just put the backups in their car. Still others take them to a neighbor's house. The idea is to just get them elsewhere.

Part of the decision of where to store backups and archives depends on your data's sensitivity. If you work with sensitive data, store your backups and archives in a secure off-site location. For sensitive data, a bank safety deposit box may be the best solution.

Backups save lives . . . er, I mean, your data

A company I worked for about 20 years ago was large, and my department was in the corner of the top floor of our building. One morning we came to work to find that a tornado had caught our corner of the building and peeled the roof back. Nobody was hurt, but the damage to our department was extensive. With the roof peeled back, the rain poured in. All the acoustical tile was soaked, and it dropped from the ceiling onto the desks. The computers were ruined, as was our work. Fortunately, our department had a policy of daily backups. Employees were responsible for backing up their own PCs, and each employee would take the backup home at night. We were down for a couple of days while the building was fixed, but we were able to get right back to work as soon as we had access to working computers.

Part III
E-Mail and the Internet

The 5th Wave   By Rich Tennant

"He saw your laptop and wants to know how much Amazon.com charges for spears."

In this part . . .

In addition to helping you manage information you might receive when using the Internet, this part zeroes in on dealing with spam, organizing your e-mail, and identifying virus and spyware infections.

Chapter 8

Tackling E-Mail Overload

Ahhh! Modern conveniences — what did we ever do without them? Can you imagine life without a copy machine? How about life without telephones, computers, or air conditioning? How about without electricity, running water, or indoor plumbing? (Don't laugh — when I was a kid about 35 years ago, I remember visiting relatives in Tennessee who had no running water and no indoor plumbing. It made for interesting visits for this city boy.)

We take many modern conveniences for granted; we just figure they've always been there and always will be. In another few years, e-mail will fall into that category. Even today it's hard to believe how much e-mail has changed the tempo and tenor of business life (and personal life, as well).

E-mail is the convenience we love to hate. We complain when it's slow, we complain when it flakes out, and we complain when we get too much. This is a sure sign that e-mail tends to be a focus of much of our daily routine. Because of that focus, it often contributes to the clutter and the general disarray in which you find your computer systems. E-mail pours in, sometimes messing up your filing system or even bringing your operating system to its knees.

This chapter focuses on ways you can tackle the huge influx of e-mail (including spam) you undoubtedly receive every day. If you're one of those fortunate few who only get a dozen (or fewer) e-mails a day, you probably don't need to read this chapter — your management issues are so light that there's little chance e-mail is cluttering your system. If you're like me, however, you need all the help you can get dealing with the hundreds you receive each day. If you're in this camp, read on! You're bound to find something to help in your quest to become clutter free.

Using Different Accounts to Manage and Reduce E-Mail

E-mail accounts are a dime a dozen these days — or cheaper! You're not limited to a single account, as it used to be. You can set up accounts with your ISP, your company, your business associates, your relatives (if they run their own mail server), and the eternally springing free-account companies.

Even with all the flexibility, you may wonder whether you really need all these accounts. The answer is a resounding maybe: Maybe you should set up multiple accounts, if it helps you manage the load better. The following sections examine some of the issues involved in making the decision.

Managing incoming mail

I work from my home office. (The surroundings are comfortable, but the commute is a killer.) Rather than have my business mail sent to my home, I have a post office box. This allows me to segregate my incoming mail: business goes to one place and personal goes to another.

I encourage you to consider getting different e-mail addresses for the same reason. By using different accounts, you can use one for business purposes and another for personal purposes. You don't have to stop there: You can get as many e-mail addresses for as many purposes as you want. Your e-mail client can then be set up to check all your accounts and deliver your mail to appropriate folders in your client.

For instance, you could have separate accounts for general business mail, incoming orders, family correspondence, mailing lists, and e-mail publications. If you provide support for other people, you can set up accounts for your various support tasks. The management benefits are obvious:

✔ You can tailor your addresses to the purpose of the account, such as orders@widgeco.com.

✔ You can delegate order processing to someone else and set up that person to access the orders account. (You don't even have to let people know not to send their orders to your general business account. The public senses no interruption in service because they continue to use the same address.)

While multiple accounts make it great to divvy up your incoming mail by purpose, it can also increase your spam load. Each account can receive its own full measure of spam, and obvious business addresses, such as orders@widgeco.com, are easy for spammers to target. Make sure you think through the consequences of adding e-mail accounts before doing so.

Reducing unwanted mail

If you creatively use multiple e-mail accounts, you can actually decrease unwanted mail drastically. As you find out later in this chapter, any e-mail account is vulnerable to receiving spam. With multiple accounts, you can turn the table on the spammers — at least for a while.

Consider a scenario where you have three e-mail accounts: primary, secondary, and disposable.

- **Use a *primary account* that you publicize to your friends and business acquaintances.** Because you publicize it, this account is the one where you fight most of your spam-related battles.

- **Set up a *secondary account* to use only when your primary account is unavailable.** Don't publicize this one. Give it out only if someone needs to send you something and your primary account is disabled or unreachable for some reason.

- **Create a *disposable account* for online commerce or for participating in public forums or mailing lists.** It doesn't matter if you start getting spam on this account because you can always close it and get another.

Primary accounts are typically business related, but they can be personal. You get them through your office, your ISP, or your Web hosting company. Your secondary account should be one you get through a different ISP. For instance, if your primary account is through your office, then your secondary account could be through your ISP. The idea is for the account to be on a different network than the primary account. That way, if the primary goes down, chances are good that the secondary is still available.

A good place to get disposable accounts is through the free e-mail account services on the Web, such as Hotmail, GMail, or Yahoo!. You can set up one quickly and disconnect it just as quickly.

When you decide to no longer use a disposable account, go through the process of shutting it down. If you just abandon the account, spam continues to accumulate in the inbox, which means that the ISP needs to store the messages on its hard drives. For your one account, that may not be much of a problem. Multiply it by 100,000 or so abandoned accounts, and storage needs become large. Help conserve resources by shutting down instead of abandoning the account.

Psychology 101: Don't Answer That Phone . . . er, E-Mail

I saw a commercial the other day for a well-known pizza company. The scene opens with a bunch of guys sitting in a living room. One guy says, "Watch this," and then rings a little bell. A dog, in the other room, jumps up and runs in to answer the bell. The guy makes a comment about the stupid dog. Then, the doorbell rings, and all five guys run to answer the door. The parallel with the dog's behavior is purposely pointed out.

Pavlovian responses are elicited by many things in life: Provide the right stimulus and people behave in a predictable way. If the doorbell rings, we hurry to open the door. If the telephone rings, we drop everything to answer it. If new e-mail is announced, we drop everything to read and respond.

If you want to be more productive with your computer, break this bad habit. With full-time high-speed access to the Internet, users routinely leave their e-mail clients running all the time, automatically checking at a regular interval. When the mail arrives, they look it over to see if something needs their immediate attention.

I'll bet you would be upset if someone kept calling you on the phone every 10 minutes, trying to sell you something or get your opinion or tell you a joke. At the end of the day, you would complain that you were frustrated and that you got nothing done because of all the interruptions. Yet, users allow the same thing to happen with their e-mail. Every 30 minutes, 15 minutes, 10 minutes, or 3 minutes they check for new e-mail. Every check is an interruption, as surely as if someone had knocked on the door or called on the phone. Focus is lost, attention is demanded, and productivity goes down.

If you want to reclaim your workday, turn off your e-mail client and keep it off until you're ready to focus on addressing your e-mail. If you schedule your e-mail activities, you give yourself larger blocks of time for other work, where you won't be interrupted.

If you prefer not to turn off your e-mail client, then at least configure it so that it doesn't automatically check for e-mail or so it checks for e-mail only every hour or so. How you configure automatic checking depends on the e-mail client. To make the change in Outlook 2003, follow these steps:

1. **Choose Tools➪Options.**

   Outlook displays the Options dialog box.

2. **On the Mail Setup tab, click the Send/Receive button.**

   Outlook displays the Send/Receive Groups dialog box, shown in Figure 8-1.

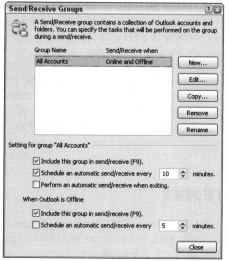

Figure 8-1:
The Send/
Receive
Groups
dialog box is
where you
configure
automatic
mail
checking.

3. **Make sure the Schedule an Automatic Send/Receive Every *N* Minutes check box is selected.**

4. **Specify a time length in the Minutes control.**

   Set the Minutes control to something like 60 minutes or more. If you prefer, clear the Schedule an Automatic Send/Receive Every *N* Minutes check box. Mail is then checked only when you click the Send/Receive button in Outlook.

5. **Close all the dialog boxes.**

You can use the controls in the Send/Receive Groups dialog box to configure Outlook to check different e-mail accounts at different intervals. For instance, you might have it check your personal account every three hours, but check your orders account hourly. Just use the New button to create a new group, assign accounts to that group, and then configure how often that group's e-mail accounts should be checked.

Why You Get Spam

Everyone knows what *spam* is — unsolicited e-mail that usually tries to sell you something. If you purchased something from Amazon.com and Amazon sends you an advertisement, then the message is probably not spam (unless you've opted out of receiving such e-mails — I further discuss opting out in "Purchasing addresses"). If you get an advertisement from someone you've never heard of, that message probably is spam.

I've had the same e-mail address since January 1997. I get more than 500 spam messages per day on that account. I am not alone. Many people get hundreds of unsolicited e-mail messages every day. Dealing with the literal deluge of spam can be a challenge for any computer user.

Spam gets sent to an e-mail address for any number of reasons. The simplest reason is because a spammer has your e-mail address. (That seems sort of obvious, doesn't it?) You may wonder how that spammer ever got your e-mail address in the first place. They get addresses in three main ways: harvesting, guessing, and purchasing.

Harvesting addresses

Harvesting is done automatically by software. Computer programs used by spammers look through Web pages with the express purpose of garnering e-mail addresses. If an address is found, the program "harvests" the address by adding it to a database. This database then sends messages.

Spammers harvest e-mail addresses not only from Web pages but from other public sources, as well. Your address could be used in a message forum, on a newsgroup, or on a friend's Web site. If you doubt your e-mail address can be harvested, just do a Google search for it. Put your address in quotation marks and search for it at Google. When I did that with my e-mail address, Google returned 725 matches for awyatt@dcomp.com. Take a look at Figure 8-2. If Google is able to find and index your e-mail address, spammers are able to do it, as well.

You instigate another method of harvesting. If you send a funny story, via e-mail, to 20 friends and put all their addresses in the To: or Cc: message lines, some of those friends may forward the story to a bunch of their friends. The addresses that you sent the message to now show up in the body of the forwarded message. The message continues to be forwarded, and after about five forwards, there could be a hundred or so e-mail addresses in the forwarded e-mail. These addresses are very easy to harvest. You may trust your friend to not send you unsolicited e-mail, but do you trust your friend's friend's friend's friend's friend? (Probably not.)

Guessing addresses

Some spam-sending software is very good at guessing correct e-mail addresses. Sometimes called a *dictionary attack*, the guessing works like this:

1. A spammer creates a list of words that serve as a dictionary. The dictionary may contain common words, such as *webmaster, info, sales, retail, customerservice, manager, admin, help,* and so on.

2. The spammer's software then connects with your mail server and uses the words as potential e-mail accounts. When the software connects to the widgeco.com mail server, it tries these addresses: webmaster@ widgeco.com, info@widgeco.com, and so on.

3. The mail server at widgeco.com tells the spammer's software whether the address is valid. If the address is valid, the spammer adds the address to its database of known good addresses.

Obviously, the dictionaries used by a spammer's software are much more complex and comprehensive, but you get the idea — the software tries different addresses until it finds those that are good.

Closely related to the dictionary attack is a different method of guessing addresses. If your name is John Smith and your name appears on your company's Web site, the spammer's software can try to put together probable e-mail addresses for you. Based on your name, the software could try jsmith, johnsmith, john.smith, johns, john, smith, j.smith, or any other permutation of your name. When the software tries these addresses, your mail server politely responds whether each guess is good or bad. If the guess is correct, the address ends up in a spammer's database.

Figure 8-2: Searching for your address on Google is a good way to determine your harvesting vulnerability.

Spam isn't a treat

"Have you got anything without Spam?"

"Well, there's Spam egg sausage and Spam. That's not got much Spam in it."

"I don't want ANY Spam!"

Most people feel like the Graham Chapman character in the original Monty Python Spam skit: We don't want ANY spam. And still we get it. Morning, noon, and night, you get spam, undoubtedly served up by a cadre of brainless, horn-helmeted

Vikings, singing the virtues of Spam as they shovel yet another helping your way.

Dealing with spam has developed into its own area. Much of this chapter provides an introduction to some things you can do to combat the problem, but is not an exhaustive treatment of the topic. For more detailed information on the topic, see *Fighting Spam For Dummies*, by John R. Levine, Margaret Levine Young, and Ray Everett-Church (published by Wiley).

Purchasing addresses

The third method that spammers use to get your address is by purchasing it. In my daily serving of spam, I routinely see advertisements offering "39 million Internet e-mail addresses on a single CD." These addresses have been collected in other ways, but if I was a spammer I could purchase the addresses and use them for my own messages.

Call me odd, but purchasing a list of e-mail addresses through spam sent to me seems sleazy. Legitimate e-mail address purchasing exists. Many direct marketing companies sell e-mail addresses that are gathered quite legitimately.

Consider this scenario: You purchase a product from company A and your e-mail address is added to its database. You don't notice that company A's privacy policy states that you may receive notices (advertisements) from them "and its affiliates." This means that company A may send you messages, but also that company A may sell your address to other companies. Those companies can then send you messages and sell your address to still other companies. Before you know it, you're on the list of "39 million Internet e-mail addresses," and receiving spam on a regular basis.

When you visit a commercial Web site, look for a check box that allows you to "opt out" of receiving e-mail from company A or its affiliates. Unchecking the affiliate-related check box is always a good idea. And unless you want e-mail from company A, check the appropriate check box to opt out of future messages.

Tactics for Limiting Spam

In the real world of the Internet, there's nothing you can do to make sure you never get spam. Such thinking is unrealistic. If you have an e-mail address, you *will* receive spam sooner or later. However, a few guidelines can help limit the amount of spam you receive:

- **Use an address that isn't easily guessed.** The addresses jsmith@widgeco.com or jsmithb@widgeco.com are much easier to guess than josmi27th@widgeco.com. If you place a few numbers in the middle of your e-mail address, it cannot be guessed nearly as easily. (Don't place the numbers at the end or beginning; place them in the middle. Numbers at the beginning or end are too easy for spammers to guess.)

- **Don't give out your address.** The more places you use your e-mail address, the more likely your address will end up on someone's list. If you don't want your address to get around, be very, very selective about who you give it to.

- **Don't use electronic greeting cards.** Chances are good that you've received electronic greeting cards before. Everyone seems to like them and they're much easier to send than the paper-and-stamp variety. Unfortunately, many greeting card companies (but not all) are spammer collection points. If you enter your e-mail address (or that of a friend) into a greeting card form, it ends up in a database. That address is then often sold. Before you know it, you (and your friend) start getting spam like crazy.

- **Use throwaway addresses for online commerce.** Earlier in this chapter you discovered how to use multiple e-mail addresses as a tactic for dealing with a flood of e-mail. Come up with a throwaway address to use for your online commerce needs for a while; never use your primary address for e-commerce. When the throwaway address starts to be over-run by spam, throw it away and get another address for that purpose.

- **Don't use autoresponders.** When it comes to business e-mail accounts, many people use a "gone on vacation" autoresponder for those times they are out of the office. If you send them an e-mail, you get a message back stating that Sue is on vacation and can't answer your message right now. Sue not only lets you know she's gone, but also lets spammers know they have a live, valid address. If Sue gets spam, the spammer (or an unwitting victim, if the reply-to address is forged) gets a message indicating Sue's mailbox is open for business, even if Sue is on vacation.

- **Don't click Remove My Name links.** This has been one of the general rules for dealing with spam for a long time. You may think that it's okay to click such links now that the highly publicized CAN SPAM legislation is in place. Wrong! There's no guarantee that the spammer feels he is subject to U.S. laws in the first place or that he is being on the up-and-up. Only click such links for mailing lists you specifically signed up for or for companies with which you have a longstanding relationship.

✔ **Don't reply to spam.** You never know if the e-mail's return address really belongs to the spammer. (Many spam messages have forged e-mail addresses as return addresses.) If you do get through to a spammer, they often view your address as proof of a live e-mail account. If they're unscrupulous enough to send you spam, what makes you think they'll take your return response seriously?

If you have Windows XP SP2 installed on your system and you use Outlook Express (not Outlook), you'll love a new feature that can help reduce one way that spammers get your address.

Spammers sometimes try to validate an e-mail address by sending you an e-mail that includes a reference to a picture back on their server. Sometimes the picture is so small — perhaps consisting of a single pixel — that you can't even see it. When you view the e-mail, the picture is loaded and "displayed," and the spammer's server now knows that your e-mail address is valid. Bingo! You start getting more spam than you wanted.

Outlook Express, with SP2, blocks external pictures, refusing to load them just by viewing a message. (The latest versions of Outlook have done this for some time.) Instead, you can selectively download images on different messages by using the new External Message Information Bar. The result, over time, is that you will hopefully get less unwanted spam.

Implementing Spam Filters

The proliferation of spam has lead to a proliferation of spam filters. An entire industry has built up around the idea of preventing unwanted e-mail from getting to your inbox. The following sections examine the types of filters available, as well as the technology they use.

Types of filters

Let's see . . . there's a HEPA filter, a reverse-osmosis filter, an activated charcoal filter, and an infrared spectrum filter. Yup. That should just about cover it. Implement all these and you'll have cleaner air, cleaner water, cleaner charcoal, and a cleaner spectrum. (Who doesn't need a cleaner spectrum?) But you won't have a cleaner inbox.

I'm positive — it's false!

One of the problems with filtering technologies is the concept of false positives. A *false positive* happens when a message is incorrectly identified as spam. If your spam filter ever had an e-mail newsletter or sales receipt quarantined (or deleted), then you've experienced a false positive.

Makers are constantly trying to improve their filters because false positives destroy confidence in the program. If you have to examine your quarantine folder to see whether it contains mail it shouldn't, you may question the filter's value. After all, examining your quarantine folder all the time isn't much different from wading through all the spam in your inbox.

When looking for an e-mail filter, consider the following:

- ✔ **ISP-provided spam filters:** Some ISP's provide spam filtering as part of their e-mail service. This is common practice from providers such as AOL, Hotmail, MSN, Juno, and Yahoo!. Typically, these providers provide filtering by default, without you needing to do anything. Their programs provide a junk mail folder, where e-mail suspected of being spam is automatically quarantined.

- ✔ **Integrated client spam filters:** More and more e-mail programs are including their own filtering methods. Some are very good, but others have a way to go. For instance, Microsoft's Outlook 2003 includes a good built-in junk filter. If you don't have the latest version of your e-mail client, you may want to check with the publisher to get it.

- ✔ **External client spam filters:** A wide range of third-party software packages filter spam. These generally act as an intermediary between your mail server and mail client. The program is not a part of either, but instead weeds out suspected spam before delivering e-mail to your client.

- ✔ **Server-based filters:** Many companies — large and small — maintain their own mail servers. These companies may also implement server-based filters to try to stop both inbound and outbound spam. These filters are different than those you may use on your desktop; it filters all mail, for all mail server users.

Each type of filter has its pros and cons. You get the most control with spam solutions installed on your local computer, whether those solutions are integrated into your e-mail client or implemented through a third-party solution. On the other end of the spectrum, you have very little control over filters used by your ISP or implemented on your mail server.

No rule says you can't use more than one filter at a time. For instance, your company could have a server-based filter installed, and you could supplement that with a desktop filter. You should intelligently choose the solution that is right for your needs.

If you choose a filter that runs on your desktop computer, make sure you pick something that has been well-reviewed by other users. (Don't rely on the publisher's hype.) Some scum-sucking lowlifes hawk e-mail filters that are nothing but spyware. You think you got it bad with e-mail? Wait until you get a good dose of spyware on your system. (You find out more about spyware in Chapter 10.)

Types of filter technology

Regardless of where the filter is installed (on your machine, by the ISP, or on your mail server), all filters use the same general approach. Four predominant filtering technologies exist:

- ✔ **Rules-based:** The most prevalent type of anti-spam technology is *rules-based filtering.* Each incoming message is examined to see whether it meets specific conditions. The rules are used to determine whether a message has a certain set of phrases, a certain quantity of keywords, or other identifiers commonly associated with spam.

  For instance, a rules-based system may be programmed to identify a message as spam if it contains a lot of uppercase words, sexually explicit words, or wording normally associated with advertisements (such as *free, discount, buy now,* or *money back*). If the rules are met, the message is either refused, deleted, or quarantined, depending on how the filter is designed.

- ✔ **Bayesian:** Another type of technology — one that is relatively new — is called *Bayesian filtering.* This type relies on complex statistical analysis. You essentially "train" the filter to know what you consider to be spam. The more training you give the filter, the greater its accuracy. Well trained, these filters do an amazing job of identifying spam and have a low incidence of false positives.

- ✔ **Blacklists:** *Blacklists* identify known spam sources. Some spam filters allow you to create your own blacklist or use one created by other people or companies. Incoming e-mail is compared against the list. If there's a match, the e-mail is quarantined or deleted — you never see it.

- ✔ **Whitelists:** The opposite side of the coin is a *whitelist.* These lists identify e-mail sources that you consider legitimate. If you place a source on the whitelist, e-mail from that source is automatically passed through to you.

Unfortunately, blacklists and whitelists sometimes work against each other. This is particularly true if your ISP or network administrator maintains a blacklist. The list could be used by the ISP's spam filters or by those implemented on your local network. If you're also using your own spam filter, placing something on your whitelist does not guarantee you'll get e-mail originating from that source. Instead, the e-mail could be filtered out by those further up the line. Your filter never gets a chance to say the message is okay. If you get into a situation of dueling lists, contact your ISP or network administrator and let her know to whitelist the same sources you have. That way, you get the e-mail you expect with no problems.

Blacklists and whitelists can be based on the message sender, the sender's domain, or the sender's IP address. The most accurate lists are created via IP addresses. An *IP address* is the unique numerical Internet address of the sending server. If you identify the IP address, you can black- or whitelist all e-mail that originates with that server, regardless of who it's from.

Combating Spam with a Challenge/Response System

Besides run-of-the mill filters, another spam-fighting tool is known as a *challenge/response (C/R) system.* C/R systems are not technically filters; they're blocking systems. No analysis is done on the message to see whether it meets a set of criteria. Instead, a C/R system is analogous to one huge list system. Everyone in the world is assumed to be on a blacklist, so everyone must also respond to a "challenge" in order to be removed from the blacklist.

Because most spam is generated by machines and the return addresses on most spam are forged, C/R systems are very attractive. They ensure that the person sending the e-mail is real. A C/R system works like this:

1. John Doe sends you an e-mail.

2. The C/R system intercepts the e-mail.

3. The C/R system returns a message to John, asking him to visit a Web page.

4. When John gets to the Web page, he is asked to enter a password or type in something he sees onscreen.

5. John provides the requested information and clicks a Submit button.

6. The C/R system ensures the proper information was provided. If so, then John's address is marked as a verified sender and his e-mail is passed on to you.

John's e-mail never makes it through if he never correctly answers the C/R system's challenge; the message is deleted after a specified period of time has elapsed.

A wide variety of C/R systems are available. Some run on your desktop, others are available as Internet resources. One popular Internet-based C/R system is Spam Arrest, which you can find at `www.spamarrest.com` (see Figure 8-3), and another is MailBlocks at `www.mailblocks.com`.

Figure 8-3: One of the most popular challenge/ response systems is Spam Arrest.

Chapter 9

Organizing Your E-Mail

*Y*ou're unique. (Some would say that is a good thing.) It follows that unique people receive unique e-mail. It also follows that unique people use e-mail for unique purposes. One person uses it to conduct business, while another keeps in touch with Aunt Mildred and Uncle Buck. Still another uses e-mail to keep tabs on far-flung members of her Purple Iguana Lovers' Club.

Fortunately, e-mail is flexible and most e-mail clients are quite adaptable when it comes to organizing all your business, personal, and extracurricular social messages. Figuring out how to use those tools can be a bit taxing — just *one more thing* to add to the repertoire [sigh] — but well worth the effort.

This chapter focuses on the ways you can use your e-mail client to help organize your e-mail load. E-mail is such a big part of most people's lives that establishing good habits and tackling remedial organizational chores can reap immediate benefits.

A wide variety of e-mail clients are available. Most clients accomplish the same basic tasks: checking your e-mail, allowing you to download it, and providing ways to manage what you receive. Different clients accomplish these tasks in different ways, however. The examples in this chapter cover how to do specific tasks using Outlook. These examples are just that — examples. If you use a different e-mail client, you can probably accomplish the same task, although you may need to search around a bit to find out exactly how. (The use of Outlook shouldn't be considered a rebuff of the client you use. Outlook is used in the examples for the sake of example only.)

Using Folders Effectively

In Chapter 7 you discover how to use folders to help organize the data on your hard drive. I don't know of a single e-mail client that doesn't allow you to use folders to organize your e-mail. In fact, folders are a great boon to keeping your incoming e-mail uncluttered and under control.

Don't confuse e-mail folders with file folders on your disk drive. Conceptually, they're similar to each other only in that each allows you to organize information. While some e-mail clients may use file folders to store your e-mail, many do not. The folders are maintained within the client as a logical structure, with no relation to file folders on the hard drive.

Rather than leaving all your e-mail in your inbox, give some thought to how you can organize it using folders. For instance, you could have a folder for your work-related e-mail or a folder for each project you're working on. You could also create folders for family e-mail, hobbies, and other categories.

You can configure most (if not all) e-mail clients to display available folders onscreen. The folders in Outlook are part of the Navigation pane. When displayed, the pane is at the left side of the program window, as shown in Figure 9-1.

Figure 9-1: The Navigation pane in Outlook is handy for working with folders.

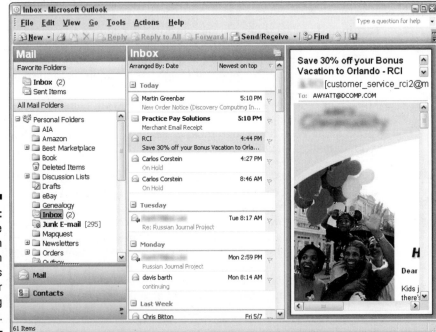

The Navigation pane (or its equivalent) is helpful when working with folders. You can easily drag messages from one folder and drop them in another or move entire folders. To create an e-mail folder, simply right-click an existing folder and choose New Folder. Name the folder and start using it to store messages.

Smart Move: Using Mail Rules

One of the most helpful things I found in Outlook is the ability to establish rules related to incoming message processing. For instance, I'm on a couple of mailing lists for right-handed computer geeks who happen to be Geminis. (Don't ask. These are very select groups and you can't join — so there!) I get a couple dozen e-mails per day from the lists, but I don't need to review them all the time. To deal with this influx, I create a *mail rule* that causes Outlook to move all of those specialized e-mails into their own folder. The benefit is that I can then pay attention to that e-mail when I have the time and inclination, rather than dealing with it every day.

You can create similar mail rules for any number of purposes. If you can define how a particular piece of e-mail should be treated based on any number of characteristics, you can set up a rule for Outlook to process it.

 Several e-mail clients allow you to create mail rules. The concepts presented in the following sections can help you understand what mail rules do, but if you use something other than Outlook you must look at your own e-mail client to see how to define and use rules.

Creating a rule

Creating a mail rule can be quite easy. Suppose you receive e-mail through two accounts: jsmith@widgeco.com and orders@widgeco.com. You want the e-mail that comes to the orders account to automatically be moved to a folder named (appropriately enough) Orders. Follow these steps to set up the appropriate rule:

1. **Choose Tools⇨Rules and Alerts.**

   Outlook displays the Rules and Alerts dialog box, with the E-mail Rules tab selected.

2. **Click New Rule.**

   The Rules Wizard dialog box displays, as shown in Figure 9-2. From here you can pick one of the more common types of rules (those generated by templates) or you can select the Start from a Blank Rule radio button (which gives you the most versatility).

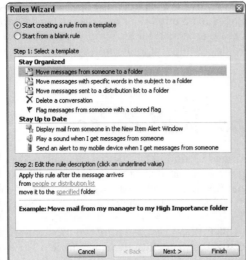

Figure 9-2:
Use the
Rules
Wizard to
design a
rule.

3. **None of the predefined templates describe moving mail from a particular account to another folder, so select the Start from a Blank Rule radio button.**

The dialog box changes and the choice Check Messages When They Arrive is selected.

4. **Click Next.**

The Rules Wizard asks you to specify what conditions make the rule applicable to the incoming mail. See Figure 9-3.

5. **Because you want to move e-mail that comes through a specified account (orders@widgeco.com), select the Through the Specified Account option.**

The area at the bottom of the dialog box changes to reflect the selected condition.

6. **At the bottom of the dialog box (under Step 2: Edit the Rule Description), click Specified (the underlined word).**

Outlook displays a dialog box that shows all the accounts you have set up in Outlook.

7. **Using the drop-down list in the dialog box, choose the account that uses the orders@widgeco.com address. Then click OK.**

The word Specified (which you clicked in Step 6) is replaced with the account name you selected.

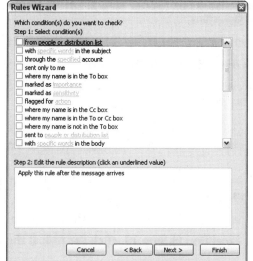

Figure 9-3:
Pick criteria
for incoming
e-mail.

8. **Click Next.**

   The Rules Wizard asks you to specify what you want done with a message that meets your criteria. See Figure 9-4.

9. **You want Outlook to move messages, so select the Move It to the Specified Folder option.**

   The area at the bottom of the dialog box changes to reflect the desired action.

Figure 9-4:
Decide
what to do
with e-mail
meeting
your
criteria.

10. **At the bottom of the dialog box (under Step 2: Edit the Rule Description), click Specified.**

    Outlook displays a dialog box that shows all the folders available.

11. **Choose a folder, as desired, and click OK.**

    The word Specified (which you selected in Step 10) changes to reflect the name of the folder you selected.

12. **Click Next.**

    The Rules Wizard asks you to specify any exceptions to this particular rule.

13. **If you can think of any exceptions, click the check box next to the exception's description.**

    The bottom of the dialog box changes to reflect the exception you chose.

14. **If you specified an exception in Step 13, click the link at the bottom of the dialog box.**

    Outlook displays a dialog box where you can select the exception details.

15. **Pick a check box and click OK.**

    The wording in the dialog box updates to reflect the completed exception.

16. **Click Next.**

    The last step of the Rules Wizard displays, as shown in Figure 9-5.

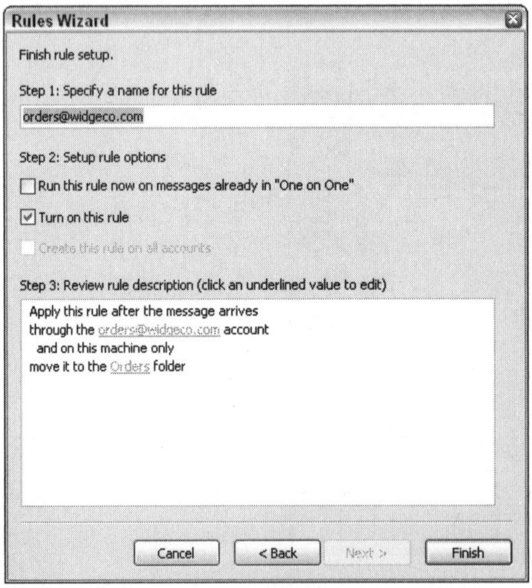

Figure 9-5:
Wrapping
up the Rules
Wizard.

17. Specify a descriptive name for your rule and click Finish.

If desired, you can run the rule on the current folder. In most cases you don't need to select this option; just finish out the Rules Wizard.

With your rule completed, it runs automatically every time e-mail is received. If anything comes through the orders@widgeco.com account, the rule moves the message automatically to the Orders folder.

Rearranging the rules

After you get the hang of creating rules, you may get a whole passel of them. (I think *passel* is the proper group nomenclature for rules; it certainly sounds better than "a gaggle of rules" or "a pride of rules.") When you have your passel defined, they show up in the list of rules when you choose Tools⇨Rules and Alerts; see Figure 9-6.

Notice the wording at the top of the list of rules: Rule (Applied in the Order Shown). Normally, this isn't a problem. But say you have two rules that could apply to the same message. Perhaps you have a rule that moves orders to one folder, and another that moves anything containing the word *sample* to a different folder.

What happens if a message through the orders account contains the word *sample?* Do you want it moved to the Sample folder or to the Order folder? Exactly what happens depends on the order in which your rules occur in the rules list. You need to make sure that the rules occur in the order you want them processed.

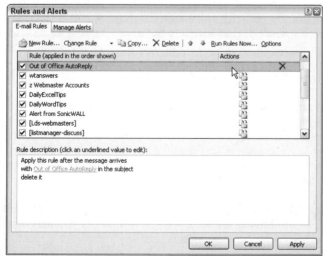

Figure 9-6:
You can
define quite
a number
of rules in
Outlook.

To move a rule up or down the list of rules, click the rule and use the up and down arrow buttons on the toolbar.

Sometimes rules conflict with each other. If you have an order that deletes a message and the subsequent order would have moved the same message to a folder, Outlook may generate an error when it processes the rules. The only solution is to think through your rules and make sure you remove any that obviously conflict with each other.

Deleting a rule

Anarchy rules! (Oops, another oxymoron.) If you decide you no longer need to follow rules, and you don't want Outlook to suffer under the tyranny of rules (even if you created them), you can delete rules.

Follows these steps to delete a rule:

1. **Display the Rules and Alerts dialog box by choosing Tools⇨Rules and Alerts.**

2. **Select the rule you want deleted.**

3. **Click the Delete button or press the Delete key.**

    The rule is removed from your system.

Deleting E-Mail Regularly

I just checked — I officially have a gazillion old e-mails in my e-mail client. (Lest you doubt my veracity, the e-mail database is currently 315MB.) The sad thing is that most of that e-mail is not in my Deleted Items folder, but in other organizational folders I set up to help manage my e-mail over time.

I think it's time to do some housekeeping.

I suspect I'm not alone in needing to clean out e-mail. Over time, it tends to accumulate like barnacles on the hull of a ship. Individually, each barnacle doesn't slow down the ship much, but in aggregate, they can seriously degrade the performance of the vessel. Old, collected e-mail messages can similarly burden your system almost imperceptibly, decreasing response time and increasing system overhead.

The primary reason e-mails accumulate is phobias. Phobias about throwing them away. The following sections cover a few points you may want to consider concerning deleting messages.

Determine a cutoff point for e-mails

Fine wines and some actors get better with age. E-mail doesn't. Its primary purpose is immediacy. As your messages get older, they lose immediacy and their associated value. You may determine a cutoff point of 30, 60, or 90 days. When an e-mail reaches that age, just delete it. (Or archive and then delete it, as I discuss later in this chapter.)

Empty the Deleted Items folder

When you press the Delete key, you may think the message is gone and you don't need to worry about it again. You'd be wrong. On most clients, the message is simply moved to a Deleted Items folder, where it awaits a specific command to be permanently removed.

You unclutter your system and improve its responsiveness by simply emptying the Deleted Items folder on a regular basis. If you're using Outlook or Outlook Express, just right-click the folder and choose Empty Deleted Items Folder. (If you prefer, choose Tools➪ Empty Deleted Items Folder.)

You can also set up Outlook to automatically clear the folder for you. Follow these steps:

1. **Choose Tools➪Options.**

   Outlook displays the Options dialog box.

2. **On the Other tab (shown in Figure 9-7), select the Empty the Deleted Items Folder Upon Exiting check box.**

   With this option selected, the Deleted Items folder is automatically emptied whenever you exit Outlook.

3. **Click OK.**

Empty the junk mail folder

Many e-mail clients (and many online e-mail systems) have a folder where suspected spam is automatically stored. If you have a high volume of spam, delete that folder's contents often. Depending on your spam filter, you may also have a quarantine folder, which I recommend that you check and empty often.

Figure 9-7:
Configure
Outlook
to auto-
matically
empty the
Deleted
Items folder
for you.

Many e-mail clients (and spam-filtering software) can be configured to auto-matically empty your junk mail or quarantine folder. For instance, the junk e-mail filter in Outlook 2003 allows you to permanently delete junk e-mail as it's detected. To enable Outlook's junk e-mail filter, follow these steps:

1. **Choose Tools⇨Options.**

   Outlook displays the Options dialog box.

2. **On the Preferences tab, click the Junk E-mail button.**

   Outlook displays the Junk E-mail Options dialog box shown in Figure 9-8.

3. **Select the Permanently Delete Suspected Junk E-Mail Instead of Moving It to the Junk E-Mail Folder option.**

   Don't you love check boxes that have paragraph-size descriptions of what they do? With this option selected, an incoming suspect message is deleted on the spot.

4. **Click OK.**

If you configure your client or spam filter to automatically delete suspected spam, those messages are gone. If someone calls you and says they sent you something, you have nowhere to look if it was trashed. Unless you're very confident in your filter's work, you may want to let the spam pile up in the junk folder or quarantine area until you explicitly review and delete it.

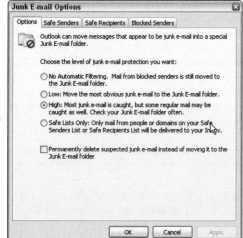

Figure 9-8:
Outlook can,
if directed,
auto-
matically
delete junk
e-mail.

Watching Out for Attachments

E-mail messages aren't just for sending text anymore. People attach all sorts of things to their messages. Many of the messages I get every day have attachments. As I'm writing this book, I send manuscript to my editor as an attachment. The edited manuscript comes back to me as an attachment. This makes transporting information easy and convenient, but attachments are problematic for two reasons.

The first reason is that there are good attachments, not-so-good attachments, and downright bad attachments. Everyone gets attachments that fall in these three categories:

- ✔ **Good attachments:** Manuscripts flying back and forth through the ether fall in the good attachment category.

- ✔ **Not-so-good attachments:** Funny pictures (visual jokes) that get sent around the Internet like chaff in the wind probably are in the not-so-good attachment category.

- ✔ **Bad attachments:** The viruses, worms, and Trojan horse programs that are often sent as attachments of innocent-looking messages are defi-nitely bad attachments, and something you need to look out for.

You need to carefully review messages with attachments as you receive them so that you don't open a bad attachment. I discuss viruses, worms, and Trojan horses — and how to protect yourself from them — in Chapter 10.

The second reason attachments are problematic is that they take up a lot of space and can quickly clutter up your system. Plain text e-mail messages don't take up much space at all, but messages that include attachments are larger, require more time to transmit, and take up more storage space. Some e-mail clients store attachments as part of the actual e-mail, in a specialized database. Other clients store the attachments in a temporary folder, waiting for you to determine what to do with them. I recommend that you determine the fate of messages with attachments as quickly as possible. If you don't need the message (or its attachment), delete it right away.

If you send attachments, chances are good that those attachments are taking up double the space on your hard drive. When you attach a file to a message, the file is copied by the e-mail client, along with your message, to the Sent Items folder. The upshot is that you have one copy (the original) where you expect it and another copy (the attachment) in your e-mail client. Check and delete messages from your Sent Items folder on a regular basis.

Archiving Valuable E-Mail

The concept of archiving should be part of any e-mail organization campaign. Most e-mail is of no value after a short time. (Some e-mail is of no value before you even get it.) You may need to keep other e-mail, however, for historical purposes. Archiving comes in handy here.

In Chapter 7 you find out how to archive files on your computer system. Archiving e-mail messages is very similar. The idea is to move the old-but-I-need-to-keep messages out of your primary mailbox into some other area where you can access them.

Several approaches exist for generating archives from your e-mail, ranging from using the e-mail program's own archiving capabilities to creating your own solution. I cover these approaches in the following sections.

Enabling built-in archives

Most e-mail clients include some facility for archiving your messages. Archiving capabilities are typically date based, which means you can automatically archive messages that are older than a particular date. For example, Outlook allows you to configure its AutoArchive capabilities in the following manner:

1. **Choose Tools⇨Options.**

   Outlook displays the Options dialog box.

2. **On the Other tab (shown earlier in Figure 9-7), click the AutoArchive button.**

   Outlook displays the AutoArchive dialog box shown in Figure 9-9.

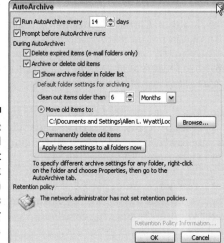

Figure 9-9:
Control
what
Outlook
does when
it archives
older
messages.

3. **Use the controls in the dialog box to specify how you want archiving performed by Outlook.**

   If you get an average amount of e-mail, archiving every two weeks (the default) should be sufficient. You should make sure the other settings result in moving older items to the archive folders and deleting them from your regular inbox area.

4. **Click OK twice to close all the dialog boxes.**

Outlook (and some other e-mail clients) allows you to specify archiving on a folder-by-folder basis. In Outlook, just right-click a folder and choose Properties. In the dialog box, use the AutoArchive tab to configure archiving for the specified folder.

Some online e-mail systems also include ways to archive messages. Normally, this involves simply moving your older messages out of your regular folders and placing them in some archive folder.

Some online e-mail systems limit the amount of e-mail you can archive. If you try to surpass the storage limit, the system may either delete your oldest messages or start refusing to accept new e-mail. You should not allow your archive folder to become a catchall. Make sure you periodically clean it out.

Using the Mailbox Cleanup tool in Outlook

Outlook 2003 includes a helpful tool for managing your e-mail. Appropriately titled Mailbox Cleanup, the tool allows you to see the size of your mailbox, archive or delete old items, and get rid of your deleted items.

To start the tool, choose Tools⇨Mailbox Cleanup. Outlook displays the Mailbox Cleanup dialog box, shown in Figure 9-10. The Mailbox Cleanup tool doesn't provide any features you cannot accomplish through other menu selections — all it does is put those features on a single dialog box so that you can easily access them.

On the Mailbox Cleanup dialog box, I get the most help from the Find button. You can easily search for older items or items larger than a specific size. When you click Find, Outlook runs the Advanced Find feature using the parameters you specified.

For instance, I often search for items larger than 500KB and then delete them. In the Advanced Find dialog box — where the results are shown — simply right-click an item you no longer want and then choose Delete.

Figure 9-10:
Use the
Mailbox
Cleanup tool
to perform
routine
house-
keeping
chores.

Rolling your own archive process

One good way to create archives is to get the messages completely out of your e-mail client and into a standard file format. Most e-mail clients allow you to export messages to a text file. You can archive a message by exporting it to a text file and deleting the original message. The text file can be archived as you would archive any other file on your hard drive.

Some e-mail clients allow you to create macros to automate regular tasks. Outlook is one such client. (If the thought of macros gives you the heebie-jeebies, then you may want to skip the rest of this section.) To help with my archival needs, I wrote a macro that archives and then deletes selected messages:

```
Sub SaveStuff()
    Dim oMailItem As MailItem
    Dim iMsgCnt As Integer
    Dim J As Integer
    Dim sFileName As String
    Dim dSent As Date
    Dim sBase As String

    sBase = "f:\archives\"
    'Save and delete each of the selected e-mail messages
    iMsgCnt = Application.ActiveExplorer.Selection.Count
    For J = iMsgCnt To 1 Step -1
        Set oMailItem =
            Application.ActiveExplorer.Selection.Item(J)

        If oMailItem.Attachments.Count = 0 Then
            dSent = oMailItem.SentOn
            sFileName = sBase & Format(dSent, "yyyymmdd-
            HhNnSs") & ".txt"
            oMailItem.SaveAs sFileName, olTXT
            oMailItem.Delete
        End If
        Set oMailItem = Nothing
    Next J
End Sub
```

To use the macro, select a group of messages that you want archived and run the macro. It steps through all of those selected and then saves them, in text format, in the designated folder. The sBase variable designates the target folder for the archives. If the message has an attachment, the macro does not archive or delete the message.

Chapter 10

Banishing Internet Villains

· ·

In This Chapter

▶ Detecting and removing viruses

▶ Understanding and eliminating spyware

▶ Dealing with pop-up advertisements

▶ Keeping your system free of potential problem programs

· ·

As Sarah, little Timmy, and Crusty Bob hunkered down beneath their wagon, the marauding outlaws circled the camp and looked for the right moment to attack. Sarah and little Timmy cowered in fear, waiting for the attack to begin (and hoping for a rescue). Little did the outlaws suspect that Crusty Bob was well protected, just holding his Acme ZX-31 rocket launcher at the ready but always out of sight.

When you fight the good fight to keep your system free from viruses, spyware, and pop-ups, you may feel like Sarah and little Timmy. With the right information and tools, you can begin to feel more crusty, just like old Bob, lying in wait for the unsuspecting bad guys.

This chapter addresses some of the bad things that can infect and affect your system by virtue of your connection to the Internet. If your system has ever been infected with a villainous virus, suspicious spyware programs, or a plethora of pop-ups, you know that not only can your system get cluttered up quickly, but it can also become downright unusable in a hurry.

Applying the information in this chapter helps you reclaim your system and productivity while maintaining your sanity.

This chapter provides some good guidance on how to begin cleaning and protecting your system from the bad stuff. Please don't consider this chapter the end-all and be-all of this topic, however. If you need to deal extensively with viruses, spyware, and pop-ups, consider reading books that focus just on those topics. *Computer Viruses For Dummies,* by Peter H. Gregory, and *Fighting Spam For Dummies,* by John R. Levine, Margaret Levine Young, and Ray Everett-Church (both published by Wiley) are a couple of good places to start.

Uh-Oh! Do 1 Have a Virus?

Thousands of viruses are out in the wild. The phrase *in the wild* means that the virus is not in a lab or on a single computer, but loose and propagating around the Internet. Each of these *viruses* is a program designed to do different things to computers. Some viruses are nuisances that display annoying but otherwise harmless messages. Others are programmed to destroy data or attack specific computer networks across the Internet.

Just like people develop symptoms that indicate when they're sick, computers do as well. ("Quick! Call the doctor; Junior seems to have some sort of a bug!" When my kids got sick, some sort of telltale sign always appeared — lethargy, achy pains, fever, sweating, and nausea were sure signs that Junior was coming down with something.) The broadest possible sign of a virus-infected computer is that the computer just doesn't behave like it used to. Perhaps it reboots all the time or its files disappear or strange messages pop up. All of these (and more) are signs that you may have a virus.

Essentially, you have two ways of handling viruses:

✔ Search for and eliminate a virus after it's already on your computer by downloading and running a virus checker.

✔ Prevent a virus from getting onto your computer in the first place by installing anti-virus software.

I explore each option in the following sections.

Finding viruses on your computer

The best way to find out whether you have a virus is to use one of the free virus checkers available on the Web. I have had success with HouseCall from Trend Micro. To use it, just follow these steps:

1. **Go to** `http://housecall.trendmicro.com/`, **which is shown in Figure 10-1.**

2. **Click the Scan Now link.**

3. **When prompted, provide your country and click the Go button.**

   The site downloads a small program that actually scans your computer. Depending on your security settings, you may need to give Windows the go ahead to install the program.

4. **After the program is downloaded, specify which drives you want scanned and click the Scan button.**

   As the drives are scanned, you see an update of how many files are checked and how many infected files are located.

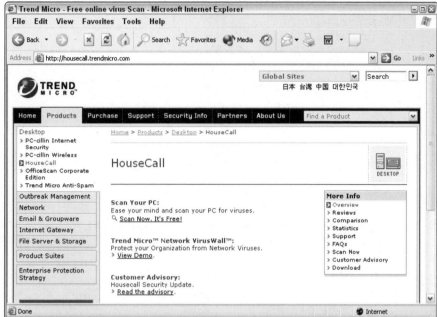

Figure 10-1:
Trend
Micro's
HouseCall
can do a
scan on
your system
for viruses.

If HouseCall finds a virus on your system, it offers to remove it for you. Accept this offer — you really don't want those buggers to stay on your system.

Not all virus checkers catch all viruses — too many are out there to catch! For that reason, you may want to seek out some other online sites to see what they have to offer. Another good one to try is AVG from Grisoft (www. grisoft.com/us/us_dwnl_free.php). The process is generally the same: You go to the virus checker's Web site, where you may have to provide some basic information before downloading and running the checker. Easy as pie.

Blocking viruses

The best way to avoid virus infection is to catch viruses as they arrive at your computer. This means that you should use anti-virus software to protect your system. While you can use the online scanners (covered in the previous section) to check your system, *anti-virus software* provides better coverage. It hooks into your operating system and checks everything coming to and (in some cases) everything leaving your computer. Online scanning systems can't do that.

A wide variety of anti-virus programs are on the market. Some of the most popular follow:

✔ **McAfee VirusScan Professional:** This is the home version of the same technology used in many corporate networks.

```
http://us.mcafee.com/root/package.asp?pkgid=145
```

✔ **Norton AntiVirus:** This product is one of the true old timers. (Is Peter Norton even still around?)

```
www.symantec.com/nav/nav_pro/
```

✔ **eTrust Antivirus:** A well-designed solution from the folks at Computer Associates.

```
www3.ca.com/Solutions/Product.asp?ID=156
```

✔ **F-Secure:** An award-winning anti-virus provider, with solutions for home, small business, and network users. This is not the least-expensive anti-virus software, but many consider it the best.

```
www.f-secure.com/virus-info/
```

✔ **Panda Software:** This relative newcomer is making a splash and offers three solutions.

```
www.pandasoftware.com
```

Literally scores of other vendors are selling anti-virus solutions. Before you settle on one, spend some time looking around, checking features, and reading reviews. Make sure that you purchase from a reputable vendor — viruses and spyware have been known to masquerade as anti-virus solutions.

After purchasing or downloading your selected anti-virus software, follow the publisher's instructions on how to install it on your system. Most programs are fairly similar in this area — you run an installation program or insert the program's CD-ROM in your system, follow the on-screen instructions, and are protected before you know it.

Virus software is only as good as your latest signature upgrade. All virus software depends on signature files, which help the software identify a virus. If the signature files are out of date, the virus software offers no protection from the latest viruses. Most vendors provide an annual subscription service that allows you to automatically download the latest and greatest signature files so that you're protected at all times.

Sizing Up Spyware

Spyware is a relatively recent "innovation" in malicious software. *Spyware* is a broad term that includes software that tracks what you do on your computer, information that may be delivered to someone else or to a company that collects such information (normally the spyware's developer). Spyware can use this information to display advertisements on your system (harmless but annoying) or to get unauthorized access to your computer or its data (a serious security issue).

Technically, spyware is a subset of a larger category of software called *malware,* which is a contraction of the phrase *malicious software.* Many people use spyware as a synonym of malware, as I have chosen to do in this book. Malware is often broken down into other categories such as *adware* (software that sends you unwanted ads or pop-ups), *browser hijackers* (software that takes over your browser), *dialers* (software that reroutes your dial-up Internet account), and many other categories.

In this book, I use the term *spyware* to refer to any malicious software that doesn't include viruses, worms, or Trojan horse software.

Identifying spyware

Not all spyware displays advertisements on your system, so it's not always evident that you have spyware on your system. Some types of spyware quietly and secretly track what you do on your computer — gathering information such as your passwords, credit card number, personal data, and online behavior.

Obviously, spyware compromises your system's security. It can also adversely affect Windows and make your legitimate software less stable. As of this writing, over 400 spyware programs have been identified on the market. Some are sold as commercial PC surveillance programs, system recorders, parental control software, or spouse monitors. If you see an advertisement for software that lets you know what your employees, children, or spouse are doing on the Internet, you're viewing an advertisement for spyware.

Many other spyware programs are "out there"; most are installed without people even knowing it. You could have spyware installed on your system if you notice any of the following symptoms:

- **Flickering screen:** If your computer screen flickers periodically without apparent reason, spyware could be the cause. Many spyware programs — particularly those used in office environments — periodically take screenshots and store them. While the screenshot is being made and stored, the screen can flicker.

- **New browser toolbars:** Some spyware installs its own toolbars in your browser. If you don't know where the toolbar came from, chances are good that it came from spyware.

✔ **Unexplained disk activity:** Information gathered by spyware is often stored in log files on the local computer. These files are periodically sent to a remote system. While the files are accessed, the drive activity light may remain on for extended periods. (If you don't have a lot of memory on your system, Windows could do a lot of disk access on its own.)

✔ **Sluggish system:** If your system starts responding slower than you remember, spyware could be the cause. Running spyware (it is, after all, a program) takes time normally spent running your other programs.

✔ **Low system resources:** Windows lets you know when it detects that your system resources (typically memory and disk space) are getting low. If you start seeing warnings about your system resources, it could be due to poorly written spyware consuming the resources normally allocated to other programs.

✔ **Inability to change home page.** If your browser's home page suddenly changes to a page different from what you chose, you could have a browser hijacker on your system. If you cannot change the home page to one you want and have the change remain, you're infected.

✔ **Unwanted advertisements.** If you see pop-up or banner ads appear on-screen, you may have spyware installed. (Believe it or not, you shouldn't need a pop-up blocker if your system is free of all spyware.)

Don't think that a single symptom is a "sure sign" you have spyware on your system. Other things could be causing individual symptoms. For instance, if your system doesn't have a lot of memory, Windows can spend quite a bit of time swapping memory to a disk file. This causes lots of disk activity, which is one of the symptoms listed. In general, the more concurrent symptoms you have, the greater the chances you have spyware on your system.

If you suspect you have spyware, the first rule is to not panic. Don't start deleting files left and right, thinking you're solving the problem. You probably aren't, and may be making matters worse. A little later in this chapter you discover how to remove spyware.

Getting to know spyware

Even if you haven't experienced the previously outlined telltale signs, it's important that you know about spyware. In this section, I explore the following questions, the answers to which can help keep your computer safe from this Internet villain:

How does spyware get installed on my computer?

Is spyware a serious matter?

Where can I find reliable information about spyware?

How does spyware get installed on my computer?

Believe it or not, you typically install spyware yourself — you just don't realize it. The following list highlights places you may unwittingly pick up spyware:

- ✔ **Popular file-sharing utilities:** Kazaa and LimeWire, to name just two, often include spyware installed automatically when you install the utility.

- ✔ **Innocuous-looking software:** Spyware may be included with software that reports the day's weather forecast or that synchronizes your PC's clock. These programs entice you with something neat, but you also unknowingly install spyware.

- ✔ **Less-than-scrupulous Web sites:** Visit the site and your browser attempts to download and install a driver that is nothing but spyware. The browser lets you know what it's doing, and you can refuse to install the "driver," but every time you load a page at the Web site, you're asked over and over again if you want to load the driver. If you give in and say yes, spyware is installed on your system.

Many spyware companies claim their software is installed legitimately because they include information in the software license agreement that indicates their intent to collect and use information. Reading the license agreements of all downloaded software is very important — *before* you install it on your system.

Is spyware a serious matter?

Many people view spyware as nothing more than an annoyance. Granted, it is annoying — but there's more. Imagine, for a moment, that spyware monitors your browsing, detects when you're shopping online, and then transmits your credit card information to a hacker. From there the hacker can use your credit card without your knowledge or steal your identity.

Reports are starting to emerge concerning people who have lost jobs or spent time in jail due to spyware. If you have spyware on your computer system at work and it brings up pornographic ads, you could easily lose your job — if your boss assumes you've been visiting those sites.

In May 2004, *Wired* magazine ran an online news story about Jack (not his real name) and how he spent time in jail because of spyware that loaded child pornography onto his computer. Someone saw the never-ending pop-ups on his system and reported him to the police. When they raided his home and found the pornographic images on his system — put there, according to Jack, by spyware — he was convicted as a sex offender and sentenced to jail. Jack's case may be extreme, but spyware on your system is a serious matter that you need to address as soon as possible.

The legal side of spyware

In some instances, spyware is actually legal. For instance, your employer can use spyware to monitor how employees use work computers. Courts have ruled that such monitoring is completely legal. You may be tempted to think that your company doesn't trust you if it utilizes spyware. Your employer, on the other hand, has a huge liability for whatever happens on the company computer systems. If the company is liable, then it has a right to monitor and protect the system that carries the liability.

The bottom line is that you should be aware that spyware may be installed on your work computer and that it's perfectly legal. Check with your IT department to determine whether your company uses spyware and how you can detect and remove other spyware without damaging the monitoring software that IT has in place.

Where can I find reliable information about spyware?

The number of spyware programs is increasing, as is the number of sneaky ways for spyware to get on your system. Because the battlefield is changing so rapidly, you need a reliable source of information regarding spyware.

I routinely recommend the following two sites:

- ✔ **SpywareGuide:** This site has some great educational tools, along with descriptions of all the identified spyware programs.

    www.spywareguide.com

- ✔ **SpywareInfo:** This site features a weekly newsletter about spyware, along with helpful forums and software.

    www.spywareinfo.com

Eliminating spyware

Spyware is notoriously hard to remove. In that respect, spyware is very similar to a virus — both can actively thwart your efforts to remove them. Spyware programs often install themselves in several places on your system and include methods for "healing" themselves. In other words, if you don't get rid of all the spyware, it reinstalls itself from the pieces and parts you missed.

You could seriously cripple your system if you start deleting files willy-nilly. Spyware often hooks itself deeply into your operating system. Deleting the wrong files could make the system unusable. My son's system became infected with spyware when he put a file-sharing program on his computer. I started deleting the spyware and then couldn't boot the computer. Ultimately, I needed to do a complete operating system reinstallation.

If you have functioning anti-virus software on your system, it may detect many of the spyware programs that vex you. Some spyware programs use the same tactics Trojan horse software uses, and therefore are vulnerable to detection and removal by anti-virus software. If you suspect undetected spyware on your system, a number of detection utilities are available. The best free program I have seen is Spybot Search & Destroy (`www.safer-networking.org`).

To run Spybot Search & Destroy, follow these steps:

1. **Go to** `www.safer-networking.org` **and download Spybot Search & Destroy.**

   The latest version as of this writing is 1.3 and it's approximately 4.2MB.

2. **Double-click the icon to install the software.**

3. **Run the program by choosing Start⇨All Programs⇨Spybot - Search & Destroy⇨Spybot - Search and Destroy.**

   The main program window, shown in Figure 10-2, appears shortly. The interface for Spybot S&D is very easy to understand and use.

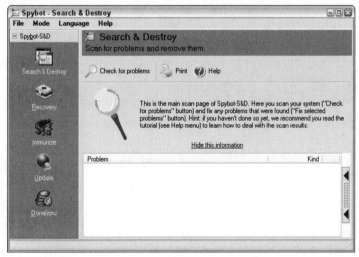

Figure 10-2:
Get ready to
check for
spyware.

4. **Click Check for Problems.**

   The program runs through thousands of permutations of spyware programs that could be on your system.

   Depending on your number of files and hard drives' sizes, letting Spybot S&D run its course can take a good amount of time. On my system, it ran for almost 12 minutes. When it was finished, the program had discovered traces of spyware in several places on my computer; you can see them in Figure 10-3.

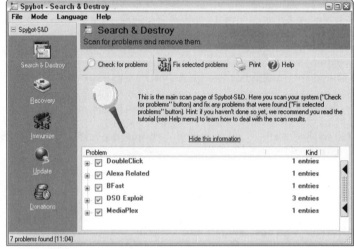

Figure 10-3:
Any trace of
spyware is
called to
your
attention.

5. **Select which things you want the program to correct (by selecting the check box beside each item) and click Fix Selected Problems.**

   Most problems are solved through deletion, but Spybot S&D automatically creates a Windows XP system restore point before doing anything else. This helps in case the spyware deletion causes problems; you can then use Windows XP to restore the system to its condition just before the restore point was set.

6. **When Spybot S&D is done, exit the program and restart your system.**

   You should notice a difference in performance right away.

Don't get hijacked!

An annoying variation on spyware that is becoming more and more common is the *browser hijacker*. This type of pest loads into your system and constantly modifies your browser so that you can't change your home page. Every so often it may even switch the page you're viewing, pointing to someplace you don't want — such as a porn site.

You can eliminate some browser hijacking by following the steps that rid your system of spyware. Other hijackers are particularly nasty and need special attention. One tool that is particularly good at removing hijackers is CWShredder. Go to its Web site for more information on this tool and to download it for free):

```
www.spywareinfo.com/~merijn/
         index.html
```

Blocking Pop-Ups

Everyone has seen *pop-up ads* — small advertising windows that appear onscreen seemingly out of nowhere. One or two popping up now and again is an annoyance; several constantly popping up cripples your system. Where do these pop-ups come from? It has been my experience that most are the result of installed adware (a type of spyware). The software delivers ads with the hope you click a link and purchase something. Trouble is, if you get five, six, or more adware programs — each delivering pop-ups — getting anything done is hard.

Throughout this section I discuss *pop-up blockers* (which can eliminate most pop-up problems) and a relatively new type of pop-up ad that appears directly within your browser's window — the Flash pop-up ad. Knowing that many people block pop-ups, advertisers with larger budgets are turning to TV-type commercials, written in Flash.

Employing pop-up blockers

If you have lots of pop-ups on your system, first get rid of the spyware on your system. (See the earlier section, "Eliminating spyware.") If your pop-ups go away after the spyware is gone, you have no problems — just keep your system clean. If they don't go away or if pop-ups at some Web sites just bug you, I recommend investigating pop-up blockers.

Pop-up blockers do just that — they block pop-ups. Recently other products integrated them. For instance, it's not unusual for anti-virus software to include a pop-up blocker. Google even includes a pop-up blocker in its popular toolbar.

Google toolbar = spyware?

Some people consider Google's toolbar slick spyware, and with good cause. The Google toolbar has a tight integration not just with your system, but also with the folks back home in Googleland. With its advanced features enabled, the toolbar sends information to Google computers about every page you visit in your browser. (Google states this in its privacy policy.) The biggest difference between regular spyware and Google's toolbar is that you can uninstall the Google toolbar much easier than you can regular spyware.

We always did like that boy

Every once in a while I visit my inlaws, who live about 700 miles away from us. One of my regular duties (as the resident computer geek in the family) is to "fix" their computer from all the ills it has garnered since my last visit. The last time I visited, my mom-in-law told me that the computer has a few advertisements that pop up and that they bother her. I told her I would take a look.

When I started the computer, everything looked normal. Within 45 seconds, though, all heck broke loose. (Things are really, really bad when heck breaks loose.) There were pop-ups appearing about every 15 to 20 seconds. Even with good hand-eye coordination, they made the system almost unusable. I was closing windows so often that I thought I discovered a new video game.

My first tack was to disconnect the computer's connection to the Internet. That did away with the ads because they couldn't download, but the computer slowed to a crawl as the system went searching for ads (through the missing Internet connection) and then timed out.

The solution was to run Spybot Search & Destroy (see the "Eliminating spyware" section), which identified about a dozen spyware programs on her system. After I deleted those and restarted the system, all the pop-up ads disappeared.

If you've installed SP2 for Windows XP, your copy of Internet Explorer already has a pop-up blocker installed and active. If you aren't using SP2 and want to use a pop-up blocker, check your anti-virus software first to see whether it includes one. If not, others are on the market. Check out System Mechanic Professional at `www.iolo.com` (first mentioned in Chapter 6), which includes a pop-up blocker. I have also heard good reports about Popup Ad Filter from Meaya Software (`www.meaya.com`), a low-priced product that's capable of filtering out even the toughest pop-ups.

Be careful not to download and use just any pop-up blocker. Some of them are nothing more than adware disguised as pop-up blockers. Make sure your blocker is from a reputable company and that the product receives good reviews.

Blocking Flash ads

Flash is a content-presentation system developed by Macromedia. It's pretty slick, easily allowing developers to create animations and video presentations. If you prefer to leave your commercials on the TV, you can configure your browser so that your computer doesn't display any ActiveX content at all. (ActiveX is a technology that includes, among other things, Flash files.)

Several programs are designed to block Flash advertisements. In fact, some commercial pop-up blockers also stop Flash ads. If you don't use a blocker but are looking for a freeware solution for Flash ads, consider using No! Flash (`www.geocities.jp/baryonlee/noflash/`), written by Barry Lee. It has received good reviews for some time now.

The usual warnings concerning editing the Registry go here. Be careful; if you delete or change something you shouldn't, you could make your system unusable.

If you're comfortable editing the Windows Registry, you can disable Flash yourself by following these steps:

1. **Choose Start⇨Run.**

   Windows displays the Run dialog box.

2. **In the Open box, enter** regedit **and click OK.**

   The Registry Editor window displays.

3. **Using the Registry tree at the left side of the editor, locate and select the HKEY_LOCAL_MACHINE\SOFTWARE\Microsoft\Internet Explorer\ActiveX Compatibility\ key.**

   This key controls how Internet Explorer works with ActiveX components, including Flash.

4. **Choose Edit⇨New⇨Key.**

   A new key appears in the Registry tree, with the name of the key ready to be changed.

5. **Name the new key** {D27CDB6E-AE6D-11CF-96B8-444553540000}**.**

   Include the brackets and everything between, exactly as shown. When done changing the name, the key should still be selected, as shown in Figure 10-4.

6. **Choose Edit⇨New⇨DWORD Value.**

   A new value appears within the key, at the right side of the Registry editor. The value name is ready to be changed.

7. **Name the new value** Compatibility Flags.

   When done changing the name, the value should still be selected.

8. **Choose Edit⇨Modify.**

   The Edit DWORD Value dialog box appears, as shown in Figure 10-5.

9. **Change the Value Data field to** 400.

   Make sure you leave the Base setting as Hexadecimal, as shown in Figure 10-5.

10. **Click OK.**

11. **Close the Registry Editor.**

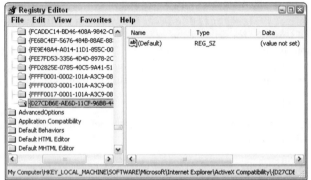

Figure 10-4:
Add a new
data key to
the Registry.

When you restart Internet Explorer, it no longer runs Flash advertisements (or any Flash content). If you later want to re-enable Flash, just delete the data key you created in Steps 4 and 5.

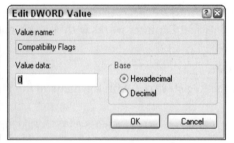

Figure 10-5:
Edit the
value
assigned to
the DWORD
value.

Non-Pop-Up Pop-Ups

When is a pop-up not a pop-up? When it's from the messenger! Windows has a background service called the *messenger service,* which allows geek-type people to talk to each other across a network. Messages can be sent easily and quickly, from computer to computer. Primarily, the service was for network administrators to send messages to people on their networks.

Somewhere along the way, advertisers found out that you could send messages from one machine to another across the Internet. Don't confuse this with e-mail messages; messages that use the messenger service show up on the screen in a Messenger Service dialog box.

You don't need special software to disable these messages. Unless your network administrator says you must have the messenger service turned on, you can turn it off by following these steps:

1. **Open the Control Panel on your system.**

2. **Double-click the Administrative Tools applet.**

   If you're using the Control Panel's task view (the default in Windows XP), click Performance and Maintenance to see the Administrative Tools option.

3. **Double-click the Services icon.**

   Windows opens a dialog box that lists services that either are running or can run on your system.

4. **Scroll through the list and double-click the Messenger service.**

   Windows displays the Messenger Properties dialog box shown in Figure 10-6.

Figure 10-6:
The
Messenger
Properties
dialog box
allows you
to control
when and
how the
service
runs.

5. **Using the Startup Type drop-down list, choose Disabled.**

   The default startup type is Automatic, which means the service is run whenever needed. You don't need it, so disable it. This informs Windows not to start the service next time you start your system.

6. **If the Service Status is Started, click the Stop button.**

   The messenger service is stopped and the Service Status changes to reflect this.

7. **Click OK and close all open dialog boxes.**

Resisting the Lure of Trinkets

I remember the amazement I felt when I first hopped on the Internet in early 1995. With a background in computers, publishing, and information systems, I was agog at what I saw. I was, to borrow a well-worn phrase, like a kid in a candy store.

Many people have this same reaction to the World Wide Web. They spend hours browsing around, looking at this thing or that thing, peering into far-flung places that were previously inaccessible. Like a kid in a candy store, new Internet users want to pick up and try every new thing they see, ohhing and ahhing all the while.

It's a fairly safe bet that the neighborhood candy store is a safe place. Unfortunately, the World Wide Web is not a safe candy store. People are out there who want, for no discernable reason, to feed you things that harm your computer.

You need to resist the urge to download, install, and try out every new trinket that you find on the Internet. Some trinkets may include spyware; others may include things that damage your system.

I make it a personal rule to never download a program unless

(a) I know the developer to be reputable.

-or-

(b) The program received good reviews from others, without charges of being harmful.

If I don't know the developer, I also do one other thing — I read the vendor's privacy policy and license agreement. The privacy policy is important because it governs what the vendor does with information about me. The license agreement is important because it often gives hints regarding whether its software does things on my system that I don't want.

This last point — about the license agreement — is particularly important. License agreements may include important tidbits that indicate what you're agreeing to do if you allow a vendor's software on your system. Look for phrases that indicate the vendor's right to collect data from your system and share your information with their *partners* or *display advertisements*. Unless you like spyware, this type of phrasing is a dead giveaway that you don't want the software installed.

Chapter 11

Managing Internet Information

*T*he phrase *information superhighway* is synonymous with the Internet. With every passing month, the Internet handles more and more information, speeding that information to all corners of the globe — even to your corner.

Yes, your little corner of the globe receives its fair share of Internet information. The Internet applications you use invariably clutter your computer with different files — sometimes hundreds or thousands of files. Knowing what these files are and how to manage them can be a big help toward keeping your system in top form.

In Chapters 8 through 10, I show you how to manage e-mail and keep your system safe from the harmful effects of the Internet. This chapter addresses some of the ways you can manage the information your little corner receives, without ending up cluttered.

Are Cookies a Reason for Worry?

Seasoned Web mavens often refer to *cookies* when discussing the Internet. To those less seasoned, the term *cookies* conjures up thoughts of tasty chocolate chip or (my favorite) snickerdoodles. Those mavens you're eavesdropping on aren't talking about their favorite recipes, though; they're discussing something much less flavorful and much more controversial. Many Web sites include programming code that writes small files on your computer when you visit. Before you run off screaming, "How dare they do that!" it's helpful to understand what cookies do and what they don't.

First of all, cookies are not insidious programs destined to suck the life out of your computer. In fact, *cookies* aren't programs at all — they're data. (Viruses and other life-sucking things are not related to cookies. See Chapter 10 for more information.) Cookies store data necessary for the Web site you're visiting to customize your experience in some way.

For instance, I run a couple of e-commerce sites that use shopping carts. As people browse my sites, they can add items to their shopping carts prior to checking out. The items added to a shopping cart are actually stored in a cookie on the user's system. After the shopper pays for the items, the cookie is left behind on the user's system.

Another example is when you visit sites like Amazon.com. When you visit the site after purchasing something, you see recommendations for different products that may be of interest to you. Amazon recognized you because the last time you visited, it wrote a cookie on your system that contained information about your purchases and interests. When you visited again, that information was accessed and used to generate the new recommendations.

Cookies are, without exception, harmless. Some people consider them controversial because they think cookies are used to gather personal information. That's not entirely true — cookies don't gather information on some far-away site; they remain right on your system. In fact, if any information gathering happens at all, it's done when you first provide your personal information at a site.

Still, some people don't like the idea of cookies being on their systems. Recognizing this, Internet Explorer provides ways to delete and block cookies. In addition, you can use third-party software to more effectively manage any cookies you allow on your system. The following sections describe different ways you can slice, dice, and otherwise deal with cookies, all with the goal of decluttering your system.

Blocking cookies

If the idea of anyone storing anything, of any nature, on your computer drives you absolutely nuts, you may want to block cookies completely. Using Internet Explorer, you can both block and minimize the cookies stored. Follow these steps:

1. **In Internet Explorer, choose Tools➪Internet Options.**

   IE displays the Internet Options dialog box, probably with the General tab selected.

2. **On the Privacy tab (see Figure 11-1), use the slider control at the left side of the dialog box to specify the way you want to limit cookies on your system.**

Figure 11-1:
Internet
Explorer
allows you
to specify
how cookies
should be
accepted.

IE allows you to set any of six acceptance levels:

- **Block All Cookies:** Blocks all cookies from being written, and existing cookies cannot be read.

- **High:** Allows only a tightly controlled set of cookies.

- **Medium High:** Blocks some first-party cookies and most third-party cookies.

- **Medium:** Restricts some first-party cookies and most third-party cookies. (Differs from Medium High by restricting, not outright blocking, some first-party cookies.)

- **Low:** Accepts all first-party cookies, and only a tightly controlled set of third-party cookies.

- **Accept All Cookies:** The door is wide open — any and all cookies are free to jump in your cookie jar.

If you don't mind cookies, use the Accept All Cookies setting. If you're more persnickety, choose Medium or Medium High. As you tighten the restrictions on cookies, you increase the likelihood that you might not be able to use some Web sites; some sites rely on cookies to work properly.

3. Select an acceptance level and click OK to apply your choice.

When setting your privacy level, the slider you use in Step 3 can specify a full range of settings. Most of the nuances between settings has to do with how Internet Explorer handles first-party versus third-party cookies. *First-party cookies* are those that are written on your system (or read from your system) by the actual page you're visiting. A *third-party cookie* is one that is read or written by a site other than the one you're visiting — for instance, by a pop-up advertisement.

Other programs on the market can block cookies. A popular one is ZoneAlarm, a personal firewall program. One of its features is alerting you if someone tries to save a cookie on your system; you can block it so it isn't saved.

Managing your cookies

Unfortunately, Windows XP and Internet Explorer don't provide much versatility when it comes to managing cookies. Sure, you can

- ✔ List cookie files (browse to the folder on your system where the cookies are stored)
- ✔ Limit what cookies are accepted (see the previous steps)
- ✔ Delete all the cookies on your system (see the following section)

but these options don't really count as management except by the most liberal of definitions. Good management practice dictates that you can do cool things such as examine individual cookies and make deletion decisions on a case-by-case basis. Any number of cookie managers is available, and most are *freeware* (available at no cost) or *shareware* (available at a low cost after a short trial period).

One tool I find particularly useful is Cookie Pal, provided as shareware by Kookaburra Software (`www.kburra.com`). The software allows you to block different cookies, but uses a more intuitive interface than what is provided in Internet Explorer. In addition, it works seamlessly with a wide variety of browsers, not just IE.

I typically have no beef if sites want to deposit cookies on my system; the vast majority are no problem at all. Periodically, however, I like to look through what's already there and perhaps clean up the clutter by removing cookies from sites I either don't recognize or don't plan on visiting again in the near future. Cookie Pal works great for that purpose, allowing me to see who put what on my system and delete it if desired.

Deleting all cookies

Cookies tend to collect and collect and collect over time. I checked one of my systems and it has over 600 cookies — and I had deleted all cookies on that system only about four months ago!

Saving your cookies

Cookies are nothing but files stored on your system. If you know where the goods are stored, you can display the folder they're in and back up the files, as desired.

If you plan on deleting all of them, it's a good idea to back them up first. Backing up your cookies enables you to restore one of them if you find that you have unanticipated problems at a Web site you visit often. Simply open the

folder in which your temporary Internet files are located; the cookies are clearly marked. You can then copy them to another directory or to removable media — floppy or Zip disk — before deleting.

If you need help figuring out where the temporary Internet files are stored, see the section titled "Finding the cache," later in this chapter.

Internet Explorer provides a way to delete all the cookies on your system, all at once. Before you rush to delete them, however, remember that cookies can serve a good purpose — they make using some Web sites fast and easy. If a cookie contains a site's username and password, for example, deleting the cookie means you must re-enter that information the next time you visit the site.

To delete all your cookies, follow these steps:

1. **In Internet Explorer, choose Tools➪Internet Options.**

   IE displays the Internet Options dialog box shown in Figure 11-2.

Figure 11-2:
Get ready to toss your cookies.

2. On the General tab, click Delete Cookies.

A dialog box asks if you really want to delete all your cookies. (Never can be too careful, you know.)

3. Click OK.

The cookies are permanently deleted.

Negotiating Newsgroups

I've never caught the newsgroup bug, but I know people who swear by them. Through a system of bulletin board messages and replies, *newsgroups* enable people to discuss, pontificate, argue, harangue, and otherwise kvetch about anything and everything you can think of (although each newsgroup is generally restricted to one point of interest). Newsgroups have been around longer than the Web and will be here long into the future.

Thousands of newsgroups are accessible. Most dedicated newsgroupies use special *newsreader programs* that allow users to access the newsgroups, subscribe to them, and download headlines, articles, and files. Following are just three such programs:

- Agent at `www.forteinc.com`
- Digibin at `www.sixpencesoftware.com/Digibin.htm`
- NewsBin Pro at `www.newsbin.com`

Everything downloaded by your newsreader, however, can clutter your system quite amazingly. I know people who have saved their newsgroup conversations from 1998. Think about that — people are using precious hard drive space to store conversations that occurred the better part of a decade ago. These same people have all the conversations since then, as well.

The bottom line is that newsreader files can quickly fill up megabytes of storage on your system. If you aren't discerning in what you save, you'll eventually run out of space. When jumping into the wild world of newsgroups, remember a few things:

- **Minimize the newsgroups you subscribe to.** You can't subscribe to everything; there aren't enough hours in a day. Be selective about the groups you follow and you'll automatically reduce the clutter they produce. (You probably need to get a real life, anyway.)

✔ **Archive important conversations.** If you're impressed with the words of wisdom imparted by others (or amazed at your own eloquence), then archive what you want to keep. If the conversation is older than three months, however, it's a prime candidate for archiving.

✔ **Delete uninteresting threads.** Don't let old messages, downloaded in error, continue to consume space on your drive. Get rid of them as soon as you can.

✔ **Clean out old binary files regularly.** Many newsgroups allow you to download binary files — pictures, videos, audio, and so on. Sometimes the files are huge. Make sure you keep only what you really need and delete or archive the rest.

A large part of effectively managing newsgroup clutter is mastering large numbers of files. Chapter 7 presents a wealth of ideas for decreasing clutter and increasing efficiency when working with data files.

Organizing Web Favorites

I visit some Web sites over and over and over again. I check out my company's site daily. I regularly visit my bank's site to do some online banking. I go to the Discover Card site to check whether my payment was applied. I pop off to Google to check the news or do a search. I check movie times at the local theatres. The list goes on and on — I visit literally dozens of sites quite regularly, sometimes a few times each day. These sites end up in my Favorites list, where I can access them quickly and easily.

When you first install Windows (which also installs Internet Explorer), 36 different sites are deposited in your Favorites list. I consider these filler sites put there to take up space until you populate the list with your real favorites. Still, when I look at other people's systems, I find that often the preinstalled favorites are still there, taking up space unnecessarily.

In the true spirit of getting rid of clutter, I implore you to vow to delete the favorites you no longer need and organize the rest. Without the unused clutter, you can find and use your favorites quicker than ever before. In Internet Explorer, you can organize your favorites by choosing Favorites⇨Organize Favorites. The Organize Favorites dialog box is shown in Figure 11-3.

The controls in the Organize Favorites dialog box are self-explanatory. Simply select a folder or favorite and either click Delete to remove it or Rename to change its name. You can also click and drag items in the favorites list; drag them to a desired location in the list or drop them in a folder for better organizing. When you're done making changes, click the Close button. The changes are immediately reflected in the Favorites list.

A quick way to delete a favorite you no longer need is to display the Favorites list and right-click the unneeded item. Choose Delete from the context menu, and the item is removed from the list.

Figure 11-3:
This dialog box has all the controls you need to organize your favorites.

Taming Web Cache Files

If I go on a road trip of any length, it's not a pretty sight. I tend to minimize my stops, trying to coordinate restroom breaks with gas fill-ups. (With 400 miles between fill-ups, my wife variously accuses me of sadism and masochism.) I get into the fast lane, stick the car on cruise control, and crank up the tunes. (I prefer classic rock for road trips.) I nibble, snack, and slurp as I drive, often tossing spent boxes, cups, and papers into the back seat. After a day's worth of driving — sometimes 1,000 miles on a long day — the back seat is pretty cluttered (and my bladder is feeling somewhat abused). It takes a concerted effort to get both areas back into the shape they should be.

When you take a road trip on the Internet, your Web browser has a lot in common with my long-distance driving habits. As you nibble, snack, and slurp up the information you find, the browser discards pieces and parts into your computer's back seat. After a while, that back seat gets pretty messy and it needs your attention.

Web browsers maintain what is called a *cache,* an area of your hard drive where the browser stashes recently stored Web pages and, more likely, recently stored images downloaded on your Web travels. If you have a slow Internet connection, the cache is a necessity because it prevents the need for downloading graphics every time you visit a Web page. Visit once and the graphics are downloaded to the cache. Visit the site again and the graphics are loaded from the cache, eliminating the need to download them over the slower Internet connection. (The cache is less useful if you're using a high-speed connection, simply because downloading graphics takes less time.)

The problem is that if you visit 30 Web pages, each with an average of 10 graphics, you end up with 300 graphic images in your cache. Multiply that times a month of browsing every day, and all of a sudden you have 9,000 graphics in your cache. (Do you see the problem with my back seat yet?)

In the following sections you find out how to locate the cache, clean it out, manage its size, and make sure it contains only what you want.

Cleaning the cache

If you're using Internet Explorer, cleaning out the cache is relatively easy. You can do it in a couple of different ways. If you have the browser open, follow these steps:

1. **Choose Tools↩Internet Options.**

    IE displays the Internet Options dialog box. Refer to Figure 11-2.

2. **On the General tab, click the Delete Files button.**

    A warning dialog box offers to delete all your offline content, as well. For most folks, this doesn't matter — they don't browse offline. If you're in the minority that does, select the check box.

3. **Click OK.**

    IE deletes the cache files. Depending on how cluttered your system is, this can take a while. Sit back, relax, and don't be too worried if it appears your system is on vacation.

4. **When IE is done deleting cache files, click OK to close the Internet Options dialog box.**

You now have a fresh, clean cache, ready once again to be cluttered with new pictures from your Internet road trips.

You can also clean out the cache without even opening the browser — just use the Disk Cleanup tool (which I describe in Chapter 6). In a nutshell, you follow these steps:

1. **Choose Start↩All Programs↩Accessories↩System Tools↩Disk Cleanup.**

    The Disk Cleanup tool starts running. If you have multiple hard drives on your system, you're asked to choose which hard drive to analyze.

2. **Pick a hard drive and click OK.**

   Disk Cleanup looks through your hard drive, calculating how much space it can reclaim. This process may take a while. A dialog box, shown in Figure 11-4, indicates things you can clean.

3. **Make sure the Temporary Internet Files option is selected.**

   Temporary Internet files translates to what's stored in the cache. You can also pick other things to clean up, if desired. Chapter 6 includes additional information on your options.

Figure 11-4:
Choose what you want Disk Cleanup to clean up.

4. **Click OK.**

   Disk Cleanup displays a dialog box asking if you want to proceed. (I bet you know how to answer this one.)

Depending on what you asked Disk Cleanup to do, the actual cleanup can take a few minutes to complete. Cleaning out cache files this way takes no longer than cleaning from within the browser.

Finding the cache

Most normal people never worry about where their browser stores its cache files. Microsoft recognizes this and doesn't make a big deal of advertising where the cache is located. You can locate the cache by displaying the

Internet Options dialog box (in the browser, click Tools⇨Internet Options) and then clicking Settings. The resulting Settings dialog box (shown in Figure 11-5) indicates where the cache is located (next to Current Location in the middle of the dialog box).

As you examine the path name, notice that it's associated with the current user. If your computer is shared by multiple users, Windows creates a cache folder for each.

Another interesting tidbit is that Microsoft hides the cache folder. It doesn't hide it in the Settings dialog box, but it does hide it if you try to get to the folder yourself.

To see how this works, open a My Computer window for the C: drive. Double-click the Documents and Settings folder, then your account name. (On my system, I double-click the folder named Allen L. Wyatt.) If your system is like mine, you won't see a Local Settings folder in the account folder, even though the Settings dialog box says you should. The reason for this is that the Local Settings folder is configured as a hidden folder; it doesn't show up when normally viewing folders.

Figure 11-5:
Find where
the cache
is located.

To see the hidden folder, follow these steps:

1. **In the folder window, choose Tools⇨Folder Options.**

   Windows displays the Folder Options dialog box shown in Figure 11-6.

2. **In the Advanced Settings area on the View tab, select the Show Hidden Files and Folders option.**

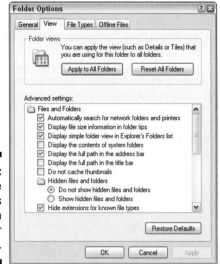

Figure 11-6:
Change
what's
displayed in
a folder
window.

3. **While you're at it (and especially if you wanna be a good geek),**
   deselect **the Hide Extensions for Known File Types and also the**
   Hide Protected Operating System Files options.

   (You might have to scroll down the list to see these options.) Deselecting
   these two options ensures that you see as much information as possible;
   with more information, you can make better decisions in the long run.

4. **Click OK.**

As the Folder Options dialog box disappears, the information in the account
folder is updated. You can now see the Local Settings folder, but the folder
icon should appear a little more washed out than other icons. This indicates
that the folder is normally hidden. You can still double-click it and then
double-click the Temporary Internet Files folder to see what's in your cache.

Changing the cache size

Internet Explorer makes a point of ensuring that your cache never gets too
big. In some respects, the cache is similar to the Recycle Bin — when its maximum size is attained, it starts deleting the oldest files to make room for the
new files.

The problem is that the cache is often set much larger than it needs to be.
The Settings dialog box (refer to Figure 11-5) has a control that indicates the
amount of disk space to use for the cache. By default, Internet Explorer

allocates 10 percent of your disk to its cache folder. This doesn't mean the folder automatically uses that much space, just that IE keeps storing files in the cache (without deleting any of them) until that 10 percent mark is reached.

Think about that for a moment — most computers these days come with at least a 20-, 40-, or 60GB hard drive. If all that space is allocated to a single drive and IE uses that drive for its temporary files, you can easily set a maximum cache size to 2-, 4-, or 6GB. Wow. If the average image downloaded from a Web site is approximately 10K, IE could store anywhere from 200,000 to 600,000 images on your system without deleting anything. Talk about clutter! When hard drives were smaller, the 10 percent rule made more sense.

You can lower the cache size by following these steps:

1. **In the browser, choose Tools⇨Internet Options.**

   The Internet Options dialog box appears. Refer to Figure 11-2.

2. **On the General tab, click the Settings button.**

   The Settings dialog box appears. Refer to Figure 11-5.

3. **Adjust the cache size via the Amount of Disk Space to Use slider or by typing a number in the text box.**

   You shouldn't hesitate to lower the cache space to 75MB. If you have a high-speed Internet connection, lower it even more — perhaps to 35MB or 40MB.

By making this simple adjustment, you save lots of hard drive space for better uses and won't hurt the overall performance of Internet Explorer.

Part IV
The Operating System

The 5th Wave   By Rich Tennant

"Can't I just give you riches or something?"

In this part . . .

In Part IV, you find out how to clean up the user interface, streamline Windows, and speed up the file system.
In addition, you discover when to update and when to get
a new system.

Chapter 12

Cleaning Up the User Interface

- -

- -

A user interface is the way that Windows communicates with you, the user. Windows allows you to tweak, prod, cajole, and otherwise beat into submission most parts of the interface. Because the interface is almost elastic, it can become a dumping ground for clutter and crud.

Your mission, should you decide to accept it (cue the *Mission Impossible* theme), is to use the same tactics of tweaking, prodding, and cajoling to beat the clutter and crud out of your user interface. This chapter shows you how — and you quickly discover it's not an impossible mission.

Master of the Desktop

In the world defined by your computer, your desktop is prime real estate. The things you place on the desktop should represent those items you work with the most. If you use the desktop properly, you won't have to resort to the Start menu that often.

Some folks' idea of prime real estate is more akin to downtown Gary, Indiana. (I don't wanna hear from any readers on the economic development council in Gary about my supposedly disparaging remarks — I used to live there!) The more icons you have on your desktop, the harder you'll find it to use your desktop the way it was intended.

Your desktop was originally intended as a place to do work. (Imagine that!) If you clutter it up with every icon under the sun, your desktop becomes a catchall, not a place to work. The solution is to clean up your desktop and allow only the most critical icons.

The following sections describe different things you can do to remedy a cluttered desktop (and make your prime real estate worth more).

Displaying the traditional desktop icons

Older versions of Windows had a few icons that always appeared on the desktop:

- My Documents
- My Computer
- My Network Places
- Internet Explorer
- Recycle Bin

Of these five, only the Recycle Bin appears on the Windows XP desktop by default. If you want to display any of the other icons, follow these steps:

1. **Right-click anywhere on the desktop.**

   Make sure you right-click the desktop itself, not on an object lying on the desktop. Windows displays a context menu.

2. **Choose Properties.**

   The Display Properties dialog box springs into view.

3. **On the Desktop tab, click the Customize Desktop button.**

   Windows displays the Desktop Items dialog box with the General tab selected, as shown in Figure 12-1.

4. **At the top of the dialog box, select the check boxes corresponding to the icons you want displayed on the desktop.**

   Conversely, you can deselect the check boxes of any icons you don't want displayed.

5. **Keep clicking OK to dismiss all the dialog boxes onscreen.**

The icons you selected should be visible onscreen, along with all the others you have.

Notice in Figure 12-1 that the Recycle Bin icon is not a selectable item. Windows prefers that it always be available on the desktop. If you're bound and determined to remove the Recycle Bin icon from the desktop, use a program such as Microsoft Tweak UI, part of the PowerToys collection. This suite of small utilities is available for free. The Windows XP Professional version is available here:

`www.microsoft.com/windowsxp/pro/downloads/powertoys.asp`

Figure 12-1:
Select the
traditional
icons that
Windows
should
include on
the desktop.

The Windows XP Home Edition version can be downloaded from here:

```
www.microsoft.com/windowsxp/home/downloads/powertoys.asp
```

After you download, install, and run Tweak UI, it presents a very sparse interface, as shown in Figure 12-2.

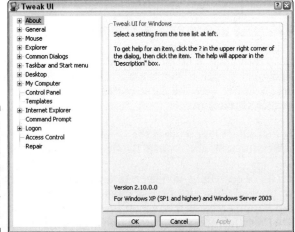

Figure 12-2:
You can use
Tweak UI
to change
many parts
of your user
interface.

To modify the traditional icons that appear on the desktop, click the Desktop item in the hierarchy at the left. At the right side of the screen you then see six icon options, as shown in Figure 12-3.

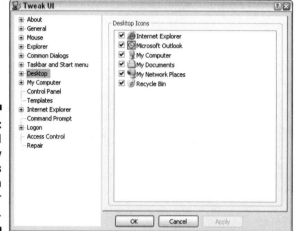

Figure 12-3:
Tweak UI can specify which icons appear on your desktop.

Notice that four of the check boxes in Figure 12-3 are the same as those shown in Figure 12-1. They serve the same purpose: to define which of the traditional desktop icons are visible. You can choose to turn off the Recycle Bin icon, as well.

You can use Tweak UI to change quite a few user interface elements. Spend some time with the program, making changes that reflect how you work (or want to work).

Renaming and deleting icons

Desktop icons can be renamed, just like any other object in Windows: Right-click the icon and choose Rename from the context menu. If you prefer, select the icon and press F2. Either way, the name of the icon is activated, and you can make any changes you desire.

To delete an icon, just select it and press the Delete key. If you prefer to use the mouse, right-click the icon and choose Delete from the context menu.

You should be careful of one thing, however: that you delete shortcuts only from the desktop. You can tell if an icon is a shortcut by looking closely at it. If a small upward-pointing arrow is in the icon's lower-left corner, it's a short-cut. You can delete these left and right without any real consequences — the program, folder, or file pointed to remains on the computer. (You're only deleting a reference to the program, folder, or file, not the actual item.)

If no small upward-pointing arrow appears in the lower-left corner of the icon, then the icon represents the real thing. Deleting the real thing may be something you want to do, but it may not — think through your action to make sure. If you do, delete away! If you don't, consider moving the icon to a different folder on your system so it's still accessible, but doesn't clutter your desktop.

Running the Desktop Cleanup Wizard

The folks in Redmond absolutely love wizards. (Those nutty Microsofties; perhaps they attended Hogwarts while growing up.) Scores of wizards are installed with Windows XP. One such wizard is the Desktop Cleanup Wizard.

The wizard doesn't do anything big or fancy, but it does help get your desktop back under control by examining all the shortcuts on the desktop. If a shortcut hasn't been used within a specific period of time, it's moved to a folder called Unused Desktop Shortcuts. (The wizard creates the folder, on your desktop, if necessary.)

By default, the Desktop Cleanup Wizard is run once every two months. (Well, once every 60 days — but who's picking nits?) You can turn off the automatic run, if desired. Follow these steps to change when the wizard is run or to run it manually:

1. **Right-click an empty area of your desktop and choose Properties from the context menu.**

   Windows opens the Display Properties dialog box.

2. **On the Desktop tab, click the Customize Desktop button.**

   Windows displays the Customize Desktop dialog box.

3. **Either select or deselect the Run Desktop Cleanup Wizard Every 60 Days check box.**

   If you want the wizard run automatically, make sure the check box is selected. If not, then make sure it's clear.

4. **Click the Clean Desktop Now button.**

   The Desktop Cleanup Wizard welcome screen appears, as shown in Figure 12-4. Working through the wizard is quick and painless.

5. **Click Next to begin the wizard.**

   A list of desktop shortcuts that haven't been used in 60 days appears. Brand new shortcuts — which, by definition, have never been used — are also included in the list.

Figure 12-4:
The first
step of the
Desktop
Cleanup
Wizard.

6. Select or deselect a check mark next to each shortcut and click Next.

Shortcuts with a check mark are moved to the Unused Desktop Short-cuts folder; those without remain unchanged. After you click Next, you see a screen (shown in Figure 12-5) that shows you all the shortcuts you're going to move.

Figure 12-5:
Getting
ready to
move the
shortcuts.

7. Click Finish to move the shortcuts.

The folder is created (if necessary) and the shortcuts are moved. You can then close all the open dialog boxes.

If you later decide that you need one of the shortcuts moved to the Unused Desktop Shortcuts folder, open the folder and drag the shortcut back to your desktop. You can also delete the folder (and its contents) at any time, just as you would any other folder.

A word on themes and screensavers

Windows allows you to use different themes and screen savers for your system. Some people find it hard to resist the allure of a tropical background, dancing cursors, animated icons, or infinitely propagating walls.

Fun stuff, but be aware of its dark side. This dark side is rooted in the fact that any processing done on a computer uses resources. That includes even the most mundane things — a blinking cursor, a wagging-tail animated dog, spinning icons, or elaborate system sounds.

Themes that rely on glitz and screen savers that rely on motion or 3D effects look great, but they also consume lots of resources. If the computer is dedicating resources to that, it can't devote those resources to some other program you may be running on your system. Thus, the glitz, glitter, and wow effect can bog down your system and make your main computing tasks slower than they need to be.

This isn't to say that you should never use themes and screen savers — just know how they can affect your system. With all the information, you can make a decision that is right for your needs.

If you decide you like glitz and glitter over raw processing muscle, you gotta check out the Windows interfaces offered at www.stardock.com. Very cool!

Ordering the Menu System

I've been to some restaurants where the menu could almost be classified as a novella. Page after page described in sumptuous detail exactly how the chef proposes to increase my weight and decrease my wallet's weight. In fact, sometimes it takes longer to read the menu than it does to eat the meal.

Sometimes I feel the same way when it comes to the menus in Windows. I know that my productivity is dropping when I find myself spending more time reading menus than using programs.

Fortunately, you have complete control over the way menus work in Windows. The next several sections explain how you can exercise your control, assert your organizational acumen, and reclaim some of your lost productivity.

Picking a Start menu layout

The Start menu in Windows XP is quite a bit different from the Start menu in previous versions. Fortunately, you can select the traditional form of the Start menu, if you prefer. To do so, follow these steps:

1. **Right-click the Start menu button and choose Properties from the context menu.**

   If you prefer, you can also right-click a blank area of the taskbar and choose Properties. Either way, Windows displays the Taskbar and Start Menu Properties dialog box shown in Figure 12-6.

2. **On the Start Menu tab, select the radio button that corresponds to the type of menu you want to use.**

   As you click each radio button, the preview image in the dialog box changes to approximate what your Start menu will look like. The Start Menu option is the Windows XP version and the Classic Start Menu option is the traditional version.

3. **Click OK.**

Figure 12-6:
You can easily choose the type of Start menu you want to view.

Customizing the Start menu

It's a good thing Windows allows you to customize the Start menu. Most everything you do in Windows is funneled through the Start menu in one way or another, so customizing it can help you match the menu to the way you want to work.

The Start Menu tab of the Taskbar and Start Menu Properties dialog box has two Customize buttons (refer to Figure 12-6). Which version of the Start menu you select dictates which button is active. If you select the Windows XP version of the Start menu and click Customize, the Customize Start Menu dialog box appears, as shown in Figure 12-7, offering these options:

- ✔ **The General tab:** Contains controls that allow you to specify essentially what appears on the left side of the Start menu. You can pick the icon size, the number of programs displayed, and what Internet and e-mail icons are displayed.

- ✔ **The Advanced tab:** Features options that have to do primarily with the right side of the Start menu. Different controls indicate which of the right-side options should be displayed and which shouldn't be.

Figure 12-7:
You can change quite a few options for the Windows XP Start menu.

If you select the traditional (Classic) Start menu and click Customize, the Customize Classic Start Menu dialog box appears, as shown in Figure 12-8. The options in the Customize Classic Start Menu dialog box are quite a bit different from those available when customizing the Windows XP Start menu. (This makes sense — the menus are entirely different from each other.) This dialog box provides these areas:

- ✔ **Start Menu:** The buttons at the top of the dialog box allow you to add or remove items from the Start menu. You can also use the Sort button to arrange the menu items. The Advanced button displays only the Start Menu folder, which contains shortcuts and other icons for the Start menu.

- ✔ **Advanced Start Menu Options:** Check boxes at the bottom of the dialog box control a different aspect of how menu information displays. You can experiment with the choices and select those that best reflect how you want to use the Start menu.

Figure 12-8:
Customize
the tra-
ditional
version of
the Start
menu.

Moving items in the All Programs list

The Start menu is just the gateway; it's nothing but a doorway to the menu selections that lie just out of your reach. The real menu selections, of course, are visible when you choose All Programs from the Windows XP Start menu or Programs from the Classic Start menu. Both selections (Programs or All Programs) display a menu hierarchy composed of groups and actual program selections.

The items in the All Programs list are probably not in the order that best reflects how you work. In a perfect world, the menu items you use most often would be listed at the top of the menu, with the less popular options listed lower.

If you want to move things around on the All Programs list, feel free to do so. All you need to do is click a menu item and drag it to whatever position you want. When you drop it, the item appears at the new location and can be immediately used.

Creating your own program groups

A great way to organize the items in your All Programs list is to create your own program group and place menu items within it. Follow these steps to create the group:

1. **Right-click the Start button and choose Open from the context menu.**

   Windows displays the Start Menu folder window.

2. **Double-click the Programs folder.**

   The Programs folder contains many of the items visible when you click All Programs on the Start menu.

3. **Create a new folder in the Programs folder.**

   Right-click a blank area in the folder and choose New, Folder. You can name the folder anything you want.

4. **Close the folder window.**

This folder now appears as a program group in the All Programs list. You can move shortcuts, folder, and files into the new folder; they appear as options within the program group. Use the technique described in the previous section to do the actual moving.

Effectively Using the Taskbar

The taskbar, at the bottom of your desktop, is where you keep tabs on your work. Each project you work on is considered a task, and the taskbar shows what tasks are currently active.

Windows uses the taskbar for quite a bit more information, as well. If you customize it effectively, you can use Window's user interface quicker and easier than ever before.

Birds of a feather . . .

. . . flock together (and sometimes leave a real mess on your car). One of the really cool features available in Windows XP is *task grouping,* which allows those birds to freely flock, without leaving their calling card behind.

When I start opening a lot of programs, folders, or files, my taskbar starts looking downright scary. Each task gets narrower and narrower, until I can no longer understand what the task is supposed to do.

Task grouping comes in handy here. You can instruct Windows to group tasks so that similar tasks use a single taskbar button. For instance, if I have five different Word documents open at the same time, the individual tasks are collapsed to a single button, as shown in Figure 12-9, instead of displaying five buttons. The taskbar button indicates how many individual tasks were collapsed into the single button. In Figure 12-9, I have five Word documents active, indicated by the numeral 5 sandwiched between the Word icon and Microsoft Word on the taskbar button. Click the down arrow to see a list of the individual tasks.

Figure 12-9:
Grouping
tasks saves
space on
the taskbar.

Indicates how many tasks are grouped together

Click to see a list of the individual tasks

Task grouping won't make your system run faster and it won't free up resources (such as memory or hard drive space). What it does is unclutter the taskbar so you can find tasks quicker and easier. After you get used to task grouping, you become more productive when you have lots going on at the same time.

To make sure task grouping is enabled, follow these steps:

1. **Right-click any blank area of the taskbar and choose Properties.**

   The Taskbar tab of the Taskbar and Start Menu Properties dialog box appears, as shown in Figure 12-10.

2. **Make sure the Group Similar Taskbar Buttons check box is selected and click OK.**

   That's it; task grouping is immediately in play.

Figure 12-10:
Task
grouping is
a good
productivity
tool.

Cleaning the notification area

The area at the far-right side of the taskbar is known by many names. Traditionally, it's called the *system tray,* but it's also been referred to as the *task tray* or simply the *tray.* With the release of Windows XP, it's going by the name *notification area.* Sometimes I think Microsoft has people sitting around thinking up new terminology and looking for ways to change old terminology. I guess if I had a billion dollars in the bank, I could hire people to routinely and perpetually change terminology, as well. Go figure. Regardless of what you call it, the notification area contains a bunch of icons representing a program running on your system right now. You can click the Show Hidden Icons button (to the left of the icons in the notification area) and expand the notification area so that you can see all the icons it contains.

If you don't want Windows to hide icons in the notification area, right-click a blank area of the taskbar and choose Properties from the context menu. On the Taskbar tab of the Taskbar and Start Menu Properties dialog box, clear the Hide Inactive Icons check box.

You can help unclutter your system if you examine the icons in the notification area and remove those you don't use regularly. Because each represents a currently running program, removing the icon represents shutting down the program and therefore freeing the resources that program was using.

If you want to close one of the programs, try right-clicking its icon. You see a context menu, and a Close or Exit option may be on the menu. Select the icon and it should disappear from the notification area.

To prevent the associated program from reappearing the next time you start Windows, configure things so the program doesn't automatically run. You can do this in two ways.

The first approach is to run the piece of software in question and try to make the change there. Somewhere in all the software configuration information, a control should appear that determines whether the program displays the notification area icon. The wording used in the control could be just about anything — it could reference the system tray, the tray, or the notification area. It could also reference automatically starting when you start Windows.

When you find the configuration setting, change it and then restart Windows. If the change worked, the icon should no longer be visible in the notification area.

What's really running?

Not all currently running programs have icons in the notification area. Some have tasks on the taskbar and others may not show any outward icon at all. (Windows can run many programs at the same time.)

If you want to see everything running in your system, right-click a blank area on the taskbar and choose Task Manager from the context menu. In the Task Manager dialog box, examine the Processes tab to see all the programs running right now.

When you see what's running, take a look at the column labeled Mem Usage. This column indicates how much memory is allocated to each item. Cluttered systems have many processes running, even if they aren't being used. If something is running, it is using resources that may best be used for something you really need.

If it didn't work, you have to try the second approach by following these steps:

1. **Right-click the Start button and choose Open from the context menu.**

   Windows displays the Start Menu folder window.

2. **Double-click the Programs folder.**

   The Programs folder contains many of the items visible when you click All Programs on the Start menu.

3. **Double-click the Startup folder.**

   The Startup folder contains shortcuts to some of the programs that run automatically when you start Windows. Among these shortcuts may be one for the pesky program that appears in the notification area.

4. **Delete the shortcut for the program you don't want to automatically run.**

   Deleting the shortcut means that the associated program won't run when you next start Windows.

5. **Close the Startup folder window.**

6. **Repeat Steps 1 through 5 — except this time choose Open All Users in Step 1.**

7. **When you're done, restart Windows to determine whether your actions fixed the problem.**

If despite these steps you cannot stop the program from starting and depositing an icon in the notification area, refer to information on the System Configuration Utility described in Chapter 13.

Cleaning Up the Control Panel

The Control Panel (shown in Figure 12-11) may not be the real brains of your Windows system, but it's a place where you can do some serious poking and prodding on the brain. You display the Control Panel by choosing Start⇨Control Panel.

Windows doesn't hold clear title to the entire Control Panel. In fact, other programs can add applets to the Control Panel. It's particularly common for applets to be added whenever you install new hardware drivers. For instance, I have third-party (non-Windows) applets in my Control Panel that were added by the installation program for my network card and my audio card.

Over time, your Control Panel can get quite cluttered with applets. This can make it harder to zero in on what you need to do. If your Control Panel contains applets that you never use, consider removing them. Doing so is quite easy: Just use the Windows Search feature to find all the files on your system that end with the .CPL file extension. (These files are Control Panel applets.) When you search, most of the applets are in the C:\Windows\System32 directory, but duplicates could appear in other directories. If you double-click a .CPL file in the Search Results window, the applet is opened — the same as if you double-clicked the applet in the Control Panel.

To remove an applet from the Control Panel, identify the .CPL file you want to remove and move that file to a temporary folder on a different drive or to a removable disk. That way you can operate Windows for a while without the applet and return the .CPL file if you have problems. If you get along just swimmingly without the applet, delete it or archive it, according to your mood for the day.

Figure 12-11: The Control Panel contains applets that allow you to configure, tweak, and poke your system into submission.

Chapter 13

Streamlining Windows

. . . .

In This Chapter

▶ Minimizing your Windows installation

▶ Tweaking performance options

▶ Making use of the Microsoft System Configuration utility

▶ Enhancing stability with the latest drivers

▶ Getting rid of unneeded DLLs

▶ Disabling unnecessary system services

▶ Using System Restore

. . . .

*W*hen you installed Windows XP, you probably thought it was pretty cool compared to your older version. (If you were like me, you didn't think it was terribly cool until you got used to the intricacies of the new user interface.) Windows XP works faster, smoother, and more reliably than any of its predecessors.

Still, Windows XP — out of the box — is comparable to a solidly built family sedan. That may fit your style for a while, but you may eventually want to grab a hammer, a blowtorch, and a can of Bondo so you can tinker with the car to make it more sporty.

Likewise, you can streamline Windows in a zillion ways to improve its perfor-mance. In fact, entire books have been written on the subject. This chapter focuses on some of the performance tweaks you can apply and tools you can use to declutter your system and make it perform better. This approach isn't the be-all end-all; you need the dedicated books for that. I can, however, guar-antee that if you apply the information in this chapter, your system can run faster and smoother than before. (Keep that Bondo away from the monitor.)

Installing Just What You Need

A good case can be made for the proposition that Microsoft wants Windows to be all things to all people. ("Resistance is futile. You will be assimilated.") With every new operating system version, more bells and whistles are added.

The reality is that you don't need all those bells and whistles. You should carefully select what bells and whistles you install on your system. Paring down Windows to just what you need frees up hard drive space and makes your system run faster. In other words, your system becomes less cluttered.

Most people don't actually install their own operating system. It either came installed on their computer or some geek from the IT department took your system away and brought it back with Windows magically installed.

Fortunately, uninstalling Windows XP components isn't that difficult. Follow these steps:

1. **Choose Start⇨Control Panel.**

   The Control Panel magically appears on your screen.

2. **Click Add or Remove Programs.**

   If you're using the Control Panel's Classic view, double-click the Add or Remove Programs applet. In either case, the Add or Remove Programs window appears.

3. **At the left side of the window, click Add/Remove Windows Components.**

   The Windows XP Setup program starts running. Shortly you see the Windows Components Wizard shown in Figure 13-1.

   Note the Total Disk Space Required statistic at the bottom of the window. Your goal is to get this figure as low as possible, without sacrificing what you really want to do with Windows.

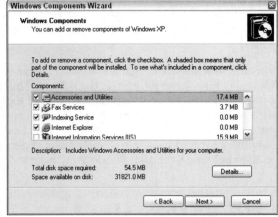

Figure 13-1: You can remove a number of Windows' pieces and parts.

4. **Pick and choose what you want installed.**

   For instance, most people don't need Fax Services or Internet Information Services. Deselecting the check box beside these two saves you over 19MB of disk space right off the bat.

5. **For more information about a particular option, select an option and click the Details button.**

   You can continue clicking the Details button to display more information about what you can remove. For instance, if you choose Accessories and Utilities, you can click Details to see that you can choose to avoid installing either Accessories or Games. If you choose Games, you can click Details to choose which games you don't want installed.

6. **When you're satisfied, click Next.**

   When you're just removing components, you shortly see the final wizard screen.

7. **Click Finish.**

You probably don't need the Windows installation CDs if you're removing features. You do need them, however, if you try to install features. Either way, it's a good idea to have the CDs close by.

Perhaps it's the pragmatic ogre coming out in me, but if you're using your computer in a business environment, you really don't need to have games installed. After all, games aren't considered business for most companies. You can free up over 12MB of disk space just by uninstalling the Microsoft-installed games.

Setting Performance Options

Talk about performance options and most guys think about supercharging their car. Microsoft, single-handedly, is trying to change that perception. When Microsoft uses the phrase *performance options,* it wants you to think about making your computer run faster. Windows even has a configuration area where you can set performance options for your system. It's pretty hard to track down, unless you know where to look. I'm gonna show you where to look.

To display the Performance Options dialog box, click Start, right-click My Computer, and choose Properties. If your system is configured to have a My Computer icon on the desktop, you could right-click it, if you prefer. Either way, the System Properties dialog box flashes into view. In the Performance area of the Advanced tab, click Settings. Windows displays the Performance Options dialog box shown in Figure 13-2.

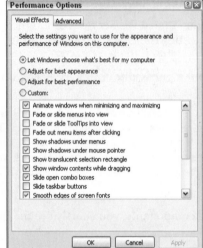

Figure 13-2:
You can
change how
Windows
handles
visual
effects.

Two tabs are in the Performance Options dialog box, each covering distinct areas of performance. Each tab is discussed in its own section, following.

Understanding visual effects

I bet you never gave much thought to the visual effects used in Windows XP. Most people don't; the effects are very subtle. Just little things, like shadows in key places or screen objects that slide smoothly or fade into obscurity as they're no longer needed.

Visual effects, like these and so many others, can rob a system of its performance. If you've got a fast system with plenty of power, you may be able to spare a few processor cycles without any ill effect. On older systems, those with slow graphics cards, or those with limited memory, visual effects do nothing except slow a system.

The Visual Effects tab on the Performance Options dialog box (refer to Figure 13-2) is where you control what effects you want Windows to display. Do so by selecting one of these radio buttons:

✔ **Let Windows Choose What's Best for My Computer:** By default, this is selected. Not surprisingly, some people rile at having Uncle Bill decide anything for them. If you would rather dictate what Windows does, select one of the other radio buttons.

✔ **Adjust for Best Appearance:** This options selects *all* the visual effects.

✔ **Adjust for Best Performance:** This option turns off all visual effects. This should tell you something about what they do to your system performance, right?

✔ **Custom:** To turn individual effects on and off at your will, select this option.

Advanced performance options

The less noticeable performance options are accessible by clicking the Advanced tab shown in Figure 13-3.

You can change only three things on the Advanced tab:

✔ **Processor scheduling:** For most desktop systems, you should leave the default, Programs, selected. Only select Background Services if your computer runs some critical programs as system services. (You find more information about system services later in this chapter.)

✔ **Memory usage:** The second setting controls how Windows allocates memory (RAM) to programs. For desktop systems, the Programs default is just fine. The System Cache selection is appropriate if you're running your system as a server. For instance, if your system is used as an active file or print server — in addition to doing your work — then you should select System Cache.

✔ **Virtual memory:** This setting indicates how Windows uses hard drive space for system purposes. A *paging file* is a chunk of hard drive space Windows uses for swapping programs in and out of RAM.

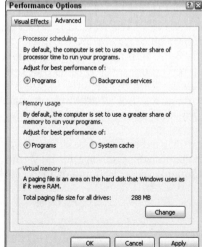

Figure 13-3: Change a couple of settings and you can match system performance to your needs.

If you want to change the paging file settings, click the Change button. For most people, the system defaults for the paging file should be fine. You can modify paging file settings with the goal of better performance, but should do so only after you understand the ramifications of making a change. You learn some more about paging files in Chapter 17, but explaining the detailed ins and outs of paging files is beyond the scope of this book; refer to a good Windows XP technical reference guide for the detailed information necessary.

Using the Microsoft System Configuration Utility

When I was a kid, I joined a secret club. (Well, it was only a secret from all those unwise enough to not eat my brand of breakfast cereal.) I got an official membership card, discovered the official handshake, and got this really cool secret decoder ring. Sometimes, I feel like there must be a secret club for Windows users, but they forgot to give me the really cool secret decoder ring. If I just had that ring, I could figure out why Windows is doing what it's doing.

If you've ever belonged to a kid's secret club, you'll understand my glee when I found out about the Microsoft System Configuration (msconfig) utility. It may not be a really cool secret decoder ring that reveals all of Windows' secrets, but it's a really cool almost-secret program that reveals what's going on whenever you start Windows.

The msconfig utility streamlines what happens when you start Windows. According to Microsoft sources, msconfig "automates the routine troubleshooting steps that Microsoft Technical Support engineers use when they diagnose issues" with Windows' configuration. (Sounds idyllic, doesn't it?)

The reality is quite simple: msconfig allows you to modify how your system starts. When Windows starts, it loads all sorts of things, from a variety of places. If your system is sluggish or you're having problems starting at all, it could be because of conflicts between different programs that run when your system starts. You correct such a condition by uncluttering the startup files. Using the msconfig utility, you can see a list of what Windows loads and individually select which of those items should load.

By its very nature, the msconfig utility exemplifies geekiness. If you're not afraid of delving into your system's innards, you may actually enjoy using msconfig. If you don't have a technical streak, you may want to steer clear of it.

To start msconfig, choose Start⇨Run. In the Open text box, type **msconfig. exe** and click OK. The program is executed and very shortly you see the System Configuration Utility program window shown in Figure 13-4.

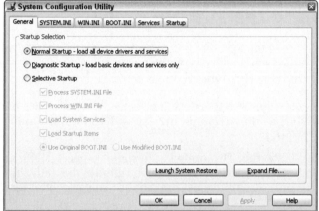

Notice that there's no menu bar for the program; everything is handled through a series of tabs. These tabs represent different aspects of how Windows starts on your system. Besides the General tab (shown in Figure 13-4), you could see a variety of others:

- **System.ini:** This tab shows the contents of the system.ini startup file. The tab doesn't contain the file text but presents the file contents in a hierarchy.

- **Win.ini:** This tab shows the contents of the win.ini file. A carryover from earlier versions of Windows, this file is used for backward compatibility with some older programs. Again, the file contents are displayed in a hierarchical manner.

- **Boot.ini:** This tab shows the actual contents of the boot.ini file. This file indicates exactly how your system should boot. On most systems the file is pretty mundane, but it becomes critical if you have multiple operating systems or different versions of Windows on the same system.

- **Services:** This tab lists all the services that Windows can start. (Windows services are discussed a bit later in this chapter.)

- **Startup:** This tab lists all the programs automatically started whenever you begin Windows.

Additional tabs may be present, depending on your system's configuration. For instance, you may see tabs that contain environment or international settings.

Modifying the startup process

The General tab on the System Configuration Utility dialog box (refer to Figure 13-4) allows you to specify, in the most general way, how your system starts. Three options are available on the tab:

- **Normal Startup:** With this default selected, Windows goes blithely on its way, loading all the programs, drivers, and services it was instructed to load.

- **Diagnostic Startup:** This option is, in some respects, similar to starting your computer in safe mode. When you choose this radio button, Windows only loads the most basic of its many potential services and drivers.

  Normally, you choose Diagnostic Startup only to get rid of all the potential problem areas in one move. If your system starts problem-free with Diagnostic Startup selected, you would then move onto Selective Startup to narrow the problem even further.

- **Selective Startup:** This option enables you to make choices regarding which startup files are processed. If you deselect one of the check boxes under this option, then the corresponding startup file is skipped when Windows starts.

If you're experiencing startup problems, follow these steps:

1. **Choose Start⇨Run, type** msconfig.exe **in the Open dialog box, and click OK.**

   The System Configuration Utility program window appears.

2. **Deselect all the check boxes under Selective Startup and click OK.**

   (The boot.ini option is not a check box; you won't be able to change it.)

3. **Restart Windows.**

   You should have no problem.

4. **Go back to msconfig, select the first check box (system.ini), and click OK.**

5. **Restart Windows again to see if your problems crop up again.**

   If your problems crop up, you know the problem is in system.ini. If they don't crop up, then you know system.ini had no problem.

6. **Repeat the process until you've selected all the check boxes one at a time, restarting Windows after each.**

   Through this iterative process, you can determine which startup file is causing problems. You won't yet know which command in the file is causing problems, but you'll know where to look closer.

Modifying startup files

Windows uses a bunch of startup files. You can see these files (system.ini, win.ini, boot.ini, and so on) through msconfig, where you can also modify their effect on the startup process. (See the preceding section.)

Figure 13-5 shows the msconfig tab for the system.ini file. Notice that the information on the tab is shown in a hierarchical manner, with check boxes. The information presented on the boot.ini tab is similar to this. Many of the older Windows startup files (such as system.ini and boot.ini) are organized into sections. Each section begins with a keyword, on a line by itself, surrounded by brackets. Each file section contains individual Windows configuration commands.

The hierarchical display shown in Figure 13-5 represents the section of the startup file. The check boxes beside each section name allow you to indicate if you want that section processed when Windows starts. By selectively turning off different sections and restarting Windows, you can determine which section of the startup file may be causing your problems.

If a section name has a plus sign to the left, clicking it displays the contents of that particular section. Again, use check boxes to determine whether Windows should process a command line.

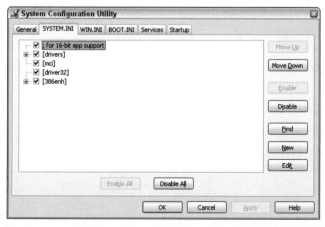

Figure 13-5:
Startup
files are
displayed in
a hier-
archical
manner.

It's important to remember that msconfig doesn't actually edit the startup files; it simply allows you to select which parts are processed. Once you identify a problem area, open the file in Notepad and make the edit.

Be very careful when it comes to modifying the boot.ini file. In fact, you should not modify it unless you know absolutely what you're doing. If you mess up the file, your system won't boot — period. That means you won't even be able to get back to msconfig to fix it. Be careful!

Modifying what is started

Perhaps the most informative tab in msconfig is Startup, shown in Figure 13-6. This tab lists programs that automatically run every time you start Windows. Most of these programs end up as icons in the taskbar's notification area (see Chapter 12), but some run and leave no outward sign that they're active in memory.

Each startup item has a check box next to it; you can turn off the program next time you start Windows by deselecting it. The really helpful thing about the Startup tab is the Location column. Studying this column can disclose where the actual command to run a program is located.

For instance, if the Location column for a startup item shows Startup, the command is in the user's Startup folder. To see the folder, right-click the Start button, choose Open, double-click Programs, and then double-click Startup. The shortcut or program should be in that folder.

Similarly, if the Location column contains Common Startup, the command is in the Startup folder maintained for all users. To display the folder, follow the same steps just covered, but choose Open All Users instead of Open.

Figure 13-6:
The Startup
tab lists
all the
programs
that auto-
matically
run when
Windows
starts.

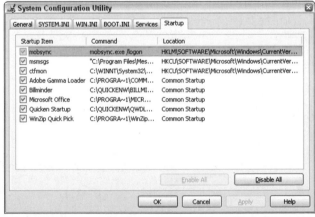

Finding programs in the Startup folders is not particularly difficult; I show you how to do that in Chapter 3. Tracking down programs that run because of entries in the Windows Registry is more difficult. The msconfig Startup tab makes this easier because the Location column can indicate a Registry key that contains the program's startup command.

If you want to remove a startup command from the Registry, doing so is not for the feint of heart — the Registry can be quite daunting. Refer to Chapter 20 for the necessary information on working with the Registry.

Using msconfig's Startup tab, you can select which programs should be started when you begin Windows and which shouldn't. Deselect the check box for any programs you don't want started and then reboot. If problems crop up, you can also go back to msconfig, select the check box, and restart.

Working with the Latest Drivers

Drivers rule! Device drivers do, anyway. Without device drivers, devices are little more than expensive works of art — nice to look at but not terribly productive. *Device drivers* provide an interface between the operating system and a piece of hardware. Information moving from Windows to the device (or vice versa) travels through the driver, so it's critical to make sure that the drivers work properly.

Unfortunately, drivers often clutter systems unnecessarily. Installation programs often take the shotgun approach to compatibility: Install every possible driver for the device, even if only one of them is ultimately used. The extra drivers take up space and make your system more complex than it needs to be.

The following sections discuss how you can make sure you have the latest (and safest) drivers and how you can remove drivers, if necessary.

Checking a driver's signature

For Windows to function properly, all the pieces and parts that make it up must work together flawlessly. (Trust me; it has thousands of parts.) If a problem crops up with one little part, then Windows becomes unstable and can behave erratically — or not at all.

Historically, device drivers are a weak spot in the thousands of pieces that make up Windows. Microsoft has no control over many device drivers, relying upon third parties to create the drivers necessary to support its hardware and software. Some developers do a good job; others don't.

To help mitigate the problem, Windows created something called the Windows Hardware Quality Lab. This lab tests different hardware designed to work with Windows. If the hardware (and its attendant drivers) passes the battery of tests, then the driver is granted a digital signature. This signature is essentially a mark of quality assurance, signifying that the driver has passed the tests and can be relied upon.

This does not mean that unsigned drivers won't work; it just means that those drivers don't have Microsoft's stamp of approval. Windows XP even has a tool that allows you to see whether the various drivers in your system are signed.

To run the File Signature Verification utility, follow these steps:

1. **Choose Start⇨Run, enter** sigverif.exe **in the Open box, and click OK.**

   The welcome screen for the utility, shown in Figure 13-7, appears.

Figure 13-7:
Get ready to
check file
signatures.

2. **To use the program in simplest way, just click Start.**

   The program can take quite a while to run through its tests; it checks a large number of folders and directories. When the scan is completed, you see a summary screen like that in Figure 13-8. Note that in this case 3,100 files were located, but only four of them were unsigned. Those four are shown in the summary.

   Figuring out what the unsigned drivers do can be frustrating. After all, how are you supposed to know what acpdf207.dll does or whether it's necessary to have mdiui.dll on your system?

3. **Do a Google search for the driver's name.**

   Chances are good that you'll find results that indicate more information about the file. You can then decide whether to keep or remove it.

4. **To see a full report of all the drivers checked, click the Advanced button (refer to Figure 13-7), display the Logging tab, and click View Log.**

The log file can be mind-numbingly long, but you get a real sense of geek pride when you successfully wade through it.

5. **When you finish using the File Signature Verification utility, click the Close button to exit the program.**

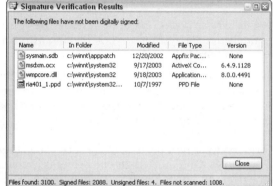

Figure 13-8:
A summary of unsigned drivers.

The File Signature Verification utility isn't limited to checking drivers. You can use it to check other files, as well. For instance, you might want to check all executable files (ending in .EXE) to see if they're signed. You can check other files by clicking the Advanced button, available when you start the File Signature Verification utility (refer to Figure 13-7). You then see the Advanced File Signature Verification Settings dialog box, shown in Figure 13-9. Click the Look for Other Files That Are Not Digitally Signed radio button and set the search options in the bottom of the dialog box. When you click OK, you're returned to the starting dialog box, where you can click Start to perform the search.

Figure 13-9:
Search for signatures on other types of files.

Checking for updated device drivers

If you find unsigned drivers (see the preceding section) or you experience problems with a signed driver, you may want to look for updates. Similar to other software programs, drivers are updated periodically to fix problems in older versions. You can update drivers in two ways:

- Update Windows; its *service packs* (major updates to the operating system files) routinely update system drivers. Dealing with Windows updates is covered in Chapter 15.

- Check the hardware manufacturer's Web site if a third party developed the driver. For instance, if you have an Epson printer, go to the support section (generally where you find driver updates) of the Epson Web site, download the appropriate driver, and then install it.

When downloading drivers from third parties, make sure you get the driver version designed for Windows XP. If more than one driver is available for Windows XP, check the descriptions to figure out which one is best for you. (For instance, one driver may work best if you have a particular service pack installed.) If you download and install drivers intended for other operating systems, you run the risk of making your system unstable.

Removing device drivers

Like rabbits on overdrive, device drivers tend to multiply and multiply quickly. Every new piece of hardware you install adds one or more drivers. Many pieces of software add drivers. These drivers normally end up in the Windows folder (or one of its subfolders) and stay there way too long. Even if you remove the hardware or software, one or more drivers will probably remain behind.

If you have nothing better to do one afternoon, spend some time identifying and removing unneeded drivers. (You might also want to remove unsigned drivers if you know you can get a later, signed version.) The most common file extension for drivers is .DLL, but drivers can have other extensions, as well.

Start by using the File Signature Verification utility, which I describe in the earlier section "Checking a driver's signature," and looking at the full log file it creates. Look at the unchecked files — often drivers you no longer need. You can do a search on Google to determine what the driver does and then make an executive decision to delete it.

Be careful removing drivers — if you delete a critical one by mistake, you may make your system unstable. Instead of deleting it, move the driver to a temporary folder and then restart your system. If you find the driver was necessary, you can move it back to its original location.

Going on a .DLL Diet

The most common file extension for drivers is .DLL. That does not mean, however, that all .DLL files are device drivers. To the contrary, many .DLLs are used for other purposes. *Dynamic link library* (DLL) is a type of file format that allows common code snippets to be shared between the operating system and multiple programs. The original idea of .DLL files was to reduce the overall resources necessary for the code, just by sharing.

Such economy was necessary in the early days of Windows because hard drivers weren't as large and memory wasn't as plentiful. As hard drives became larger, memory more plentiful, and Windows bigger, .DLLs also became a bigger problem. My Windows XP system, with all my production programs loaded on it, has over 5,600 .DLL files.

Just think about that for a moment — over 5,600 .DLL files that need to be tracked and swapped in and out of memory. Tracking and swapping aren't the biggest problems, however. The big problem is keeping all the .DLLs updated. If I update one program, it wants to update the .DLLs that it uses. If other programs use some of those .DLLs, the updated .DLLs may "break" the other programs, which are not expecting a change.

The result is a greater chance for system instability — different programs, over time, become more prone to crashing and malfunction simply because of updating .DLL files. This condition even has a name: .DLL hell. Microsoft has worked hard over the last couple of versions to minimize or eliminate .DLL hell. Windows XP is much more stable than its predecessors, in large part because of the way it handles .DLL files.

This is great for you, the user. (Increased stability is always better.) It doesn't change the fact that having 5,600+ .DLL files on a system is common.

The solution lies in recognizing that not all of those files are necessary. The files accumulate over time — new programs (and their .DLLs) are installed; the .DLLs remain when the programs are removed. Orphan .DLL files are not individually a problem, but collectively they contribute to an astounding amount of clutter. This makes the operating system work harder and eats up more disk space than should be eaten.

The task devolves to the user (that's you) to figure out what .DLLs can be removed from a system, and then doing so. Obviously, sifting through 5,600+ .DLLs to figure out which ones should be deleted is not something you want to do manually. That's why programs exist to handle it for you.

I haven't seen a good standalone .DLL-winnowing program. Instead, the feature is typically built into a larger software package. You often find the feature in the following types of packages:

✔ **Registry cleaners:** These types of programs search through the Windows Registry, looking for ways to tidy it up. In so doing, they often make a list of deletable .DLL files. (Registry cleaning software is described in more detail in Chapter 20.)

✔ **Uninstallers:** Programs that specialize in uninstalling software have begun to spring up. These programs many times do a much better job of removing program remnants — including .DLL files — than the built-in uninstallers provided with the software.

✔ **Disk cleaners:** These utilities were developed specifically to look for unused files (including .DLL files) that can be removed from a system.

Any number of programs could be suggested to perform these tasks. You should figure out which one you think would benefit you most (I tend to like Registry cleaners) and then search for one that makes sense. You can often find good shareware versions on the Internet. Just make sure you look for good reviews (and possible awards) on any program you consider using.

Shut Down Unused Services

Even when you think no programs are running in Windows, some probably are. Some run in the background, without you ever knowing it, doing work required to support other programs or to accomplish assigned system tasks.

When Windows is installed, it comes with a whole raft of services that can be started on demand. The problem is other programs can start the services without your knowing it. If those other programs are malicious (such as spyware, discussed in Chapter 10), then those services can be used toward ends you would never approve of.

Because services can be started without your knowledge, they represent a vulnerability. To get rid of this vulnerability, you need to identify the services you never use or need and configure them so that they cannot be run. You can accomplish this task in a couple of ways, which I discuss in the following sections.

If you're familiar with UNIX or Linux systems, the equivalent to Windows services are *daemons.* Both do exactly the same thing — run in the system background.

Services in the Computer Manager

The Computer Manager is a very powerful administrative tool, but few people know about it. It allows you to manage a passel of things, such as disk drives, devices, and (fortunately for you) services. To start the Computer Manager and see which services are installed, follow these steps:

1. **Click the Start button.**

   Windows displays the Start menu.

2. **Right-click the My Computer option and choose Manage.**

   If your system is configured to have a My Computer icon on the desktop, you could right-click it. Either way, Windows opens the Computer Management window. The window shows a hierarchical display of tools and features on the left of the screen.

3. **If Services and Applications has a plus sign (in the hierarchy), click it.**

   The tree is expanded, and you see a number of items under Services and Applications.

4. **Click the Services option in the hierarchy.**

   A long list of services appears at the right side of the screen, as shown in Figure 13-10. Pay particular attention to the Status and Startup Type columns. The Status column indicates if a service is currently running. Each running service is noted as Started in the Status column.

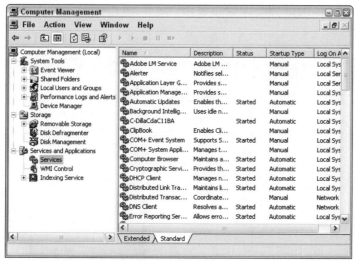

Figure 13-10: Windows XP includes quite a few available services.

The Startup Type column can contain one of three values:

- **Automatic:** The service is started whenever Windows is started.
- **Manual:** The service is started manually, explicitly by you or by another program that needs the service.
- **Disabled:** The service cannot be started.

Most of the listed services are optional, but don't start disabling services willy-nilly. Examine the description of a service or even do a Google search on the service name. Seeing a service's full description often helps you decide if you want to disable it.

5. **Widen the Description column, if desired, or click the Extended tab at the bottom of the services list.**

   The display changes to show the full description of the selected service at the left. See Figure 13-11.

6. **If you don't want a service to be started, double-click its name.**

   The service's Properties dialog box appears.

7. **On the General tab, you can change the Startup Type to Automatic, Manual, or Disabled.**

8. **Click OK after making your choices and then close the Computer Management window.**

If you use the Disable Startup Type for a service, then it cannot be run. If another service depends on the disabled service, then the other service may fail. You can see which other services depend on the one you're changing by clicking the Dependencies tab in the service's Properties dialog box.

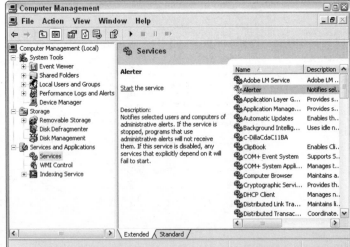

Figure 13-11: Displaying the extended version of the services list can be helpful.

Services in msconfig

Earlier sections of this chapter cover how to use the Microsoft System Configuration (msconfig) utility to track down problems and remove clutter from your system. You can use the utility to identify services that you may want to shut down.

Click Start➪Run and enter **msconfig.exe** in the Open text box. When you click OK, the program window appears. The Services tab shown in Figure 13-12 reveals the same services listed in the Computer Management window (refer to Figure 13-10), with an additional column: Essential. If Microsoft considers a service essential to Windows' operation, the word Yes appears in this column. You should not disable these services.

Remember that msconfig does not allow you to start and stop services. You can disable services only so that they don't run when the system is next started. For this reason, you may want to open both the msconfig utility and the Computer Management window at the same time. That way you can review services in both windows, at the same time, and make educated decisions about which to disable.

Figure 13-12:
The msconfig Services tab lists all the services in your system.

Putting System Restore to Work

"Set the Wayback Machine, Sherman." With this simple command, Mr. Peabody would get ready to travel through time with his boy, Sherman. They would take improbably jaunts through history, explaining the events and saving the day, all in an animated cartoon of under five minutes.

Who knew, when *Peabody's Improbable History* debuted in 1959, that when Windows XP debuted over 40 years later it would include its own Wayback

Machine, appropriately (and geekily) named System Restore. You can use System Restore to turn back the clock and restore your system's condition to a simpler, happier time.

System Restore is enabled, by default, on Windows XP. The utility periodically takes snapshots of the condition of each drive and stores that snapshot in case it's later needed.

To understand how you might need System Restore, consider the scenario where your system is running fine when you install a new piece of hardware and three new programs that use that hardware. About a week later you discover that one of your older and less-used programs is giving you fits, even though it worked fine before. In addition, Windows now crashes once in a while (which has a tendency to elicit a catechism of four-letter words).

System Restore shines here, allowing you to turn back the dial (always critical on the Wayback Machine) to a point in time before the hardware and software were installed. Presto! Your system operates without the problems introduced by who-knows-what-part of the new hardware and software.

Configuring System Restore

System Restore is turned on by default on your system. Windows XP allocates disk space on each hard drive to store System Restore information. Because Windows tends to allocate lots of space for this purpose — far more than you really need — you may want to modify the amount of space.

Click Start, right-click My Computer, and choose Properties. If your system is configured to have a My Computer icon on the desktop, you could right-click it instead of going through the Start menu. Either way, the System Properties dialog box flashes into view.

The following options are found on the System Restore tab (shown in Figure 13-13):

✔ **The Turn Off System Restore check box:** Use this option to disable System Restore completely. (If you have more than one drive, the option is called Turn Off System Restore On All Drives.) There really is no reason to do this, as the feature does not slow system performance in the least. The check box should be deselected.

✔ **Disk Space Usage area:** Windows typically attempts to set aside 12 percent (the maximum) of a drive's space for System Restore. If you have a small drive, this should be fine. If you have a large drive, the amount is probably too much. Adjust the slider control to allocate about 1500MB. You can allocate less, but doing so means storing less System Restore information.

✔ **Status area:** If you have more than one drive, you see a list of all those drives at the bottom of the dialog box. The word *Monitoring* in the Status area indicates that System Restore is available and working on that drive. If you select a drive and click the Settings button, you can either turn off System Restore for that particular drive or configure the amount of disk space allocated to the feature.

If your system has only one drive (as shown in Figure 13-13), use the main dialog box to turn on or off System Restore and to set the amount of disk space usable for restores.

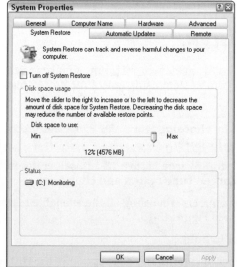

Figure 13-13: System Restore is configured for each drive in a system.

Setting a restore point

System Restore functions based on the concept of restore points. A *restore point* is a snapshot of a system's state at a given point that's stored automatically by System Restore on a regular basis. In addition, Windows sets a restore point whenever you perform a Windows update or install an unsigned device driver. In addition, some third-party utility programs set restore points before changing your system.

You can manually set a restore point whenever you feel the need, such as before installing new hardware or software or editing the Registry. Windows allows you to store multiple restore points for each drive, up to the amount of space you allocated for use by System Restore.

Follow along to manually set a restore point:

1. **Choose Start⇨All Programs⇨Accessories⇨System Tools⇨System Restore.**

   The System Restore window appears, as shown in Figure 13-14.

2. **Select the Create a Restore Point radio button and click Next.**

3. **Enter a description for the restore point and click Create.**

   In a few moments you're notified that the restore point is created. Pretty easy, huh?

Reverting to history

If System Restore allows you to save a restore point, it makes sense that it also allows you to restore your system using one of the stored restore points. Just follow these steps:

1. **Start System Restore by choosing Start⇨All Programs⇨Accessories⇨ System Tools⇨System Restore.**

2. **In the first program window (see Figure 13-14), select the Restore My Computer to an Earlier Time option and click Next.**

   A really cool calendar appears, revealing all the available restore points. The calendar is shown in Figure 13-15.

3. **Click any date shown in bold.**

   The right side of the screen shows the description of the restore points available for that date.

   Depending on the amount of space you have allocated to System Restore, you can have quite a few restore points available.

4. **Pick the restore point desired and click Next.**

5. **When prompted, confirm that you want to do a restore.**

   When you confirm your desire, System Restore sets another restore point before actually doing the restore you want. It does this so that you can undo the restore you're about to do if need be. How cool is that!

After a reboot, your system behaves exactly as it did when the selected restore point was set.

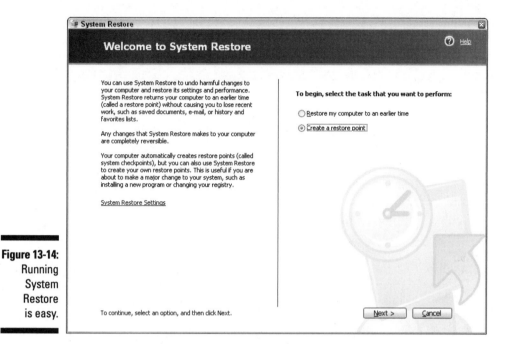

Figure 13-14:
Running
System
Restore
is easy.

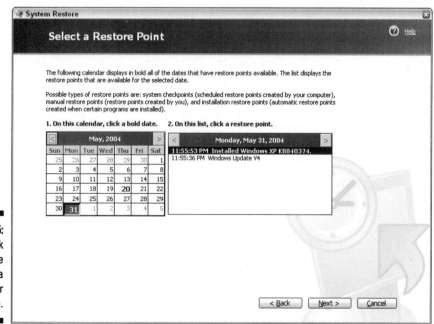

Figure 13-15:
You can pick
a restore
point from a
calendar
interface.

Chapter 14

Speeding Up the File System

· ·

In This Chapter

▶ Making sense of file systems

▶ Converting from one file system to another

▶ Removing disk fragmentation

▶ Checking a disk for errors

▶ Choosing whether to compress your disk

· ·

*I*n geekspeak, a *file system* is the organizational method that the operating
system uses to store information on a disk drive. Read that sentence
again; it's not as intimidating as it probably sounds. If your eyes still glaze
over a bit when you think about file systems, back up a moment and think
about something a bit more mundane. Walk into your kitchen, breathe deep,
and take a look around. You probably have a refrigerator, some cupboards,
and some counter space. All of these areas can be used to store stuff.

In our kitchen, we store the glasses in the cupboard to the right of the sink,
where they're handy. We store pots and pans in a lower cabinet, near the stove.
We stack our plates in another cupboard, and our bowls right next to them.
One cupboard (which I am afraid to open) contains a wide assortment of plas-
tic storage tubs and an even wider assortment of lids that don't match. One of
the drawers is dedicated to silverware, and another to dishtowels. A holder on
the countertop is full of miscellaneous wooden spoons and spatulas.

Our kitchen is not unique; we store things in there because we use them to
prepare food and do other tasks in the kitchen (like exotic chemistry experi-
ments and impromptu smoke-alarm tests). The idea is that over the years
we've devised a way to store things that makes it easy for us to later retrieve
those things.

Similarly, your operating system needs to organize a hard drive so that it can
easily store and retrieve things. This is the whole basis of a file system — it
defines how the operating system stores and retrieves those things.

Just as you need to periodically examine your kitchen to determine whether
things can be organized better, this chapter helps you look at your file system
to look for better ways.

Which File System to Use?

Windows XP supports two primary file systems, which go by two typically geeky acronyms: FAT and NTFS. Judging by the acronyms alone, you might think that NTFS is better than FAT. After all, it has more letters (it must be 33 percent better), and it doesn't have the mnemonic baggage that *fat* does.

While some people may consider the case closed after such an astute analysis, other, more solid reasons are available for using one file system versus the other. The following sections introduce the two file systems and then you discover some guidelines for making your choice.

The FAT file system

FAT is an acronym for *file allocation table*. This file system has been around, in one form or another, since the introduction of DOS in 1981. Because it has a long, long history, FAT is supported by all versions of Windows, including Windows XP.

Two variants exist: FAT (or FAT 16) and FAT 32. FAT 32 was introduced with Windows 95 (SR2) and is still supported in Windows XP. The difference between the two is in how they allocate space for internally tracking files and the size of the hard drive partitions they can access.

FAT 16 can access drive partitions up to 2GB and can store only up to 512 entries in the root directory. (This has to do with the file system's internal structure and how it tracks files.) FAT 32 can access drive partitions up to 32GB in size and has no limit on the number of files that can be stored in the root directory. (Find out more about the root directory in Chapter 7.)

If you choose to format a drive using FAT, Windows XP automatically uses the FAT 32 standard. In addition, any floppy disks formatted by Windows XP automatically use the FAT system.

The NTFS file system

NTFS is an acronym for *new-technology file system*. The file system was introduced with Windows NT. (The NT in Windows NT stands for *new technology*, so NTFS is the file system for Windows NT.)

When the engineers at Microsoft looked at the FAT file system used in DOS systems, they wanted to change how information was stored on a hard drive. In fact, they had to change it to meet some of the demands placed on the file system by Windows NT systems.

Windows NT systems were designed to be used in a networked environment — something never intended for FAT systems. (A *networked environment* is one in which multiple computers are connected in some sort of network.) Wider information accessibility meant greater concern for security and a potentially greater number of people accessing the data. FAT systems just weren't robust enough for such an environment.

The NTFS file system has grown over the years since Windows NT was introduced. NTFS can now access drive partitions up to 2TB in size. (That's two terabytes, or 62.5 times larger than the largest partition accessible by FAT 32. Considering that the largest hard drive I can find on the shelf at my local computer store is 300GB, NTFS can handle the load just fine.)

Making your choice

The default file system for hard drives in a Windows XP system is always NTFS. In most situations, this will work just fine for you, and you should accept this default when formatting. Some other nuggets are worth considering:

- ✔ If your system must be accessed by multiple operating systems (for instance, you have a dual-boot capability on your system), then you should use a FAT 32 operating system.

- ✔ If your hard drive partition is very small (256MB or less), then FAT 32 is a fast and efficient choice.

- ✔ If the hard drive partition is small and you want its data to be accessible if you boot to a floppy, use FAT 32.

- ✔ If you need to store very large files on your system (such as big databases or multimedia files), then you should use FAT 32 or NTFS.

- ✔ If you need increased file security or you share your data with others over a network, use NTFS.

Changing File Systems

Most Windows XP systems that begin as Windows XP systems (they've never had an older version of Windows on them) are formatted using the NTFS file system. If your system was upgraded a couple of times over the years and finally matured to a Windows XP system, it may use the FAT or FAT 32 file system.

If that's what your system uses and you don't have a specific need for it, you could benefit by converting to NTFS. The benefit is realized through better disk performance and better data security.

It's a good idea (actually, an excellent idea) to back up your data before you do any file system conversion.

Seeing what file system you use

Most people don't give their file system a second thought. With all this talk of file systems, you may suddenly be wondering what file system you have. To figure this out, follow these steps:

1. **Click the Start button.**

   Windows displays the Start menu.

2. **Right-click My Computer and choose Manage.**

   If your system is configured to have a My Computer icon on the desktop, you could right-click it. Either way, Windows opens the Computer Management window. The window shows a hierarchical display of tools and features on the left of the screen.

3. **If a plus sign is next to Storage (in the hierarchy), click it.**

   The tree is expanded and you see a few items under the Storage item.

4. **Click the Disk Management option in the hierarchy.**

   A list of your disk drives appears at the right side of the Computer Management window, as shown in Figure 14-1. At the top-right you see a list of all your system's drives. The File System column indicates the file system used for the drive. (Different drives can use different file systems.)

A wealth of information is found in the Computer Management window. If you scroll left and right, you can see each drive's capacity, along with how much of that space is available. The Status column indicates whether something is wrong with a drive, allowing you to figure out if you need to take some remedial action.

Converting to NTFS

To convert an existing FAT drive to the NTFS file system, you use a program called (appropriately enough) convert.exe. You run this program from the command prompt. As an example, the following steps show you how to convert your D: drive to NTFS:

1. **Open a command prompt window by choosing Start⇨All Programs⇨Accessories⇨Command Prompt.**

2. **In the command prompt window, type** convert d: /fs:ntfs.

   If you want to convert a different drive, replace d: with the drive letter desired, followed by a colon.

Figure 14-1:
Look at your
file system
in the
Computer
Manage-
ment
window.

That's it: two steps. Conversion can take a while, so you may want to take a break, go watch a show, or go home for the evening. When the conversion is done, you should reboot your system.

Converting to FAT

Converting from NTFS to FAT is more difficult than vice versa. Windows XP doesn't include a utility that converts for you. Instead, you need to back up the data from the drive, reformat the drive, and then restore the data. Chapter 7 contains information on how to back up your system. The idea is to make sure that you have a good, reliable backup that you can later use to restore your system.

With the backup in hand, you're ready to reformat the drive:

1. **Open the Disk Management tool in the Computer Management window.**

   Follow the steps provided in the preceding section. You want your screen to look similar to Figure 14-1.

2. **Right-click the drive you want to format and choose Format from the context menu.**

   Windows displays the Format dialog box shown in Figure 14-2.

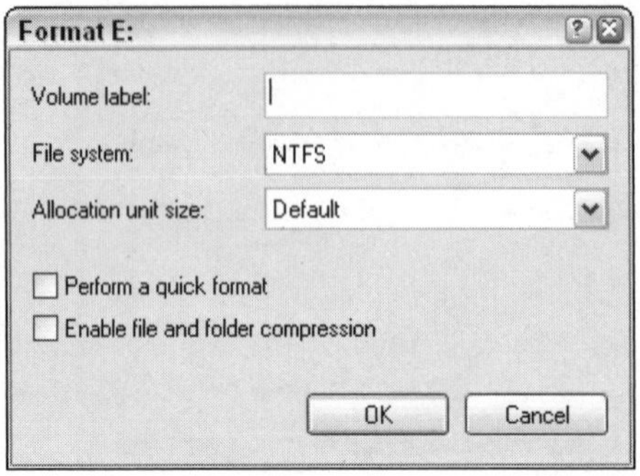

Format E:

Volume label: |

File system: NTFS

Allocation unit size: Default

☐ Perform a quick format

☐ Enable file and folder compression

OK   Cancel

Figure 14-2:
Get ready to
format a
drive.

3. **Using the File System drop-down list, choose the file system you want used for the drive — in this case, you're choosing a FAT file system.**

The size of the drive you're formatting dictates the choices available in the File System drop-down list. Only those file systems that can handle the drive you're formatting are listed.

4. **Click OK.**

Windows won't allow you to format a system drive (the one on which Windows is installed). If you want to format a system drive, you must run the Windows Setup program and format the drive from there.

Reformatting a drive erases — permanently — all the data on the drive. Do not reformat a drive unless you have backed up the data you want to keep.

When your reformatting task is complete, you should then restore the information from your backup to your newly formatted drive. The process you follow to restore the backup depends, in large part, on the way in which you created the backup. (As I discuss in Chapter 7, you have different ways to create backups of your data.) Refer to the documentation for your backup software in order to find out how to restore the data. If you created a backup by simply copying files to a different medium, copy those files back to the new drive.

Defragmenting Your Drive

How a file system stores information on a disk drive is interesting. First, it divides the available disk space into *bins* that can each contain data. Each bin is the same size as every other bin. The file system then goes about storing data in those bins. Each bin is allocated a single file; you can never store more than one file in a bin.

TIP

Third-party solutions

Many disk utility programs include disk defragmenters. For instance, both Norton SystemWorks and System Mechanic Professional include defragmenting utilities. (These examples are only two of dozens of such programs.)

Nothing is magical or inherently better about these programs — they work great. Third-party solutions may use different algorithms than the Windows defragmenter does, so they may run at a different speed. They end up with the same result: a defragmented drive.

If you're more comfortable with the user interface in a third-party product, feel free to use its defragmenter. If you don't have a third-party defragmenting utility, don't feel that you need to go out and get one; the one provided with Windows works just fine.

If a file requires more storage space than is available in a single bin, the file system grabs a group of storage bins — as many as necessary — to properly store the file. For instance, if the file requires 12 bins, the file system allocates 12 bins to that file. As more files are stored, they're placed into bins after the large file.

Later, the large file may be deleted or decreased in size. Either way, it no longer requires the 12 original bins. The file system, recognizing the file is smaller, uses only the number of bins necessary and frees the other bins for use by other files.

After a while, files can become *fragmented,* meaning that they're stored in bins all over the drive. The files are considered fragmented because the bins in which they're stored are not contiguous (right next to each other).

Fragmented files decrease the performance of Windows XP. The operating system can keep track of the files; that isn't a problem. The problem is that when a file is fragmented, it can't be read from the disk all at once. Instead, the disk drive's read head must move all over the place to gather the file from its different bins.

Recognizing that fragmentation can slow down system performance, Microsoft included a tool with Windows XP called a *defragmenter,* which basically reads through each file and moves the file to contiguous bins on the drive. After defragmentation is complete, data can be read from the hard drive faster than it was before.

REMEMBER

The very nature of defragmenting is very time consuming. You have thousands of files on your hard drive, each of which must be read, analyzed, and possibly moved around on the drive. Because of this, you should only run the defragmenter when other programs aren't running and when you have time to leave the computer. A good time is at the end of the day, when you're ready to quit working on the computer. You can let the defragmenter do its work while you're off doing other things.

To defragment a drive, follow these steps:

1. **Click Start⇨My Computer.**

   If you have a My Computer icon on your desktop, you can double-click it. Windows displays the My Computer window.

2. **Right-click the drive you want to defragment and choose Properties from the context menu.**

   Windows displays the drive's Properties dialog box. Make sure the Tools tab is selected.

3. **Click Defragment Now.**

   You see the Disk Defragmenter window shown in Figure 14-3.

4. **If you have more than one drive in your system, select the drive from those at the top of the window and click the Analyze button.**

   The selected hard drive is checked to see how fragmented its files are. Once the analysis is complete, you're notified if the drive needs to be defragmented.

5. **You can then defragment the drive or close the dialog box and click Defragment in the main Disk Defragmenter window.**

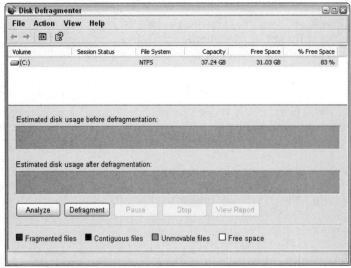

Figure 14-3:
You can work on all your drives with the Disk Defragmenter.

You should analyze your drives periodically; perhaps once every other week or once a month. You need to defragment only when the analysis reports that doing so would be helpful. A great time to defragment is after you delete a bunch of files, uninstall software, or install a large software package.

Checking for Errors

Unfortunately, disk drives have been known to develop errors. Perhaps the operating system had a hiccup when it wrote a file to disk or a file wasn't deleted correctly. Any number of errors could develop over time.

For this reason, it's a good idea to check your hard drive for errors periodically. Windows XP provides two ways to check your system for errors: disk tools and chkdsk. The following sections discuss how you can perform the necessary checks.

Using Windows' disk tools

Okay, I admit it: I'm a closet Trekkie. I don't dress in costume and go to *Star Trek* conventions, but I love to watch the shows. (All except the new *Enterprise* series — I haven't quite gotten into that one.) After a while, you get used to the characters and have a feel for how things work on the ship.

For instance, each time something went wrong with the computers in *Star Trek: The Next Generation,* Jordi LaForge (the ship's engineer) would always say, "We're running a level-five diagnostic to figure out the error." I never heard them talk about levels one through four; everything was a level-five diagnostic.

Computers don't just come up with errors in the fantasy world of *Star Trek.* Errors can develop on your hard drive. You can run your own equivalent of a level-five diagnostic by using Windows' disk tools to check, analyze, and fix any errors that crop up.

To start an analysis, follow these steps:

1. **Click Start⇨My Computer.**

   If you have a My Computer icon on your desktop, you can double-click it. Windows displays the My Computer window.

2. **Right-click the drive you want to check for errors and choose Properties from the context menu.**

   Windows displays the drive's Properties dialog box. Make sure the Tools tab is selected.

3. **Click Check Now.**

   You see the Check Disk dialog box shown in Figure 14-4.

Figure 14-4:
Get ready to
check a disk
for errors.

4. **Select either of the check boxes, as desired.**

   Clicking Scan for and Attempt Recovery of Bad Sectors provides the most comprehensive check. If you choose this option, you don't need to choose the one above it; the option automatically fixes all located errors.

5. **Click Start.**

When checking the disk, the program makes sure that the internal operating system links are uncorrupted and then works through all the files on the disk. If the program finds any minor errors, it fixes them. If it discovers anything more serious, and you opted to allow those errors to be fixed, then it works on those as well.

Checking a hard drive for errors can only be done on a drive that isn't being used. If you're using the drive (or if Windows is using the drive), then a full check cannot be completed. In that case, the program asks whether it can finish the check the next time you start Windows. If you answer affirmatively, you won't be able to use Windows until the check is complete the next time you reboot your system. (The check-upon-restart feature automatically uses the chkdsk utility described in the next section.)

Using chkdsk

Those old enough to remember DOS days may remember a utility called chkdsk. (Of course, those old enough to remember DOS may be suffering from memory loss, so they may *not* remember chkdsk.) chkdsk is short for *check disk.* It's a command-line utility that checks the operating system and disk drive for any errors, and optionally fixes them. (A *command-line utility* is one that you run, oddly enough, from a command-line. I show you in just a moment.)

The chkdsk utility is available in Windows XP. It doesn't offer anything different from the tool covered in the preceding section, but some people like using a command-line utility. To use it, follow these steps:

1. **Open a command prompt window by choosing Start⇨All Programs⇨ Accessories⇨Command Prompt.**

2. **Enter the proper commands to switch to the drive you want to check.**

   For instance, if you want to check drive E:, then type **E:** and press the Enter key. The drive you specify is made the current drive.

3. **Type** chkdsk **and press Enter.**

   Using chkdsk without any parameters runs the program in read-only mode. This means that it doesn't fix anything; it only reports what it finds. If you want chkdsk to fix errors, use the **chkdsk /f** command instead.

The chkdsk program goes through three checks before reporting its findings:

1. Checks the file system to make sure that all the file links are valid.

2. Checks the system indexes for errors.

3. Checks (on NTFS drives) security descriptors to make sure that file security is intact.

You cannot run chkdsk in fix mode on a disk that's in use. (An in-use drive is one that has files open.) If you try, the program informs you that the disk is in use and gives you the opportunity to "dismount the volume." If you instruct chkdsk to do this, all the open files on the drive are closed and the drive is made inaccessible. This could result in data loss. You should choose to dismount only if you're really sure you won't lose critical data.

If the drive is in use and you choose not to dismount the volume, chkdsk offers to perform the check the next time you start Windows. If you choose this option, the check is completed the next time you reboot.

To Compress or Not?

A few years ago, the most expensive part of most computer systems was the hard drive. As a result, people tended to have relatively small hard drives in their computers; they just couldn't afford anything more expensive.

Small hard drives meant there wasn't much room to store information. (I remember routinely running out of hard drive space on my system.) One solution to the not-enough-space syndrome was to use some sort of disk compression program. Third-party utilities started cropping up, promising to compress the information on your hard drive.

Eventually, Microsoft made compression a feature of Windows itself. Not only could you compress individual files, but you could also compress entire folders and drives. The downside, of course, is that the compression process slows down your system, overall. As information goes through the compression/decompression algorithms, information going to and from the hard drive can bottleneck.

Windows XP still has the compression feature available in it. Just because the feature is available doesn't mean you should use it, however. The historical catalyst for compression was the expense of large hard drives. Most computer systems now have large hard drives (10GB or more), and hard drives are very, very inexpensive by historical standards.

Bottom line: If you want your system to run faster, don't use disk compression.

Chapter 15

Managing Windows Updates

In This Chapter

▶ Picking the best way to get updates

▶ Determining which updates to install

▶ Removing files that uninstall updates

*W*indows XP is an amazing operating system. It consists of millions of lines of programming code, all geared toward controlling your computer the way you want.

Along with millions of lines of programming code comes the opportunity for millions of computer bugs. Windows doesn't have millions of bugs (thank goodness), due to good programmers and extensive testing before XP was released to the public.

Even so, rest assured that Windows XP *does* have bugs — there's no way around it. Windows updates come into play here. As remaining bugs are identified and corrected, the more serious bugs are stamped out with updates. As updates accumulate, they're collected into *service packs,* which provide a wholesale update to Windows.

Unfortunately, some people in the world are committed to breaking Windows or abusing your system. Such attempts typically happen over the Internet. Microsoft tries to stay on top of things, issuing patches designed to make your system more secure in an inherently insecure world.

To deal with fixed bugs and patched holes, Microsoft normally releases several Windows updates every month. To safely and efficiently deliver updates to millions of Windows users, they developed an update system that is every bit as amazing as Windows itself.

This chapter examines the different ways you can update your Windows system. You also find out which updates to install and how to remove uninstall files left behind in the update process.

The Windows world differentiates between an update and an upgrade. An *update* is a Windows XP revision. It generally includes new and improved versions of the programs and drivers you already have. An *upgrade* occurs when you actually change your operating system version. For instance, going from Windows XP Home edition to Windows XP Professional edition is an upgrade.

Getting Updates the Way You Want

Updating Windows couldn't be much easier. For the last couple of versions, updates can be downloaded from the Internet and installed directly on your machine.

Updates are available either manually or automatically. The following sections provide the information you need to understand both options.

Manual updates

It used to be that manual updates involved inserting a disk into a drive or a CD into a tray. Not anymore. Windows has an update Web site that you can visit and check for updates any time you want.

Here's a good idea: Close any files and shut down any programs you're using before updating. Under very rare circumstances, you can lose data during the update. Even more possibly the update won't complete because some component that needs updating is being used by the open program.

To manually update Windows, follow these steps:

1. **Go to the Windows update site at** `http://windowsupdate.microsoft.com,` **as shown in Figure 15-1.**

   Some people hate Internet Explorer, preferring to use a competitor, such as Mozilla or Opera. One good reason to keep Internet Explorer up to date (even if you don't use it for daily browsing) is that the Windows Update service only works with Internet Explorer.

2. **Click Scan for Updates.**

   Microsoft downloads a small program to your system. This program compares the different components on your system with what's available at the Web site.

   When the program is done figuring out what you need, a Web page appears and includes a Review and Install Updates link.

Figure 15-1:
Updating
Windows is
handled
through the
Web.

3. **Click the Review and Install Updates link to see which updates you need.**

   You can remove any of the updates, if you don't want them installed for some reason.

4. **When you're satisfied with what needs to be done, click Install Now to start the update process.**

Don't fall for it!

I just got an e-mail today that has the subject "Use this patch immediately!" It showed as being from Microsoft, and the message said

> Dear friend, use this Internet Explorer patch now!
> There are dangerous virus in the Internet now!
> More than 400.000 already infected!

Yeah, right.

I get several of these messages each week, using poor English to scare me into running the

"update" attached to the message. The problem is, Microsoft never, ever, ever sends its updates via e-mail (and they usually proofread their messages better). This e-mail carries a virus and if I run the "patch," I'll have the virus.

If you get similar messages claiming to be from Microsoft, delete them right away. They won't hurt you unless you're silly enough to run the program attached to the message.

Windows provides another way to do a manual update — a method that some people find easier than firing up their browser. Choose Start➪Help and Support to display the Help and Support Center. At the right side of the window is a task labeled Keep Your Computer Up-to-Date with Windows Update. If you click the option, the Windows Update site opens in the Help and Support Center window. The information presented is the information displayed if you use your browser to visit the site.

Automatic updates

Because updates can be delivered via the Internet, Windows XP includes a really cool feature that automatically notifies you of any updates. Called Automatic Updates, the service can download the updates and install them automatically. If you're using Windows XP SP2, the service can even download and install updates to other Microsoft products, such as Office, SQL Server, and Exchange.

To control the Automatic Updates service, follow these steps:

1. **Click the Start button.**

   Windows displays the Start menu.

2. **Right-click My Computer.**

   If your system is configured to have a My Computer icon on the desktop, you could right-click it. Either way, you see a context menu.

3. **Choose Properties from the context menu.**

   Windows opens the System Properties dialog box. Make sure the Automatic Updates tab is selected, as shown in Figure 15-2.

4. **Select or deselect the Keep My Computer Up to Date check box at the top of the dialog box.**

   This option controls whether automatic updating is active. If the option is cleared, you must do manual updates to your system. (See the preceding section for information about that.) If it's selected, Windows is able to do automatic updates and the rest of the settings in the dialog box have meaning.

5. **Of the three radio buttons in the Settings area, pick the one that most closely resembles how you want to handle automatic updates:**

   • **Notify before downloading:** The first radio button results in you being notified when updates are available, at which point you have the option to accept or decline the update. If you accept, the update is downloaded and you're notified when it's ready to install. (You can decline it again, if desired.)

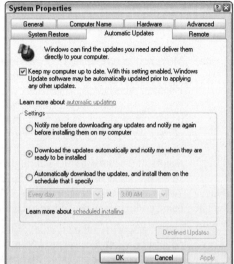

- **Notify after downloading:** The second radio button causes Windows to download all updates and store them on disk. Once downloaded, you're notified that updates are ready. Any updates you decline at that point are deleted from your disk.

- **Automatically download and install:** The third radio button tells Windows to automatically download the updates and install them without notice. With this option you can schedule updates. (If your computer is off when an update is scheduled, the update is done the next time you turn on your system.)

6. **Click the Apply button and then close the System Properties dialog box.**

You can change how updates are done or turn automatic updating off completely.

When you turn on the automatic update feature, Windows handles future updates. You should still do a manual update to check for any previous updates that you need to consider.

If you ever decline an automatic update, Windows keeps track of that. If you later decide that you want the updates you declined, display the System Properties dialog box, choose the Automatic Updates tab, and click the Declined Updates button. You can then pick and choose which of the declined updates you want installed.

Big Brother is watching . . .

. . . and his name is Bill. But don't worry — he only wants what's best for you!

Some people bristle when they hear that Microsoft sucks information from their systems. Yet, both the manual and automatic update systems do exactly that. It's unavoidable that the systems know a little bit about you, just so they can tell you what updates you need.

The information on Microsoft's Web privacy policy page says that the update process sends the following information from your system to Microsoft's computers:

✔ Windows version number

✔ Internet Explorer version number

✔ Version numbers of other Microsoft products affected by the update process

✔ Plug-and-play ID numbers of hardware devices

✔ Region and language setting

✔ Product ID and key

Microsoft assures users that it doesn't gather any information that would allow you to be individually identifiable, such as your e-mail address, name, or similar data. While you can be identified based on the product ID and key (assuming you registered your copy of Windows XP), the product information is not maintained beyond the end of the update session. Microsoft retrieves it during the update just to make sure that the version of Windows being updated is a valid, licensed version.

The company uses the information collected to determine what to offer to you in the way of updates. It also aggregates the information it receives, which allows it to determine collective information about its user base.

If you're concerned about Big Brother Bill watching you, contact Microsoft for CD updates at 800-360-7561. Of course, when you update this way, Microsoft still needs to get your name and address so they can send you the CD. (Wave hi to the cameras!)

Picking an update method

Manual or automatic? Automatic or manual? I remember learning how to drive a manual. It was a 1964 Ford Mustang. We were driving through Pennsylvania. I was fine once I got going and nobody slowed down in front of me on the freeway. Coming to a stop was interesting, however, as I would invariably forget to downshift. (My friend was *sooooo* understanding.)

Believe it or not, the decision to use manual or automatic updating is similar to my learning to drive a manual transmission car. If I forgot to push in the clutch or downshift at the right time, the car didn't work the way it should. (But it did make some very interesting sounds.) Same with Windows updates — if you set your system for manual updates and forget to update, you run the risk of your system not working the way it should.

You already know that some updates are critical — you run a security risk if you don't use them. Viruses and all sorts of bad stuff would love to find a home on your system. If you don't have the proper updates in place, you run a greater risk of providing a home to bad stuff.

For me, the easiest way to do the updates is to make them automatic. My personality insists that I like to be notified about updates rather than just having them happen, so I set my update option to the center radio button in the System Properties dialog box shown in Figure 15-2. I may even ignore the update notification for a few days at a time — but at least I know the updates are there and I can run them at any time. Take a hard look at your personality and decide which way you want to go — manual or automatic. Pick the one that means your system is the most up-to-date and works best for you.

If you've installed Windows XP SP2 on your system, then you have an additional opportunity to install any automatically downloaded updates — when you shut down Windows. If you choose to exit (by choosing Turn Off Computer from the Start menu), and there are uninstalled updates that you previously downloaded, Windows presents an Install Updates and Shutdown option. This feature allows Windows to do its security-conscious duty and help protect your system, even while you race out the door to catch up with your friends. Use it if you want to — but only use it if you're sure nobody will come in and mess with your computer while you're gone and the update is being installed.

The automatic update features are great if you have a high-speed Internet connection. If you have a dial-up connection, you probably don't want to use automatic update. You should instead configure your system for manual updates and make checking part of your weekly regimen.

Which Updates Do You Really Need?

If you install a new version of Windows XP, you may visit the Windows update site and find 30 or more updates that you need to download. Of course, doing so many updates can take a lot of time — you may wonder if you really need to do them.

The answer is an unqualified maybe. Some updates are critical, meaning you really need to do them. They include updates to the core operating system or updates that fix identified security problems.

You can easily tell which updates fall into which category. If you're doing a manual update and scan for updates, the left side of the screen shows how the available updates are categorized; see Figure 15-3.

Figure 15-3:
Windows
shows
you how
proposed
updates are
categorized.

Notice that Microsoft lists three updates categories under the Pick Updates to Install link:

- ✔ **Critical Updates and Service Packs:** These updates are the most pressing. You should update everything in this category. If you don't, you risk leaving your system vulnerable to security problems that Microsoft discovered and corrected.

- ✔ **Windows XP:** These updates are less pressing. They consist of changes to the operating system files that make up Windows XP. For instance, an obscure operational error may have come to light.

- ✔ **Driver Updates:** These updates are nice to make, but definitely not at the top of the list. They include updates to various hardware drivers, including drivers for hardware you might not even have.

As you review the proposed changes in the second and third categories, you may notice that some updates may be for programs you have installed but never use. If you know you don't need the update, don't worry about installing it.

If you have limited time, you may want to put off updating until you have a chunk of time. A good time to update is at the end of the day, when nothing else is going on. You can visit the Windows Updates site, find out what you need, and download the top one or two critical updates. Work your way through them all, as time allows, and soon your system is updated.

One update that you really, really need is the Windows XP Service Pack 2 (SP2). This service pack has a ton of updates to make your system more secure. Many of the holes exploited by spyware and pop-ups (two villains I discuss in Chapter 10) are blocked in the update. Take the time to get the service pack and install it — you'll be glad you did.

If you're using the Automatic Update service, and you configured it to notify you when changes are available, then you can check the category of proposed updates before they're installed. You can also decide to decline any updates that you feel aren't needed right away.

Getting Rid of Update Files

One of the interesting things about Windows XP is that every update is dutifully logged into the operating system and can easily be removed, if you so desire. To see the removable updates, choose Start⇨Control Panel⇨Add or Remove Programs. If you scroll to the bottom of the Currently Installed Programs list, you can see the updates, as shown in Figure 15-4.

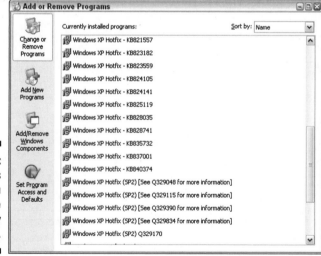

Figure 15-4:
Windows allows you to remove any updates.

Windows allows you to remove updates in case you find that it causes problems for your system. It does this by storing, on disk, files necessary to uninstall the update.

Once satisfied that an update works, you can safely delete the uninstall files. You can't do this directly from the Add or Remove Programs window shown in Figure 15-4, as that would actually remove the update — something you don't want to do.

Instead, a little trick gets rid of the uninstall files and thereby unclutters your system. To use this trick, follow these steps:

1. **Open the Add or Remove Programs window and a folder window showing the contents of the C:\Windows folder.**

   Some systems, upgraded from earlier versions of Windows, have no C:\Windows folder. In that case, open the C:\Winnt folder.

2. **Position the two windows so you can see both onscreen at the same time.**

3. **In the folder window, choose Tools➪Folder Options and display the View tab shown in Figure 15-5.**

4. **In the list of Advanced Settings, make sure the Show Hidden Files and Folders option is selected.**

5. **Close the Folder Options dialog box.**

   You should notice a bunch of faint folders at the top of the folder window, with their names shown in blue.

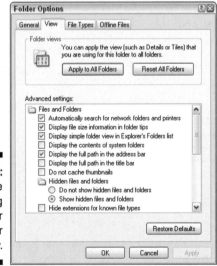

Figure 15-5:
Change the
viewing
options for
your folder
window.

6. **Select one of these faint folders; it doesn't matter which one.**

   You should be able to see the entire name (something like $NtUninstallKB823182$). This folder contains the uninstall files for a Windows XP update.

   Notice the last part of the filename, starting with KB. This portion indicates the Microsoft Knowledge Base (KB) article number in which this particular update is described. If you look to the Add or Remove Programs window, you should see an installed program that references the same KB article number. Figure 15-6 shows the two windows, side by side, in which you can see the corresponding names.

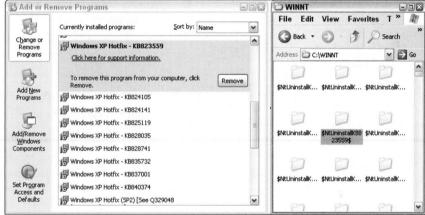

Figure 15-6:
Finding the Windows update uninstall information.

7. **After you match up two numbers, in the folder window (C:\Windows), delete the folder.**

8. **In the Add or Remove Programs window, select the update entry and click Remove.**

   You should see a notice that the uninstall files could not be located. (This makes sense; you just deleted them.)

9. **When Windows asks if you want to remove the program from the list of currently installed programs, answer Yes.**

   The list of programs is updated.

Continue this process: Locate the uninstall folders and their corresponding entries in the installed programs list. Delete the folder and remove the entry in the list. The result is a cleaner list of installed programs and quite a bit more hard drive space.

Freeing up even more disk space

If you upgraded to Windows XP from an older operating system, you're probably enjoying the new version of Windows and its features. During the upgrade, the installation program stores your old operating system files on your hard drive so you can uninstall Windows XP if you ever want to.

Once you've made the decision to stay with XP, the uninstall files do nothing but take up room on your system — a *lot* of room. Follow these steps to get rid of the uninstall files:

1. **Choose Start⇨Control Panel to open the Control Panel.**

2. **Start the Add or Remove Programs applet.**

   If you're viewing the Control Panel in Category View, just click the Add or Remove Programs task once. If you're viewing it in Classic View, double-click the Add or Remove Programs applet.

3. **In the list of Currently Installed Programs, select the Windows XP Uninstall option.**

   The list entry is expanded and a button appears at the right side of the entry.

4. **Click Change/Remove.**

   Windows starts the installer program.

5. **Choose the Remove the Backup of My Previous Operating System option, then click Continue.**

   The installer warns you that removing the backup files means that you won't be able to uninstall Windows XP.

6. **Click Yes.**

   The backup files are removed, freeing up the disk space you need.

Chapter 16

Getting a New System

. . . .

In This Chapter

▶ Knowing when a new system is necessary

▶ Determining the type of system to get

▶ Reinstalling your software

▶ Moving data from the old system

. . . .

I walked into my teenage son's room early the other day and it was trashed. Literally — junk-food wrappers everywhere, a few magazines, clothing piles (reeking of eau-de-locker), books, and some DVDs. To top things off, the dog was making himself right at home, having torn up some of the clothes and dragged in his play toys. I saw the dog looking at me (with a semi-menacing-yet-innocent smirk), and I'm fairly certain my son was actually under the pile of stuff on the bed.

That was it — the last straw — the dog was smirking and my son was being swallowed by his own detritus. Something had to be done! The most satisfying solution was to lock up the room and sell the whole thing. (The room, that is.) I'm sure we could get a new room, with an upgraded son and dog that would work better and more efficiently.

You probably have felt the same way about your computer system once in a while: You take a look around, notice how cluttered everything is, and decide it's just better to shut it down and start all over with a new system. (From personal experience, I can tell you that it's much easier to get a new computer than to get a new room, son, and dog.)

This chapter focuses on the ins and outs of getting a new system. I spend very little time actually picking out a new system; most of the information concerns confidently reaching the decision for a new system and making the transition as easy as possible.

If you're satisfied with your current system's speed and capacity but you're just tired of the clutter, you may be better off starting from scratch with your current system. Chapter 21 covers how to start over with the system you have.

When Is Getting a New System Justified?

You can find many ways to justify a new computer system. (Even more ways abound to rationalize one.) Unless you have money to burn, however, you probably don't want to abandon reason and rush out to buy another computer system. No — you need to make sure that getting a new system is the best course of action for you.

If you're thinking about getting a new computer at work, check with your IT department to see if the company has requirements that need to be met for new systems. In addition, you'll undoubtedly have paperwork to fill out. The paperwork, more than likely, includes information on how to justify a computer purchase.

My experience indicates that all the reasons for a new system boil down to only a few primary reasons:

- ✔ **A new version of your software requires a new system.** If it's time to upgrade to a new version of some critical software, the new software may require a larger hard drive, more memory, or a faster processor. Check with the software publisher to verify the new version's system requirements.

- ✔ **What you need to do has changed.** You may have taken on a new job or project that requires you to work with more or with different types of data. If your old system is no longer suitable for your new job requirements, then a new system is in order.

- ✔ **External changes require a change.** Changes in your company's computing structure may require that you get a new computer. For instance, your company may install a new network that requires increased horsepower that your current system cannot deliver.

- ✔ **Hardware has failed or become obsolete.** You may have a major computer component that dies, mandating that you get a new system. In addition, you may seek to upgrade your current system and find that the component cost is just as much as a newer system would be.

- ✔ **Clutter has ruined your system.** Clutter can absolutely ruin your system. I'm not talking about unused data files lying about; I'm talking about the type of clutter that comes from spyware, viruses, and other damaging software. If you can't clean it off, then you may need to start over from scratch. See Chapter 10 for more information about spyware.

In addition to the above considerations, you may want to upgrade your computer as a way to easily upgrade to Windows XP SP2. This newer version of Windows XP has been extensively revamped (most of the revamping is behind the scenes, away from the user's prying eyes) to be more secure. It includes changes to the operating system, Outlook Express, and Internet Explorer. Unless you specify otherwise, most new systems should come with Windows XP SP2 already installed, so you can hit the ground running.

Remember that a computer is nothing but a tool; it helps you accomplish tasks you wouldn't be able to otherwise perform. If getting a different tool (a newer computer) helps you accomplish your work faster and easier, then justifying a new system is relatively easy to do.

Getting a new computer system only makes your computing life uncluttered for a short time. Clutter happens through poor computing habits. If you're not ready to change your habits, your new system is doomed to be just as cluttered as your old. Getting a new system is a great time to make changes in your habits, however — just remember to think through how you use your system on a daily basis.

What Should You Get?

Deciding what type of new system to get depends, in large part, on your budget. If money is not a concern, reach for the sky! In fact, just walk into your neighborhood computer store and tell the on-commission sales rep that you want the top-of-the-line system. No doubt you'll get something to satisfy your every computational need and keep you happy for at least the next two years.

For most people, such an approach to a new system is unrealistic because money *is* an issue. (It's always an issue.) Before you decide what type of system you want to get, realistically figure out how much you can comfortably afford for your computer. That gives you a starting point.

You should count on your computer system to be usable for about two or three years only. After that time your software needs to change. As new versions of the software (and Windows) come out, they always require larger and faster systems. In a few years, when you want to upgrade your operating system or your software, you may need a whole new system.

This section does not provide a definitive shopping guide for computer systems; computer magazines and full-length books on the topic tackle that best. Instead, you can find some guidance here on the general types of systems to look into.

High-end systems

The most expensive systems on the market are always the high-end systems. These systems are defined by the most powerful processors, the fastest memory, the biggest memory, the fastest DVD and CD-ROM drives, and the like. Everything in a high-end system is the newest, fastest, and most powerful. (I can just hear Tim Allen's testosterone pumping as he grunts a primal "Arrrhh, arrrhh, arrrhh.")

The fact of the matter is, most people don't need high-end systems. (A lot of people *want* them, but they don't *need* them.) Typically, high-end systems are appropriate for people using software that needs lots of resources. For instance, if you use your system for video editing, architectural modeling, generating animations, or crunching large databases, then you need a high-end system. Most state-of-the-art game players can benefit from high-end systems, as well.

High-end system purchasers always pay a premium for their systems because equipment on the bleeding edge of technology always costs more. Fully configured high-end systems often cost in excess of $2,000, not including the monitor.

Before deciding to plunk down lots of your hard-earned bucks, make sure that you really need the horsepower you're trying to harness.

Mid-range systems

The vast majority of computer users are satisfied with a mid-range system. If you're writing letters to Aunt Martha (or your boss, who happens to be Aunt Martha), juggling the books, browsing the Web, or tracking your yacht club membership roster, then a mid-range system is just what you need.

Age is the primary thing that sets a mid-range system apart from a high-end system. The components in a mid-range system typically are not leading edge; they have been on the market for a while and no longer command the premium price they once did.

In addition, mid-range systems normally aren't maxed out on memory or hard drive space. In fact, if you need a mid-range system, memory and hard drive space is something to which you should pay particular attention. Get at least 512MB of memory and at least a 40GB hard drive. (Memory and hard drives are discussed more in Chapter 17.)

For your mid-range system, you should expect to pay anywhere from $1,100 to $1,500. The primary difference in price depends on whose name is on the box and how much memory and drive space you got.

If you have high-speed Internet access at the location you plan to use the new computer, get an Ethernet network card system. Many mid-range and high-end systems are shipped with Ethernet support built in, but check anyway. High-speed Internet access requires that you have a network card installed. (*Network cards* allow you to connect to a network, such as the Internet.)

Roll your own

It used to be that only dyed-in-the-wool geeks built their own computer systems. DITW geeks still do, but they aren't the only ones. Most urban areas (and some rural areas) have computer stores that build systems for you. All you do is pick the components you want; they put them together and make them work for a small fee. If you prefer, you can take the components home and put them together yourself.

Building your own system is a great way to ensure that you get exactly the type of system you want. You can even talk to the geeks on the payroll (at the store) to get the latest word on which components are better and from which to stay away. You can often save money by building your own when compared to the large commercial computer outlets. If you're interested in building your own, check out a copy of *Building a PC For Dummies*, Fourth Edition, by Mark L. Chambers (published by Wiley).

Low-end systems

Most systems priced below $1,000 are low end. Systems like this are sold by discount retailers and many mail-order outlets. If your computing needs are very limited — you need to write a letter or check e-mail — you may be able to get by with a low-end system.

Don't expect high-powered performance from a low-end system. If a system doesn't cost much money, normally it's because the manufacturer left out some things. Two things normally left out: RAM and hard drive space. True, you get some memory (a minimum amount) and a hard drive (a small one), but skimping on these two items can seriously affect a system's performance.

Low-end systems also normally skimp on the video card in the computer. Many software packages today require extremely capable video cards. For instance, some computer games (not necessarily those that require high-end systems) won't even work on low-end systems because of the video cards used.

Portable systems

More and more road warriors are finding that their mobile life makes a portable computer necessary. In fact, you might want to consider getting rid of your desktop and working solely with a portable if you often hit the road.

If you decide to use a laptop computer as your main system, be prepared to spend a bit more. Actually, you can spend a lot more when compared to a comparable desktop, but that is the price of reliability and style.

Avoid this problem!

The last time I did an installation, I ran into a problem that you can avoid. I had a software program that was an upgrade to an earlier copy I originally had on my system. I dutifully pulled the installation discs and the installation key and had them ready when the new system was up and running. I couldn't install the software, however, because it was an upgrade; an older version of the software wasn't on the new system.

The solution seems easy enough — just grab the discs for the older software version, right?

(Most upgrade installations allow you to insert the old discs to make sure you qualify for the upgrade.) Problem was, I had thrown away the original discs in the last big office purge I did, about six months before.

The bottom line was that I wasn't able to install the upgrade. You can avoid the problem if you collect the original discs of any truly upgraded software.

To figure out what type of laptop you should get, figure out whether you need a high-, mid-, or low-end system, as described in the previous sections. Once you have your system needs pegged, look for a portable computer that provides those capabilities.

Consider getting a docking station for your portable, as well. The *docking station* stays on your desktop, with your monitor, mouse, and full-size keyboard attached to it. When you're not out battling on the road, you slide your system into the docking station and instantly convert it into something more comfortable to use on a desktop.

Preparing for the New System

You've decided: You're going to get a new system. You've done your homework and figured out exactly what system you want and how you can do it. Now you need to get ready for its arrival.

Assuming you're replacing your current system, you can do some things to make the transition go much smoother. The following sections detail things you can do.

Collecting pieces and parts

As you use your computer over time, you may tend to collect what I call "pieces and parts." For instance, I have a small drawer full of installation discs and several files full of manuals. These items become very important when you get a new system.

To prepare for replacing an old system, you need the following:

- ✔ **Program inventory:** Chapter 3 provides detailed information on assembling a program inventory. You need one not only because it lets you document what's on your current system, but also because it allows you to see what you need to install on your new one.

- ✔ **Printer installation discs:** Many printers ship with discs that contain operating system drivers and monitoring software. If you plan on the new system using the printer your current system uses, then you need these discs so you can use the printer. (If you cannot locate the printer driver discs, you can probably download the driver files from the printer manufacturer's Web site and create your own disc.)

- ✔ **Software installation discs:** Whenever I tackle a replacement system, I pull out the aforementioned small drawer and start comparing the discs to what I have on my program inventory. If you're performing an upgrade, make sure to collect the *original* software discs, too. Otherwise, you won't be able to upgrade. See the nearby sidebar, "Avoid this problem!"

In addition to the installation discs, most software needs some sort of installation key or program code to work properly. As you assemble the different software discs, make sure you have the necessary codes to reinstall the software from scratch. The code may be in the software's documentation, on the CD's jewel case, or on a copy of a registration e-mail. Regardless, these pieces and parts are every bit as important as the discs.

Collecting information

To get your new computer system functioning just the way you like, collect some information about the way your current system is configured. Specifically, pay attention to how software is configured and how the network is set up.

Why can't I just swap out the guts?

In geekspeak, *swapping out the guts* means moving the hard drive from one system to another system. The hard drive, after all, has the operating system, program, and data that you used on your old system. Moving the hard drive from one system to the other could save quite a bit of time — or not!

There's an interesting thing that happens when you install Windows. The operating system takes stock of its surroundings and writes information about your system into its Registry (and a couple of other places). This includes information about your process, memory, and peripherals.

Change out your peripherals, no problem. Change the amount of memory, no problem. Change the processor? Big problem. I had a Windows 2000 system that worked great and I moved the hard drive to an upgraded system that had a much faster processor.

Bam! The system wouldn't boot. It wouldn't even alert me to a problem with the new system;

it looked dead. At least, it looked dead until I put the hard drive back in the old system, then it worked fine.

The only way to fix the problem was to wipe the hard drive, reinstall the operating system (it was a great time to upgrade to Windows XP), and start fresh. My short, planned-at-two-hour upgrade ended up taking two days. Really big hassle.

Windows XP is a little smarter — but only a little. If you have Windows XP on the hard drive, you can move the drive to a new system but still need to do a system reinstall. Your data and programs remain intact, but stick XP on the system so it recognizes the new processor.

Of course, the ironic part of this whole scenario (moving the hard drive) is that if you were able to do it successfully, you would also be moving all the clutter from your old system to your new.

Life sometimes isn't fair.

Software configuration settings

Once a piece of software is on a system (such as your current system), you configure it to work properly with other software and to reflect how you want it to perform. If you want the software on your new system to function as it does on your current system, note how you configured the software.

Seeing if the software allows you to export its configuration settings is the best way to do this. If so, you can store them on a diskette to import them onto the new system once the software is installed.

If your software doesn't allow you to export configuration settings, then you need to write down your settings for recreation on the new system. Simply display each configuration dialog box and write down what you see.

Make sure you go through all your installed software and either export settings or write them down, as appropriate.

Network settings

If your computer belongs to a network, it uses a collection of settings that specify how communication is to occur over that network. To see what network settings you currently use, follow these steps:

1. **Choose Start⇨Control Panel⇨Network Connections.**

   A window shows your different network connections.

2. **Double-click the connection used for your network.**

   You should see a Status dialog box; at the bottom is a Properties button.

3. **Click the Properties button.**

   You see the connection's Properties dialog box shown in Figure 16-1.

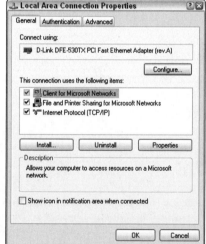

Figure 16-1:
View
network
connection
properties.

The Properties dialog box shows different clients, services, and protocols used by this particular network connection. Quite a few could be listed in the center of the dialog box.

You're interested in the Internet Protocol (TCP/IP) option.

4. **Select the Internet Protocol (TCP/IP) option and click the Properties button.**

   You see a Properties dialog box for the protocol, as shown in Figure 16-2.

   The numbers in this Properties dialog box are very important; they allow your computer to connect to either your local area network (LAN), to the Internet, or to both.

Some networks (and some Internet connections) may require that your computer be configured so that both IP and DNS addresses are obtained automatically. If set up that way, then your configuration task on the new system is very easy. If not, write down the information in the dialog box exactly as shown.

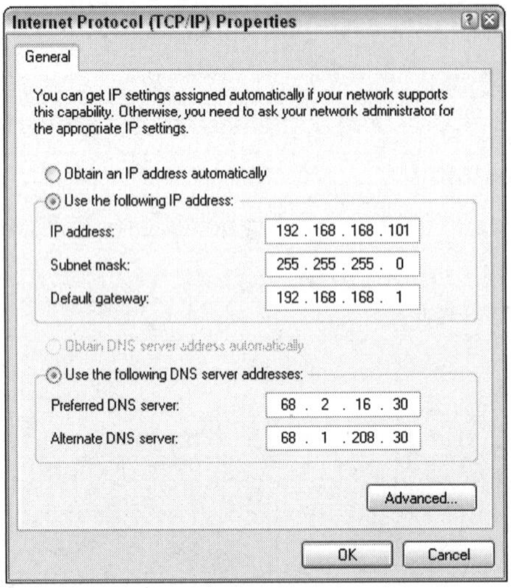

Internet Protocol (TCP/IP) Properties

General

You can get IP settings assigned automatically if your network supports this capability. Otherwise, you need to ask your network administrator for the appropriate IP settings.

○ Obtain an IP address automatically
◉ Use the following IP address:

IP address:	192 . 168 . 168 . 101
Subnet mask:	255 . 255 . 255 . 0
Default gateway:	192 . 168 . 168 . 1

○ Obtain DNS server address automatically
◉ Use the following DNS server addresses:

Preferred DNS server:	68 . 2 . 16 . 30
Alternate DNS server:	68 . 1 . 208 . 30

Advanced...

OK   Cancel

Figure 16-2: Settings for a network connection.

Reinstalling Programs

Whenever I set up a new computer system, the most time-consuming part of the process is installing software programs. I normally have to block out half a day or more to get everything installed.

Before reinstalling actual software, you should do these things:

✔ Make sure that the operating system is functioning properly.

✔ Ensure that all the peripherals (including the printer) have the proper drivers installed and can be used.

✔ Set up your Internet connection and make sure it's functioning.

To make installing software smoother, refer to the items you gathered prior to setting up the new system. (See the previous section, "Preparing for the New System.") Pay particular attention to the software inventory; use it as a checklist of programs to install. As you finish each one, check it off the list.

As you install software on the new system, focus on one program at a time. Make sure you fully install each one, start it up, and configure it before moving on to the next one. You may even want to put away any discs and manuals for each software program as you finish it up.

Transferring Data

The last step in setting up a new system is to transfer data from your old system. You probably accumulated quite a bit of data on the old system, and you probably want at least some of it on the new system.

The key in successfully transferring data is to transfer only the data you need — nothing more and nothing less. I recommend archiving the data you don't need onto a CD-ROM drive or other long-term storage medium. (See Chapter 7 for more about archiving.)

If you are unsure whether you need certain data, place it on archive CDs, separate from those you used to archive the data you are certain you don't need. Clearly mark the CDs as "don't know" data and put them near your desk. Over time, you may transfer some data from those CDs, but the rest of the data can eventually be moved into your long-term archive files.

If your system is connected to a network and you can simultaneously connect both the old and new system, then data transfer can go very, very easy. All you need to do is share drives on either the old or new system, and then copy information from one system to the other or do so via shared drives. Just drag and drop — very easy.

If you cannot get both systems set up on a network, the next easiest solution is to transfer via CD-ROM. (This assumes you have a CD-ROM burner on the old system.) Just copy the information to CD, plop it into the new system, and copy from the CD.

When you copy information from a CD-ROM to a hard drive, Windows sometimes leaves the read-only file attribute set on any of the files transferred. Once you copy a file from the CD-ROM to the hard drive, right-click the file and choose Properties. Make sure the Read-Only flag is deselected in the Properties dialog box.

If the old system doesn't have a CD-ROM burner, look for the largest-capacity medium that works on both systems. This may mean transferring data via Zip drive or even (heaven forbid!) floppy disk.

If you can get your hands on an external hard drive that connects via USB or FireWire, use it to transfer data. Copy data from the old system to the hard drive and then plug the hard drive into the new system and copy from it to the new system. The whole process is quick and painless.

Part V

Advanced Cleaning for the Truly Brave

The 5th Wave   By Rich Tennant

"Jeez-I thought the Registry just defined the wallpaper on the screen."

In this part . . .

This part focuses on implementing deep-cleaning strategies:

✔ Determine whether you need more memory or a larger hard drive

✔ Secure your system

✔ Clean up in a networked environment

✔ Work with the Registry

✔ Fix a corrupted Windows XP installation

Chapter 17

Memory and Storage

· ·

In This Chapter

▶ Understanding memory usage

▶ Determining if you need more storage space

▶ Picking an internal or external drive

▶ Looking at alternative storage devices

· ·

*W*hen I'm asked what a room needs most, I always reply that two things a room can't have too many of are electrical outlets and phone jacks. When asked the same question about computers, I always indicate two things you can't have too much of are *memory* and *storage space*.

We live in a time when both memory and disk space are cheap, cheap, cheap. You can get a gig of RAM these days for what you used to shell out for 64MB in the not-so-distant past. In addition, you can get hard drives for next to nothing. My first hard drive, for my original IBM PC, cost $3,000 and stored a whopping 30MB of data. You can get almost 3TB (that's *tera*bytes) for that same cost today — and store 100,000 times as much data!

This chapter focuses on those two essentials of any computer systems: memory and storage. Since both are inexpensive, you can easily get all the memory and storage space you need. In the following sections you discover how to determine the amount of RAM you need and whether you really need an additional hard drive.

How Windows Uses Memory

Being susceptible to the ills of time just like any other human, I love a bumper sticker I once saw. It said, "Of all the things I've lost, I miss my mind the most." As I get older, I notice that my memory isn't as sharp as it once was. What a pain. I figure it's because my mind, over the years, has become cluttered with too many unessential things. I am working on a way to get rid of those unessential items. The plan involves a marine battery and a set of jumper cables. Unfortunately, I can't seem to find anyone willing to help me test the plan.

Windows, too, relies on memory. For the most part, Windows doesn't forget things. Windows relies on two types of memory — physical and virtual. *Physical memory* is determined by the actual RAM installed in your system. In most systems, RAM is specified in multiples of 32 megabytes (MB). The majority of systems running Windows XP have at least 512MB of memory, and some may have as much as 1GB of memory.

Virtual memory is maintained by Windows in a special area on the hard drive known as a *swap file* or a *pagefile*. (It's a sad commentary on geekdom that the words *page* and *file* have been used together so often that they're now considered a single word: pagefile.) This special file is treated as an extension of your physical RAM. If a program or its data won't fit in the available physical RAM, they're stored in the pagefile.

The pagefile is also referred to as a swap file because the information in the file is "swapped" in and out of physical RAM, as the need arises. For instance, say that Excel is open on your system. You haven't opened a workbook in a while, so Windows shuffles the memory used by Excel to the pagefile. When you click the Excel task on the taskbar, Windows quickly stores another program's memory into the pagefile and loads the Excel memory image from the pagefile into physical RAM.

This may sound confusing, but it allows you to work with quite a few more programs than you otherwise could; the technology is neat. The downside to virtual memory is that relying on too much reduces performance. Face it — even the fastest hard drive is slower than the slowest RAM. If Windows spends a lot of time swapping information to and from the pagefile, it can't be doing things it should be doing.

Windows XP allows you to adjust how it uses memory relative to the programs you're running. If you need a refresher on how to modify these performance settings, refer to Chapter 13.

Determining Whether You Need More Memory

The single biggest thing you can do to increase the performance of a Windows XP system is to add memory. Most systems have less memory than they should. Fortunately, memory prices are not terribly high right now. If you can determine how much additional memory you need, then you should do the upgrade.

Windows XP provides a relatively simple way to determine how much more memory you should add. The only problem is that you have to learn a foreign language (geekspeak) to understand what's going on! (I'll do a little translation as you go along; you'll see what I mean.) Just follow these steps:

1. **Turn on your system and use it for a while: Load some of the programs you normally use, work with some good-sized files, and print a few reports.**

   The idea is to put a normal load on your system that reflects the way you use your computer.

2. **After using the system for a while, right-click any blank area of the taskbar and choose Task Manager.**

3. **When the Windows Task Manager window appears, choose the Performance tab shown in Figure 17-1.**

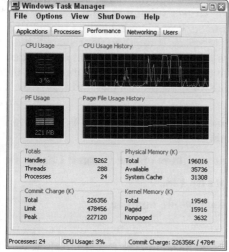

Figure 17-1: Windows monitors how memory is used.

The Performance tab has a ton of information; some of it may even be meaningful to some geek, somewhere. Most normal people look at this tab and see terms like *Commit Charge* and *Kernel Memory,* their eyes glaze over, and they quietly shut the window. You aren't going to do that, however. You only need to pay attention to a few of the figures shown. With my gentle guidance, you can extract those figures without your eyes glazing too much.

4. **Look at the Total figure in the Physical Memory area.**

   This indicates the amount of physical RAM currently installed.

5. **Look at the Commit Charge area.**

   The Commit Charge Total figure represents the amount of memory used by all the running applications, including the operating system and any services. If that figure is greater than the Physical Memory Total figure (Step 4), the difference represents how much virtual memory Windows is currently using in the pagefile. The idea is to add RAM until the Commit Charge Total is less than the Physical Memory Total.

   The Commit Charge Limit figure represents the total amount of memory available — physical and virtual. In other words, the Commit Charge Limit figure includes the Physical Memory Total figure.

6. **Subtract the Physical Memory Total figure from the Commit Charge Limit figure to determine the maximum swap file size.**

   You may want to write down this number.

7. **Look at the Commit Charge Peak.**

   This key figure is basically the Commit Charge Total's historical high. The figure represents the largest amount of total memory needed by Windows since it last started. If you can keep the Commit Charge Peak lower than the Physical Memory Total, then your system has plenty of RAM. If the numbers are reversed and the Commit Charge Peak figure is consistently higher than the Physical Memory Total figure, then your system is spending time swapping memory to and from disk. This affects your performance.

8. **Figure the amount of memory you should have installed in your system by doing this math:**

   a. **Drop the last three numbers off the Commit Charge Peak.**

   b. **Divide that number by 128.**

   c. **Round up to the next whole number.**

   d. **Multiply by 128.**

   Thus, if the figure is 577148, dropping the last three gives you 577. Dividing this number by 128 gives you 4.5078. Rounding up this number to the next whole number (5) and then multiplying by 128 gives you 640 — the number of megabytes of memory best for this system.

After you determine how much memory you need, trot on down to your local computer store and let them know. Better yet, take your computer box with you (you don't need the cables, keyboard, mouse, or monitor) so that their on-staff tech-type person can see exactly the type of memory you need. Tell them how much you need and they can help you decide how to get exactly that amount or even a bit more.

With the additional memory installed, you should notice an immediate performance improvement in your system.

Will Another Hard Drive Help?

I've developed a theory that the entire self-storage industry was built on the basis of poor individual habits. In my town, every block or two you can see self-storage facilities, with row after neat row of little garages, waiting to be filled with who knows what.

Two generations ago, people raised families of eight or more children in houses of about 800 square feet. Today, people with one or two children can't fit all their stuff into a 2,700 square-foot house with an attached three-car garage. So, rather than cull out some stuff, they go rent a storage shed so they can collect even more.

This pack-rat mentality spills over to computer use. People collect gigabytes of data and fear deleting any of it because they may, at some unknown future time, need it. Since you can't go rent a storage shed for the data, they do the next best thing and think about adding a hard drive.

If you're tempted to get another hard drive, you need to know — right up front — that more hard drive space won't solve any clutter problems. All it does is provide more space to spread out the clutter.

This being said, you can benefit from a new hard drive for a couple of reasons, as described in the following sections.

Hard drive prices continue to be low — very low. I purchased an 80GB Seagate drive a couple of days ago for the regular price of only $89.99. Right next to that was space for the 120GB Seagate drives, available on sale for only $89.99. (I would have bought the 120GB drive, but they were all sold out.) If you shop around, you can get some amazing prices on huge hard drives.

Faster speed

New hard drives are faster than old hard drives; it's a fact of life. The newer drives have rotational speeds of 7,200 and even 10,000RPM — almost twice as fast as the drives available a couple of years ago. In general, a drive transfers information faster if it can spin faster.

If you're dealing with data-intensive applications (video editing and large database crunching), then faster disk drives are a huge boon. Installing one in your system and copying your data to the drive can result in better overall performance.

Better performance

Assuming that the newer hard drive is faster than your old one, better performance is yours if you move your pagefile to the newer hard drive. (The pagefile is discussed earlier in this chapter.) You can move the pagefile to the faster drive by following these steps:

1. **Click Start, right-click My Computer, and choose Properties.**

   If your system is configured to have a My Computer icon on the desktop, you could right-click it. Either way, Windows opens the System Properties dialog box. Make sure the Advanced tab is selected, as shown in Figure 17-2.

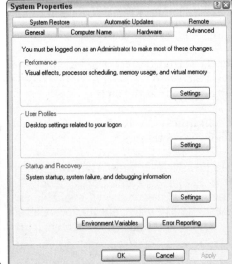

Figure 17-2: Your pagefile setting is accessed through the Advanced settings.

2. **In the Performance area of the dialog box, click Settings.**

   Windows displays the Performance Options dialog box.

3. **On the Advanced tab, click the Change button in the Virtual Memory section of the dialog box.**

   Windows displays the Virtual Memory dialog box shown in Figure 17-3. The settings in the dialog box control the location of your pagefile. At the top of the dialog box you see your system drives and how much space each drive allocates to the pagefile. You should see both your old drive and your newer, faster drive listed in the dialog box.

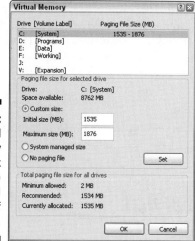

Figure 17-3:
The Virtual
Memory
dialog box
controls the
location and
size of
pagefiles.

4. **From the list of drives, select the fast drive.**

5. **In the center of the dialog box, select Custom Size and set the Initial Size equal to the Minimum Allowed setting from the bottom of the dialog box.**

6. **Set the Maximum Size just a bit larger than the Recommended setting at the bottom of the dialog box.**

   If you don't feel comfortable setting your pagefile's size, select the System Managed Size radio button. This setting allows Windows XP to decide the best size.

7. **When everything is set the way you want it, click Set.**

   The settings you specified should show up in the top portion of the dialog box.

8. **Select the old drive (probably C:) from the list at the top.**

   This drive has your current pagefile. The current drive settings should show up in the middle of the dialog box.

9. **Select the No Paging File radio button and click Set.**

   You should always have a paging file set somewhere on some drive. Thus, you need to set the new pagefile location and size before removing the old pagefile. Failure to do so could cause Windows to be unstable and perhaps unusable.

   10. **Close the Virtual Memory dialog box.**

   Windows lets you know that you need to restart your system. (Moving the pagefile is one of the few things that requires a system restart in Windows XP.)

   11. **Click OK.**

   Your system restarts.

You should notice an improvement in your system's performance after completing the preceding steps.

Choosing Between Internal or External Hard Drives

Most newer computer systems are equipped with high-speed connections, such as USB and FireWire. These connections are important when you're using peripherals, such as video cameras and printers. (Some video cameras can be plugged directly into a FireWire port so you can transfer video directly to your hard drive.)

An interesting side effect to faster connections is the emergence of external hard drives as a viable option. In the old days (by *old* I mean shortly after the IBM PC emerged), hard drives were large and couldn't fit into the computer case. Many hard drives were external, out of necessity.

Then drives started getting compact, and storing them inside the computer case became the norm. With the advent of FireWire and USB 2.0, drives are crawling back out of the computer case. External drives can be found on any computer retailer's shelves. The price for an external drive ranges from $150 to $400, depending on its capacity.

The interest in external drives is driven by two primary reasons: easy backups and easy data transfer.

Easy backups

As the amount of data on a typical PC gets larger, the ease of doing backups — even on CDs — gets harder. CDs can handle just over 600MB of data, but most hard drives are now at 40GB or more. That's a lot of CDs to use for backup!

DVDs are the answer for some people, but they're not widespread due to confusion about what encoding algorithm should be used to write data on the disc. In addition, it takes quite a bit of time to store all that data and then verify it.

An easier and faster solution is to use an external hard drive. Plug it in — normally via a USB or FireWire cable — and Windows XP recognizes it as just another hard drive. You can copy your files to the hard drive, unplug it, and store it in a safe place. The process is much faster than using either CD or DVD solutions.

Recognizing that external hard drives are being used for backups, Maxtor recently came out with a line of external drives geared toward doing them. The drives have a capacity of anywhere from 160GB to 350GB. (That's a *lot* of data.) The drive enclosure even has a button that can be programmed to do the backup for you. Plug in the drive, push the button, and the backup automatically occurs. Pretty cool!

Easy data transfer

Suppose that you work part time at an office and the rest of the time at a client's location — or even at home. If you work on the same projects in both places, synchronizing data between locations quickly becomes a big chore.

The solution is an external drive. If you store your data on the external drive, you can take it with you and plug it into all the systems (via a USB or FireWire cable). When you do, the data is immediately available and ready to use.

If you decide to move your system paging file to a different drive (using information supplied earlier in the chapter), make sure you don't move it to a removable drive. If you try to start Windows without the removable drive accessible, Windows can't create the necessary pagefile.

Alternative Storage Solutions

When considering additional storage space, many people think only of hard drives. You aren't limited to hard drives. Consider a few of these other devices:

✔ **CD-R drives:** Commonplace on most systems these days, CD-R drives make a great archival medium and are wonderful for transferring data from system to system. The thing that makes CDs so attractive is that you can get blank CD-R discs for about 25 cents each. That price is cheaper than you can get floppy disks for and much cheaper than you can get blank DVDs.

- **DVD-R drives:** Though currently less common than CD drives, DVD-R drives are becoming more common as the need to store large amounts of data becomes critical. In fact, I was shopping for graphics packages the other day, and one was available on either eight CDs or a single DVD. The hassle of swapping CDs when browsing images made the idea of purchasing a DVD drive very enticing.

- **Zip drives:** These have been around for quite a while and they remain a workhorse in many systems. Zip disks are very handy for short-term archives or for transferring moderate amounts of data from one system to another. Data capacity ranges from 100MB to 250MB (for the common system used today) to 750MB for the newest drives. The biggest drawback to the Zip drives is the price of the disks they use. The 250MB disks are approximately $10 each and the 750MB disks are about $13.50 each.

- **Flash drive:** This must be the coolest device on the market these days. This storage device is nothing but a bank of static RAM connected to a USB plug. You plug it into a USB port and it looks just like another drive. As of this writing, drive capacities range from 64MB to 512MB, so they're not huge. What makes them cool, however, is their small size. You can find drives not much bigger than a quarter, and most are about the size of your thumb. Since flash drives have no mechanical parts, they are very fast, as well.

These devices are good for a variety of purposes. Think through how you could use each of them to help reduce the clutter on your existing system.

Chapter 18

Becoming Security Conscious

* *

In This Chapter

▶ Improving the system's local security

▶ Securing a system from Internet attack

▶ Increasing security by utilizing a firewall

* *

Security is one of those things you seldom think about, until you realize that you really should have been thinking about it. That point of realization typically comes right after someone breaks into your machine, steals the data, or makes your system unusable. The ironic part of security is that once the realization occurs, it's too late to counteract the problem that caused the realization.

Whoa! I don't mean to get philosophical, but with so much "realizing" going on, you should realize that you can save yourself a lot of grief if you become more security conscious today.

Computer security is its own specialty within the larger field of computer technology. This chapter does not provide all the security answers you need, but it does provide a good general introduction to the topic. You discover some of the simplest things to make your system more secure.

Realize that if you make your system more secure, you also decrease the potential for clutter on your system. If someone breaks into your system — either locally or remotely across the Internet — it's hard to have confidence in your system again. The fact is, you don't know what programs or data the intruder placed on your system.

Let me give you an example. I had a system that was a server connected to the Internet. I felt fairly confident that the system was secure, but after a few weeks someone broke into the system. They didn't take over the machine, but they broke in through an FTP server and stored a lot of huge files on my system. These files were illegal digital copies of movies. Once I discovered the problem, I was able to delete the files, free up the system space, and shore up my defenses so the problem wouldn't happen again. You can avoid similar problems if you take a little time to increase security.

Battening Down the Hatches

The buzz about security these days is all about the Internet. Everyone is worried about all the nefarious programs that can be delivered right to your system via the Internet. Problem is, the Internet is not your biggest security problem. The biggest threat you face is to your local machine — security issues would exist even if you unplugged the network cable that leads to the Internet.

This is not to say that you shouldn't pay attention to Internet-related security; you should. Later in this chapter you find out some of the things you can do to increase security. You just need to be aware of this point:

> If you don't make your system secure from non-Internet–related threats, you're missing the most likely source of security problems that you're likely to face.

The following sections examine the biggest security threats to your local machine.

Physical security

Why it's a security threat: Studies have shown that the biggest threat to a business' data is the person who can sit down in front of the computer containing the data. If someone can sit there, think what could be accessed. For most people, unfettered access to a computer means someone can get at all the sensitive data — checking accounts, phone lists, customer transactions, letters, memos, and much more.

What you can do about it: At a most basic level, having a secure system means keeping other people from getting to your system. You can do a few things to improve the physical security your computer and its data:

✔ **Lock doors.** If the area housing your computer has a door on it, make sure the door has a lock and that you use it. A locked door puts a roadblock between your system and someone who may abuse your system.

✔ **Turn off systems.** An eternal difference of opinion exists regarding whether systems should be left on or turned off when not in use. One plus to turning them off: doing so makes it harder for people to surreptitiously use your system for short periods.

✔ **Use passwords.** Lots of advice could be (and has been) given concerning selecting a good password. Passwords are a pain for most people, but using a good password can help thwart others' access to your system.

✔ **Reconfigure booting.** Most PCs can be booted to a floppy, a CD-ROM, the hard drive, or the network. Reconfigure your BIOS so that people cannot boot your system using either a floppy or a CD-ROM. If they can do that, they can use programs on the floppy or CD-ROM to bypass security and directly access your hard drive data.

Data loss

Why it's a security threat: You have hundreds, if not thousands, of hours invested in the data on your system. The old adage is true: Time is money. So the time you spend amassing your data represents a huge investment. Losing data is a huge security risk. If you run a small business and lose your data, your business could be severely damaged.

What you can do about it: The more your investment is worth, the more important it is to back up data. Minimize the chances of damage by periodically doing backups.

Data recovery

Why it's a security threat: When you delete information from your hard drive, Windows marks as free the hard drive locations previously occupied by the data. This means the locations are once again available to store information. Notice that Windows only marks the locations as available; it doesn't actually delete data. That's right — the data previously stored on the hard drive is still there, until it's overwritten by new data. With the right tools, the data in these deleted locations can even be recovered and viewed.

What you can do about it: The accessibility poses a security threat if someone starts using your system. To avoid this problem, many disk utilities include programs that completely erase data by overwriting it with new data and then deleting it. For instance, System Mechanic (www.iolo.com) includes a program called Drive Scrubber, and McAfee's QuickClean (www.mcafee.com) includes a program called Digital Shredder. Either program — or their counterparts from other system utilities — helps ensure the security of deleted data.

If you give your system away or sell it to someone else, they can use software to access your deleted data. Make sure you use a secure deletion program like Drive Scrubber or Digital Shredder to remove all traces of your data before the old system leaves your hands.

Malicious programs

Why it's a security threat: The world is full of malicious programs. An innumerable variety of viruses, Trojan horse programs, and worms await the unsuspecting.

Some people, new to computer security, believe that malicious programs are something introduced with the advent of the Internet. Malicious programs have been around much, much longer.

Before everyone was connected to the Internet, destructive programs typically spread by people sharing infected programs. It wasn't unusual for college campuses or large companies to become infected with viruses because someone loaded a game from a floppy disk to the hard drive. Unbeknownst to the user, the game included a virus that was activated after the copying was complete.

What you can do about it: Even if you disconnect your computer system from the Internet, you can still get a virus if you allow others, including your own children, to use your computer. (I have known some people who have even disconnected their floppy drive because they don't want to chance destructive programs being introduced through that doorway.) I recommend being very selective about who you let use your computer.

You should also make sure that you have an up-to-date virus checker on your system. Such programs routinely check the content of floppy disks to make sure they contain no known viruses. See Chapter 10 for more about virus checkers.

Insecure passwords

Why it's a security threat: Passwords are one of the fundamental means of physically securing your data. Everything these days — from your checking account to your online recipe cache — seems to require a username and password. When you use obvious passwords, you make it easier for dubious folks to guess those passwords and steal your data.

What you can do about it: When selecting a password, don't use anything obvious. Things such as your name, birth date, address, or favorite sports team are all pretty obvious. You need to make sure that your password contains a seemingly random set of letters, interspersed with seemingly random numbers. In addition, passwords should be at least six characters long. (Some systems may require a password of at least eight characters.)

Beware of programs that offer to help you remember your passwords or promise to automatically fill out password information on Web forms for you. Some of these programs are proven spyware or deliver pop-up ads to your system. If you need to keep track of your passwords, do so in a small notebook that you can secure in a locked drawer. Whatever you do, don't write your password down and leave it where others can find it.

Staying Secure on the Internet

Most computer systems in the United States are connected, at one time or another, to the Internet. The Internet presents an irresistible temptation, fueled by the siren song of vast amounts of information, easy communication, and far-flung resources.

Unfortunately, the Internet also presents a security risk. When you connect to the Internet, you open a unique doorway to your system. The doorway allows you to leave your computer to wander around cyberspace, but it also allows fellow travelers to enter your computer — unless you take security seriously.

The following sections discuss some of the more common Internet-related security issues.

Using Internet zones

Internet Explorer allows you to assign different Web sites to what it calls *Internet zones*. These zones are nothing more than a way for you to categorize Web sites. Different zones have different security settings applied to them. (The different security levels for the Internet Explorer zones are described in Chapter 11's cookie discussion.)

Microsoft established four security zones in Internet Explorer:

- **Internet:** Contains all sites that you haven't assigned to a zone. The default security level for this zone is Medium.

- **Local Intranet:** For addresses either on your local computer or on your local network. The default security level for this zone is Medium.

- **Trusted Sites:** Contains sites you designate as trustworthy. The default security level for this zone is Low.

- **Restricted Sites:** Contains sites you don't trust. The default security level for this zone is High.

In my experience, most people don't use zones, even though doing so can make your system more secure. The idea behind them is that you can designate which sites you trust and which you don't. Those trustworthy sites automatically have a lower security level, which means they can store and read cookies. Those sites you don't trust aren't given this level of access.

All Web sites belong to the Internet zone unless you assign them to one of the other zones. To assign a Web site to a specific zone, open Internet Explorer and follow these steps:

1. **Choose Tools⇨Internet Options.**

   Internet Explorer displays the Internet Options dialog box. Ensure that the Security tab is chosen, as shown in Figure 18-1.

Figure 18-1:
Security
zones are
controlled
on the
Security tab.

2. **Click one of the security zones.**

   The four security zones are at the top of the page. Click the one to which you want to assign the site.

3. **Click Sites.**

   Internet Explorer displays a list of sites assigned to the zone, as shown in Figure 18-2.

   If you're working in the Local Intranet zone, click the Advanced button to see the desired dialog box.

4. **Enter the Web site's address in the Add This Web Site to the Zone text box; click Add.**

   The specified URL appears in the Web Sites list. You can remove a site from the list by selecting it and clicking Remove.

5. **Click OK.**

> Your zone changes are saved. You can close all the other open dialog boxes.

If you want Internet Explorer to verify that the server for each Web site in this zone is secure before connecting to any Web sites in this zone, select the Require Server Verification (https:) for All Sites in This Zone check box. The check box is shown in Figure 18-2.

Whenever you visit a site via Internet Explorer, its security designation is shown at the right side of the status bar. If you haven't assigned the site to a particular zone, the designation shows a small globe and the word *Internet,* meaning the site belongs to the Internet zone.

A quick way to display the Security tab shown in Figure 18-1 is to double-click the zone notation at the right side of the Internet Explorer status bar.

Figure 18-2: Modify the addresses assigned to a zone.

Harnessing SSL

One way to make transferring data safer is to encrypt it. Entire books discuss the ins and outs of data encryption. Of the many encryption methods available, perhaps the most common is SSL.

SSL is an acronym for secure sockets layer. This seemingly unassuming phrase actually hides a tremendous amount of complexity. SSL capability is built into most Web browsers, including Internet Explorer.

SSL is handled transparently for most people, meaning that you may not even be aware it's in effect. For instance, if you visit a Web site to order a product, you may be unaware that the ordering page uses SSL to encrypt the information you enter.

You can tell if SSL is in effect through two indicators:

- ✔ Look at the URL that accesses the site. Most sites begin with the http:// protocol designator. A secure site using SSL begins with https:// instead. (Notice the addition of the *s*.)

- ✔ Look at your browser for a small security icon. In Internet Explorer, a secure page has a small padlock that appears on the status bar, just to the left of the security zone designator.

Be careful when dealing with sites requesting sensitive data. If the site does not use an SSL, then your data isn't transferred to the site in a private manner. This means that your data is less secure than you may be comfortable with.

Closing down security problems

With the widespread acceptance of high-speed Internet connections, a new problem is spreading. High-speed connections such as DSL or cable modems are always on, meaning they provide a continuous Internet connection. If you leave your system turned on, your computer is constantly and continuously connected to the Internet.

In case you didn't realize it, the Internet is a two-way superhighway. You can reach out from your computer to access resources around the Internet, and people all over the world can reach out and access your computer. What!? Most people don't realize that others can access their computers. The fact of the matter is they can — and with minimal trouble. In fact, security holes and bugs in Windows XP can allow others to access your entire system.

Windows has the potential to be a secure operating system, but out of the box — as first installed — it isn't very secure. If Windows were a house, you might consider it a fairly impressive house. It locks the front door, but experienced troublemakers know they can get in through an open window.

Windows is notorious for leaving some of the house's windows open. The solution is to do a security checkup and see what weaknesses you can fix. A good place to start is with the ShieldsUP! utility from Gibson Research. This free check takes only a few minutes, but provides many ways to secure your system.

To use ShieldsUP!, visit Gibson Research at http://grc.com/default.htm. Scroll down the page just a bit and click the ShieldsUP! link. You see the first page of the ShieldsUP! check, as shown in Figure 18-3. Work your way through the checkup to discover where your vulnerabilities are and how to fix them.

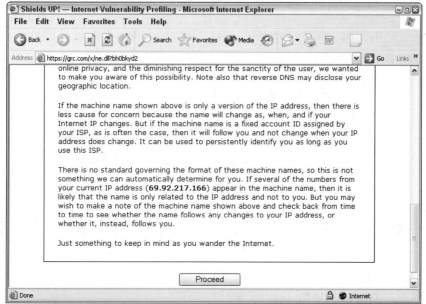

online privacy, and the diminishing respect for the sanctity of the user, we wanted to make you aware of this possibility. Note also that reverse DNS may disclose your geographic location.

If the machine name shown above is only a version of the IP address, then there is less cause for concern because the name will change as, when, and if your Internet IP changes. But if the machine name is a fixed account ID assigned by your ISP, as is often the case, then it will follow you and not change when your IP address does change. It can be used to persistently identify you as long as you use this ISP.

There is no standard governing the format of these machine names, so this is not something we can automatically determine for you. If several of the numbers from your current IP address (**69.92.217.166**) appear in the machine name, then it is likely that the name is only related to the IP address and not to you. But you may wish to make a note of the machine name shown above and check back from time to time to see whether the name follows any changes to your IP address, or whether it, instead, follows you.

Just something to keep in mind as you wander the Internet.

Proceed

Figure 18-3: Check your system for Internet vulnerabilities.

Adding Firewalls

When constructing an apartment building, a contractor often includes a firewall between apartments. This firewall is specially reinforced and retards the spread of a fire, should one start in an apartment. Similarly, firewalls exist at the front of most cars, between the passenger compartment and the engine space. The purpose of such firewalls is to provide protection for people on one side of the firewall from what may be happening on the other side. It's the same with computers. In the context of the computing world, a *firewall* is a security device that limits the effect outside people have on people inside.

Firewalls come in all shapes, sizes, and capacities. Large networks often have specialized computers that do nothing but act as a firewall. Smaller networks often have smaller, less expensive versions, and individual computers connected to the Internet can have individual software firewalls installed.

The following sections describe the firewall built into Windows XP, the most popular individual software firewall, and dedicated hardware firewalls.

The Windows firewall

Windows XP includes a firewall built into the operating system. This firewall, technically named the Internet Connection Firewall (ICF) in Windows XP and

Windows Firewall in Windows XP SP2, enables you to limit what information is communicated to and from the Internet. This firewall is ideal for those connected directly to the Internet through either a dial-up or fulltime high-speed connection.

If you have Windows XP SP2 installed on your system, the Windows Firewall is enabled and running by default. If you do not have SP2, you need to specifically turn on ICF. To do so, follow these steps:

1. **Choose Start➪Control Panel➪Networking and Internet Connection.**

   A window shows your defined network connections.

2. **Right-click the connection used for the Internet and choose Properties.**

   Windows displays the Properties dialog box for the connection. You should make sure the Advanced tab is chosen, as shown in Figure 18-4.

Figure 18-4:
Enable ICF
on your
system.

3. **Select the Protect My Computer and Network check box.**

   This check box controls whether ICF is enabled on your system.

4. **Click the Settings button.**

   Windows displays the Advanced Settings dialog box shown in Figure 18-5.

5. **Select the check boxes next to the services you want to use.**

   Each check box controls a different type of Internet protocol. For instance, if you receive and send e-mail, select the SMTP and POP3 check boxes. Different options include:

- **FTP Server:** If you're running an FTP server on your computer and you want other people to have access to it, select this check box.

- **Internet Mail Access Protocol Version 3 (IMAP3):** IMAP is a protocol used to manage mail on a mail server. Most people should make sure this check box is cleared.

- **Internet Mail Access Protocol Version 4 (IMAP4):** A newer version of the IMAP protocol, this check box should probably be cleared.

- **Internet Mail Server (SMTP):** Unless you're running your own mail server, you should clear this check box. (SMTP is used primarily by mail servers to talk directly to each other.)

- **Post-Office Protocol Version 3 (POP3):** If you use e-mail and your e-mail client doesn't use IMAP, select this option.

- **Remote Desktop:** Windows allows you to connect to other systems and remotely control them with Remote Desktop. If you don't want others to connect to your system in this manner, clear this check box.

- **Secure Web Server (HTTPS):** If you're running a Web server and it uses SSL, select this check box.

- **Telnet Server:** Telnet is a way to connect to other systems as if you're a terminal for that system. On most systems, this option should not be selected.

- **Web Server (HTTP):** If you have a Web server on your system and you want it accessible by others on the Internet, select this check box.

6. **Close all the open dialog boxes.**

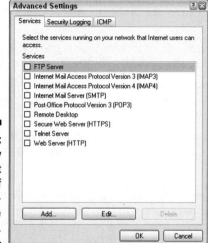

Figure 18-5:
Specify what types of communication are acceptable.

Once enabled, ICF works silently to block different types of access to your system. If a disabled type of communication is attempted from the Internet side of the firewall, ICF refuses to allow it through. If the communication is permitted (based on what you specified on the Advanced Settings tab), then it's allowed through the firewall.

Unsuccessful attempts to get through the firewall are logged in a file (stored here: C:\windows\pfirewall.log). You can review the log file anytime you need to know what's happening with your Internet connection.

The ICF is designed primarily as a personal system for your individual computer. If your computer is part of a network that already has a firewall in place, you don't need to use ICF; disable it. Check with your network administrator for more details.

ZoneAlarm

Several personal firewall programs are available, but none has garnered the market share that ZoneAlarm has. Published by Zone Labs (www.zonelabs.com), the company makes both a free and commercial version.

ZoneAlarm essentially does the same thing that the Internet Connection Firewall (ICF) does — it blocks people and programs on the Internet from getting into your computer.

Because both programs serve the same purpose, it's reasonable to ask why anyone would need ZoneAlarm when they can use ICF. Both approaches offer benefits:

- ✔ If you like visual notification of break-in attempts, use ZoneAlarm. It provides a pop-up screen every time one of these events occurs, but this feature can be turned off.

- ✔ If you want protection but don't want interruptions, use ICF. It purposely does its work silently, writing any firewall transgressions to a log file.

- ✔ If you want protection "closer" to the operating system, use ICF. It functions as an actual part of Windows XP, at a lower level than ZoneAlarm can.

- ✔ If you want protection beyond what a firewall normally provides (e-mail quarantine, pop-up blocker, cookie monitoring, and the like), purchase ZoneAlarm Pro ($49.95).

You don't need to use both ICF and ZoneAlarm; you need only one firewall. If you decide to use ZoneAlarm, make sure you turn off ICF. While there is no real danger in using both at the same time, doing so provides no benefit. (It's like putting two garage doors on the same garage — one in front of the other. It doesn't hurt but makes no sense.)

Hardware firewalls

If you're responsible for a network — for even as few as five systems — you should consider getting a *hardware-based firewall.* These are more expensive than software-based firewalls, but provide a better level of protection than you can get with products like ICF or ZoneAlarm.

Literally scores of hardware firewall products are available, and finding the right one can be time consuming. When I needed to find a good hardware firewall for my network, I did a lot of searching and settled on products made by SonicWall (www.sonicwall.com). SonicWall offers a wide range of products, suitable for all types of needs, ranging in price from about $700 to several thousands of dollars.

Sometimes firewall capabilities are integrated into other hardware devices, such as routers or proxy servers. Check with your hardware vendor to see exactly what its products provide in the way of protection.

Hardware firewalls are normally placed between your network router and the entry point for your Internet connection. For instance, if you're using a DSL line, you plug the DSL line from the wall into the hardware firewall, and then connect a plug from the firewall to your network's hub or switch (the network device to which each of your computers connects). In that way, nothing that the firewall should catch ever gets on your network — which reduces the data load on your network.

Managing a hardware firewall can be a bit more challenging than managing a software firewall, but it's not overly difficult. With SonicWall, for instance, the firewall can be managed over the Internet. (To make it secure, management can be locked for performing only from machines using specific IP addresses.) I can manage the firewall using forms presented on my Web browser, which is very convenient. Devices from other vendors may require using a serial port or some secure protocol.

If you use a hardware firewall, the systems connected to your network don't need to use their own software firewalls. This means that firewall management is done at a single point and that the network's clients have one less piece of software to master.

Checking Your Security with Service Pack 2

If you're running Windows XP SP2, you have a nifty new tool at your disposal that can give you a birds-eye view of your security standing. SP2 includes what is called the Security Center, which runs as a background process in Windows, monitoring what is going on in your system.

To display the Security Center, start at the Control Panel. You should see a Security Center applet, and if you double-click it, you see what Security Center has been monitoring:

- **Firewall:** The Security Center displays the status of the Windows Firewall (whether it is on or off) or the status of SP2-compliant firewalls from other vendors.

- **Virus Protection:** The Security Center checks to see whether you have virus protection software in place on your system. (Again, this only happens if you're using anti-virus software that is compliant with SP2.) If you do, it checks to see whether that software is up to date.

- **Automatic Updates:** The Security Center checks to make sure you're set to receive automatic updates.

If Security Center determines that you can improve your security by making changes in these areas, it provides links to recommendations on actions you can take. You should consider running Security Center periodically to make sure there are no gaping holes in your system.

Chapter 19

Cleaning House in a Networked Environment

*W*hen my children were growing up, our home was often the center of the neighborhood. It was not unusual for our children's friends to come calling at all hours of the day or night. Some of the kids would even walk right in the door without knocking. We would only hear "Hi, Mr. Wyatt!" as the child dashed through the kitchen on the way to the family room, the living room, or a bedroom.

With the continual parade of people through our home, we got used to finding the oddest things lying about. One day we'd find a shirt that didn't belong to us, another day a pair of smelly socks. A couple of times I even found pairs of pants that I know belonged to neighborhood children, and I often wondered how they got home without them.

If you have a computer connected to a network, it's possible that other network users could traipse through your system at all hours of the day or night. Just like the neighborhood kids, they may leave things behind, adding to the general clutter and making your cleaning job even more challenging.

This chapter focuses on some things you can do to help decrease the clutter on your networked system.

Getting Rid of Old User Accounts

User accounts on both your local machine and the network are analogous to passports — they allow access to various areas of the network or various resources on your system.

By careful user accounts management, you can make sure that your system and the network as a whole remain less cluttered and run smoother. The actions you can take with user accounts depend on the type of network you're a part of: client-server or peer-to-peer. (See the nearby sidebar for an explanation of these network types.) In addition, you may have different user accounts set up on your local computer.

Deleting network user accounts

On most networks, a user (such as yourself) needs an account to access network resources. This account, along with the permissions that define what your account can do on the network, is normally set up by your network administrator.

Managing different network user accounts can be a large part of an administrator's job, depending on the network size. The user accounts set up by the administrator may also affect your system and how it's utilized by others on the network.

If you belong to a client-server network and believe that other network users are abusing your system, talk to your network administrator about either changing the user's permissions or deleting the user account entirely. Little can be done to modify the account, unless (of course) you're the administrator.

Deleting local system user accounts

Windows XP is a *multiuser system,* which means that multiple people can use the same computer. This lets you set up accounts for different coworkers or family members.

Each user can add programs and create unshared files. If a user no longer needs an account on your system, his programs and files take up hard drive space that you may want to reclaim. To reclaim that space, remove the user's account by following these steps:

1. **Restart your system and log in as system administrator.**

   Windows XP created an administrator account for your system when it was set up. Since only the administrator can delete users, you need to use that account. (If your personal account was set up with administrator's rights, you can delete users when logged in under your own account. To determine whether you can do this, try. If you can't delete them, then you must log in as the administrator.)

2. **Choose Start⇨Control Panel⇨User Accounts⇨User Accounts.**

   If you're using the Classic view of the Control Panel, you need only click User Accounts once.

   Windows displays a dialog box containing all the user accounts, along with some tasks you can perform. See Figure 19-1.

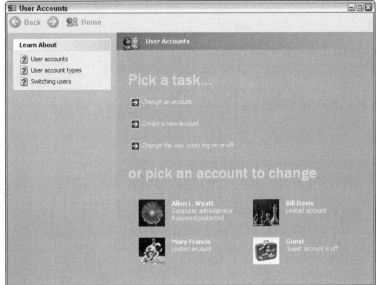

Figure 19-1:
Performing administrative tasks on user accounts.

3. **Click the user account you want to delete.**

   Windows displays a list of tasks you can perform in relation to the account.

4. **Click Delete the Account.**

   Windows asks you if you want to keep the files associated with the account.

5. **Click Delete Files.**

   Windows deletes the files. Deleting can take a while, depending on how many files were created using the account.

6. **Click Delete Account.**

   Windows finishes deleting the specified account.

Client-server and peer-to-peer

In the grand scheme of things, two general classifications of networking exist:

✔ **Client-server:** These networks rely on centralized resources, using things like file servers and print servers to manage resources. A *client* (your computer) connects to the file server to access shared files or to a print server to create printed output. In addition, client-server networks rely on a centralized repository of security information that dictates how clients can utilize the network's resources.

✔ **Peer-to-peer:** In a peer-to-peer arrangement, no centralized resource management or centralized security repository is used. Instead, the network is composed of *peers* — systems with equal authority to utilize the network. Each system on the network has the ability to make resources available to others and to define how others can use those resources. Others can use those resources in accordance with the wishes of the system doing the sharing.

Clutter happens on individual computers and it happens on networks. If you're using a client-server network, then most of the clutter happens on file servers. That type of clutter generally needs to be managed and removed by network administrators.

If you're using a peer-to-peer arrangement, then the clutter is spread across the network on whatever machine opened its doors for others. If you share resources, then your system could have clutter related to your generosity. You need to monitor the situation carefully to make sure your system doesn't become a victim of the inevitable clutter that results from your largesse.

Restart your computer after completing these steps. You don't want to stay logged in as administrator and inadvertently change other settings.

Moving Frequently Accessed Data

My home has areas accessible to different people in the family. If I want something to be accessible by everyone, I can place it in the middle of the living room or on a kitchen counter. If I want something to be more private, I can place it in my bedroom closet or in a closed-off area of my home office.

Your computer is the same way — you probably have data that you use for your programs. Others don't need to access that data. Conversely, some of your data may have wide appeal.

If you have data that others need, perform the digital equivalent of moving it from the bedroom closet to the middle of the living room. You do that by either setting up a shared folder on your system or moving the data to a shared drive accessible through your network. Moving the data to a network drive can help free up space on your local hard drive, which is a good thing.

Don't keep a private copy of data that others can change. Doing so, you run into data synchronization problems. If a coworker changes the public copy of the data file, that change isn't reflected in your private copy. Likewise, if you change the private copy, it doesn't show up in the public copy. Before long, lots of discrepancies exist between the two file versions. Solve the problem by making sure only a single copy of the data file exists. Marking a document as private or public and syncing data are concepts outside the scope of this book. If you're unfamiliar with these concepts but would like to know more, check out *Networking For Dummies*, 6th Edition, by Doug Lowe or *Home Networking For Dummies*, 2nd Edition, by Kathy Ivens (both published by Wiley).

Removing Shared Printers

You may have a connected printer that others would like to access. On a network, you can give others access to the printer; they can then print to their heart's content. Your printer becomes a focal point and you get to see more of your coworkers than you may want to.

If you find that being a print station is not for you, you can do a couple of things to help alleviate the situation. The following sections discuss how you can limit when people print and remove the shared printer completely.

Limiting shared printer hours

My most productive time of the day is early in the morning. Once I am wide awake, I find myself able to churn through work needing my attention, before the cares of the day start to eat away at my focus. If I can limit phone and e-mail interruptions, I can get quite a bit done during those hours.

If you're like me, you may want to limit interruptions during the morning hours. For instance, you might not want people to print documents to your printer before 10:30 a.m. Fortunately, Windows makes limiting the printer availability easy.

1. **Choose Start⇨Control Panel⇨Printers and Other Hardware⇨View Installed Printers or Fax Printers.**

   If you're using the Classic view of the Control Panel, instead choose Start⇨Control Panel⇨Printers and Faxes. In either case, you see icons representing the printers defined on your system.

2. **Right-click the printer you want to change and choose Properties from the context menu.**

   Windows displays the printer's Properties dialog box. Make sure the Advanced tab is chosen, as shown in Figure 19-2.

3. **Click the Available From radio button.**

   The controls for beginning and ending time become accessible.

4. **Specify a beginning and ending time.**

   Pick a time range in which you want the printer available. You can only specify a single range, with a starting and ending time.

5. **Click OK.**

When specifying the hours your printer is available, pick something that balances your needs with those of others. For instance, if you don't want people to use the printer before 10:30 a.m., you could set the beginning time to 10:30 a.m. and the ending time to 5:00 a.m. The printer would then be unavailable between 5:00 a.m. and 10:30 a.m.

Setting availability printer hours doesn't mean that others can't print to it around the clock. If someone prints outside the specified hours, the job is held in the print queue until the printer becomes available. Thus, if your printer is popular, you could see a whole rash of print jobs come through right after the starting time occurs.

Turning off shared printing

If you want to rescind your kind offer of allowing others to use your printer, turn off sharing altogether. Doing so is easy:

1. **Choose Start⇨Control Panel⇨Printers and Other Hardware⇨View Installed Printers or Fax Printers.**

   If you're using the Classic view of the Control Panel, instead choose Start⇨Control Panel⇨Printers and Faxes. In either case, you see icons representing the printers defined on your system.

2. **Right-click the printer you want to change and choose Properties from the context menu.**

   Windows displays the Properties dialog box for the printer. You should make sure the Sharing tab is chosen, as shown in Figure 19-3.

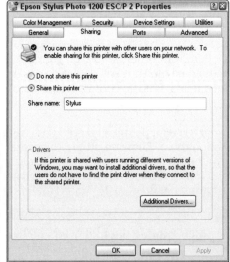

Figure 19-3: Windows allows you to specify how a printer is shared.

3. **Select the Do Not Share this Printer radio button.**

4. **Click OK.**

The printer is immediately unavailable to others on your network. If people try to print to your printer, they see an error message.

You can help others on your network by letting them know when you change the printer's shared status. When you remove sharing, others can remove the printer definition on their systems. Doing so allows Windows to remove the printer drivers previously installed. The result is that unnecessary clutter is removed from their system, as well.

Folders versus drives

Old timers like me often refer to shared folders as *shared drives* because we used to map shared folders — on someone else's computer — to drive letters on our systems. Windows doesn't require drive mapping anymore, so making shared folders synonymous with shared drives is somewhat anachronistic. That, of course, doesn't stop us from sitting in our rocking chairs on the porch of the Old Windows Users Retirement Home and discussing the "good old days." (Don't worry, Junior — you'll catch up with us old timers soon enough.)

Removing Shared Folders

Windows allows you to share data with other people on your network. It doesn't allow you to share individual files but entire directories. In other words, you aren't sharing documents, but the containers (folders) in which the documents are stored.

When you share folders on your system, people can read data from the folder and sometimes store information there. Allowing others to access data on your system can slow down your system; allowing others to place data on your system can encourage clutter. You can reduce clutter (and perhaps increase system performance) by unsharing the previously shared folder. Just follow these steps:

1. **Display the folder window containing the folder you no longer want to share.**

   You can use My Computer or Windows Explorer to display the folder. The icon for the intended folder should be shown with an outstretched hand holding the folder.

2. **Right-click the folder icon and choose Sharing and Security from the context menu.**

   Windows displays the folder's Properties dialog box, with the Sharing tab displayed like you see in Figure 19-4. Another way to display this dialog box is by choosing Properties from the context menu and then clicking the Sharing tab.

3. **In the Network Sharing and Security area, deselect the Share This Folder on the Network check box.**

4. **Click OK.**

   The folder is immediately inaccessible to others. If someone is actively using data in the folder, you may see a dialog box warning you that someone else is using your data. If you want to cut off the user's access to your data, then click OK.

Cutting off another user while she has a file open on your system can result in a corrupted data file. If possible, get the other person to exit the application (thereby closing the data file) before cutting off access.

Cutting Your System off the Network

Just because Windows allows you to share your local resources (files and printers) on a network doesn't mean you have to share them. If you want to keep your resources to yourself, you can disable sharing all together by following these steps:

1. **Choose Start⇨Control Panel⇨Network and Internet Connections⇨ Network Connections.**

   If you're using the Classic view of the Control Panel, choose Start ⇨ Control Panel⇨Network Connections instead. In either case, you see icons representing the different connections defined on your system.

2. **Right-click the connection for your network and choose Properties from the context menu.**

   Windows displays the connection's Properties dialog box, as shown in Figure 19-5.

3. **Deselect the check box next to File and Printer Sharing for Microsoft Networks.**

   This network component controls whether resources on your system are sharable with others.

4. **Click OK.**

Figure 19-5:
Changing
the network
components
used for a
connection.

After you disable file and printer sharing, nobody can utilize resources on your system. Cutting off others won't stop you from using resources on their systems, if they're sharing.

If you don't foresee a time when you'll ever share system resources with others, then you may want to uninstall the sharing component from your network. In the Properties dialog box shown in Figure 19-5, select the File and Printer Sharing for Microsoft Networks component and click Uninstall. The component is removed entirely from the operating system. If you later change your mind, you can reinstall the component by clicking Install and choose File and Printer Sharing for Microsoft Networks from the Services area.

Chapter 20

Jumping Into the Registry

● ●

In This Chapter

▶ Understanding the Registry

▶ Making Registry changes

▶ Cleaning the Registry with special software

▶ Fixing the Registry in case of problems

● ●

*I*f Windows were a sentient being, the Registry would be its central nervous system. The Registry is related to and used by virtually every program on your system and by the operating system itself. Windows checks the Registry to see how programs should be installed, accessed, used, and uninstalled. It checks to see if a program (or a user) is allowed to access different areas of the computer.

From when you first log in to when you turn off the system, the Registry is being used. In fact, much of the Windows start-up time is spent reading and checking the Registry, and virtually all of the Windows shut-down time is spent writing information to the Registry.

Even still, Windows does a pretty good job of masking the Registry's ever-present, pervasive nature. Most users go through the motions of customizing Windows and their software without the slightest hint that they're making changes to the Registry.

This chapter focuses on the Registry, giving you the info you need to make sure it's in tip-top shape. Just like your hard drive, your Registry can become cluttered with outdated information. Understanding what the Registry is, how to change it, and how to clean it can help you keep your system at its peak performance.

You can rest assured that you can live your life satisfactorily and with much joy without ever dealing with the Registry. If you don't want to know about the Registry, then skip this chapter. You find quite a bit of technical information covered here — not as much as you might find in some geek-centered book, but definitely more than your normal book for novices.

Groking the Registry Behemoth

When I was a teen, I loved the sci-fi book *Stranger in a Strange Land* by Robert Heinlein. I was not alone; during the latter half of the 1960s the book was adopted by many as a counterculture bible, of sorts. It tells the tale of a human, abducted by Martians in his infancy and raised on Mars. While a young adult, he returns to Earth. The book provides insight into his reactions to Earth's various cultures and the cultures' reactions to an earthling from Mars.

One of the terms introduced in the book is *grok,* a Martian verb meaning to totally and fully understand something, well beyond any earthly understanding. The verb made headway into the underground lexicon, and you can still hear it used at times today — like in this section's title.

Looking at and trying to understand the Registry is, for many, an exercise in frustration. With a little background, the frustration can be alleviated and you can surpass worldly understanding of what the Registry does. (After all, the Microsofties that Uncle Bill hired to develop the Registry may be human, but they were definitely raised on Mars.)

The Registry is nothing more than a hierarchical database maintained by Windows as a repository of configuration information. All the settings stored in the Registry are used by not only the operating system, but by all the installed programs. The Registry consists of four distinct parts:

- ✔ **Trees:** The major Registry divisions.
- ✔ **Hives:** Major divisions of the Registry trees.
- ✔ **Keys:** Groups of related settings within a hive.
- ✔ **Values:** The data stored within a key.

As you make changes to system settings — for instance, in the Control Panel or in various Properties dialog boxes — the new changes are stored in the Registry. Information is stored in the form of values, which are placed in keys that are determined by the nature of the placing program. Thus, if you use the Control Panel to change display settings, your information is stored in either the keys that control the desktop's appearance or the keys that control your video hardware.

Seeing the trees in the Registry forest

The Registry consists of five major trees. These *trees* comprise all aspects of the operating system:

- ✔ **HKEY_CLASSES_ROOT.** Information related to the file types and actions that can be performed on files, including shortcuts. Also includes information on file associations.
- ✔ **HKEY_CURRENT_USER.** Specific profile settings for the user currently logged on to the system.
- ✔ **HKEY_LOCAL_MACHINE.** Machine-related specifics, such as installed hardware, swap file settings, startup settings, and so on.
- ✔ **HKEY_USERS.** User-specific settings for all user profiles defined for the system.
- ✔ **HKEY_CURRENT_CONFIG.** Configuration information about the current hardware settings, such as notebooks that plug into a docking station.

The Registry has five trees, but this can be deceiving. Windows uses pointers for several keys. For instance, HKEY_CLASSES_ROOT is nothing but a pointer to the HKEY_LOCAL_MACHINE\SOFTWARE\CLASSES subkey. Likewise, HKEY_CURRENT_USER is a pointer to a subkey within HKEY_USERS. Thus, of the five trees, only three (HKEY_LOCAL_MACHINE, HKEY_CURRENT_CONFIG, and HKEY_USERS) actually represent information stored on disk.

Buzzing through the Registry hives

The first major division under each tree is known as hives; they were named as such because of their resemblance to beehives. Your Registry information is stored here on disk. According to Microsoft information, a *hive* is a discrete body of keys, subkeys, and values rooted at the top of the Registry hierarchy.

For instance, the HKEY_LOCAL_MACHINE tree contains the following hives:

- ✔ HARDWARE
- ✔ SAM
- ✔ SECURITY
- ✔ SOFTWARE
- ✔ SYSTEM

Hives are the part of the Registry either stored on disk or constructed in memory. Of the five hives here, only the first (HARDWARE) is constructed in memory when your system is first started. The other four hives utilize two separate files each.

The first file is the Registry file, which uses the same name as the hive. The second file is a log file, which uses the same name as the hive, with a filename extension LOG. Most of the hive files are stored in the c:\windows\system32\config folder but don't need to be there. (On a system upgraded to Windows XP, the files may be in the c:\winnt\system32\config folder.)

Table 20-1 shows the different hives used in the Registry, along with the files that store those hives. (If no file is listed for a hive, then the hive is created in memory every time you use Windows.)

Table 20-1	Registry Hives		
Tree	*Hive*	*Registry File*	*Log File*
HKEY_LOCAL_MACHINE	HARDWARE		
HKEY_LOCAL_MACHINE	SAM	Sam	Sam.log
HKEY_LOCAL_MACHINE	SECURITY	Security	Security.log
HKEY_LOCAL_MACHINE	SOFTWARE	Software	Software.log
HKEY_LOCAL_MACHINE	SYSTEM	System	System.log
HKEY_CURRENT_CONFIG	SOFTWARE		
HKEY_CURRENT_CONFIG	SYSTEM		
HKEY_USERS	DEFAULT	Default	Default.log
HKEY_USERS	Varies	Varies	Varies

Unlocking Registry keys

Registry hives are divided into *keys,* organizational units for Registry information. Because keys are designed to contain information, they're similar to folders on your hard drive. (This explains why the Registry Editor, presented later in this chapter, displays keys using a file-folder symbol.)

Registry keys can contain values and subkeys. In turn, the subkeys can contain additional values and subkeys. Just as directory folders can contain files and additional folders, the keys under each hive can contain values and subkeys. This organization is the basis of the Registry's hierarchical structure and means it can be presented in a tree fashion.

Appreciating Registry values

Values contain data that represent configuration settings for Windows or for a program installed on your system. For instance, a value may contain the starting position for a window or the amount of memory in your system.

Data can be of five basic types:

- ✔ **REG_BINARY:** Numeric information of any length.

- ✔ **REG_DWORD:** Numeric information limited to a length of 32 bits.

- ✔ **REG_EXPAND_SZ:** String information of any length and whose length can change over time. Normally, this data type is used for system and program variables.

- ✔ **REG_MULTI_SZ:** A series of string values, each separated by a NULL character. This data type is typically used for information lists, such as those displayed in drop-down lists.

- ✔ **REG_SZ:** A string value, of any length, that does not change. The value is static.

In addition, applications can define their own special data types. The exact type maintained for a value is determined by the purpose for which the value is used.

Editing the Registry

The Registry is a very dynamic place, with changes happening all the time. Because it contains all your system's settings and configuration information, that makes sense. In some cases, the Registry is updated automatically by Windows itself. The following list highlights the ways the Registry changes:

- ✔ **Automatically:** For instance, you may add a hardware device that Windows automatically detects. In such a case, the drivers are loaded automatically and settings are changed. The information about these drivers, the device, and any settings is stored automatically in the Registry.

  The Registry can also be changed by some action you take. For instance, you may use an applet in the Control Panel, in which case the Registry stores the change. Other changes are introduced by programs you use and settings you make in them.

- ✔ **Manually:** Windows allows you to manually change the Registry. While manual changes are tougher than changes made using the Control Panel (or other tools), the effect is the same because system settings control how Windows functions.

Differences in Registry Editors

In reading other books (or information on the Internet), you may have read that two Registry Editors are available in Windows: regedit and regedt32. In older versions of Windows, quite a bit of difference existed between these two programs. regedit was the 16-bit Registry Editor and regedt32 was its 32-bit counterpart.

Everything changed in Windows XP. Windows no longer has different programs for editing the Registry. According to the Microsoft Knowledge Base (article 141377), the primary Registry Editor is regedit. In fact, if you run regedt32, it turns right around and runs regedit for you.

The tool that manually changes the Registry is the Registry Editor. This program is not available from any of the regular Windows menus (probably due to the potential adverse consequences of misuse). Instead, start the program from the Start menu's Run option. Follow these steps:

1. **Choose Start⇨Run.**

   Windows displays the Run dialog box.

2. **In the Open field, type** regedit, **and click OK.**

   Regedit, short for Registry Editor, is the name of the Registry Editor program.

   Shortly you see the Registry Editor shown in Figure 20-1.

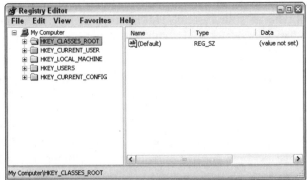

Figure 20-1:
The Registry Editor uses a hierarchical interface.

The Registry Editor window has two parts. The left displays the different trees, hives, and keys, while the right displays anything within the element selected in the left portion of the window.

The Registry Editor's hierarchical interface is very similar to interfaces used in other programs, such as Windows Explorer. If you're already familiar with the interface, you should have no problem getting around in the Registry Editor.

If you manually make changes in the Registry, you do so at your own risk. Whenever you make changes in the Windows configuration, those changes are stored in the Registry. Windows includes many safeguards to protect you from making changes that don't make sense or that may harm your system. When you manually edit the Registry, no such safeguards exist. Make sure you know what you're changing before you make the change.

Backing up the Registry

The Registry Editor allows you to export the Registry to a text file and later import the text file back into a Registry. This capability provides the means for backing up the Registry.

Before you make any changes to the Registry, you should back it up. Doing so helps you in case of a catastrophic error — like deleting an entire hive. (I've done that. It's not a pretty picture.)

To export the Registry, follow these steps:

1. **In the Registry Editor, choose the key that you want to export.**

   If you want to export the entire Registry, don't worry about this step. For a reminder of how to open the Registry, refer to the previous steps.

2. **Choose File⇨Export.**

   The Registry Editor displays the Export Registry File dialog box shown in Figure 20-2.

3. **Use the dialog box controls to locate and select the drive and folder you want used for the exported Registry.**

   Unless you're exporting a small key, don't try to save to a floppy disk. You can, however, save to a Zip disk or another capacious media.

4. **In the File Name text box, enter a name for the export file.**

5. **In the Export Range area, select what you want to save.**

   The default is Selected Branch, meaning the key you selected in Step 1. If you want to save the entire Registry, select the All radio button.

6. **Click Save.**

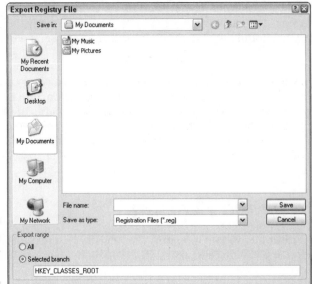

Figure 20-2:
Exporting
the Registry.

When you later decide to import the Registry file, you can do so by choosing File⇨Import. You see a dialog box that allows you to select a file. The file you specify is imported to the current Registry. If the import file contains keys or values that already exist in the Registry, the existing keys and values are over-written with the new information. Conversely, if the Registry has any items with names that don't exist in the import file, these items remain in the new, modified Registry.

Finding information

Men are always accused of being reluctant to ask for directions. When my wife and I go out driving, she knows better than to ask if I need to ask how to get somewhere. After driving around for a while (and seeing the same scenery a couple of times), she may ask if I am lost. Invariably I'll say, "No, I'm not. I've been lost before, and this doesn't look anything like it."

Such an attitude may have no huge marital consequences in real life, but it can have huge consequences if you decide to go romping through the Registry without knowing where you're going. Its sheer size and amount of information make it mandatory to know what you want to edit before you begin poking around.

Cleaning up software references

The Registry can easily become cluttered with pieces and parts of old programs no longer on your system. In your neverending quest to clean your system, you may want to remove all references to a program from your Registry. Doing so is theoretically easy, albeit time consuming:

1. **If you know the name of the program, search the Registry (using the Registry Editor's Find command) for all occurrences of the program name.**

   Make sure you start your search from the beginning of the Registry.

2. **Delete every value or key that contains the name.**

3. **Search for any program nicknames.**

   For instance, Word is often referred to as WinWord, and some Registry values reference this term *(winword)*.

If you do your search-and-destroy mission after you uninstall the unwanted software, you may be surprised at how many references still remain.

It's not unusual to browse through the Control Panel, find a new capability, have it catch your imagination, and then make some changes based on your discovery. Not so with the Registry. Though you can snoop through the Registry, the chance of intuitively finding something to change is remote. Thus, you must know what you want to do before you start your editing trek.

Many times you can determine what you should edit by reviewing an application's documentation or talking to a program's technicians. Unfortunately, no comprehensive guide exists to possible Registry entries, and anyone who claims to have a comprehensive guide is yanking your chain.

When you do want to find information in the Registry, the biggest help is the Registry Editor's search command:

1. **With the Registry Editor open, press Ctrl+F or choose Edit⇨Find.**

   The Find dialog box opens, as shown in Figure 20-3.

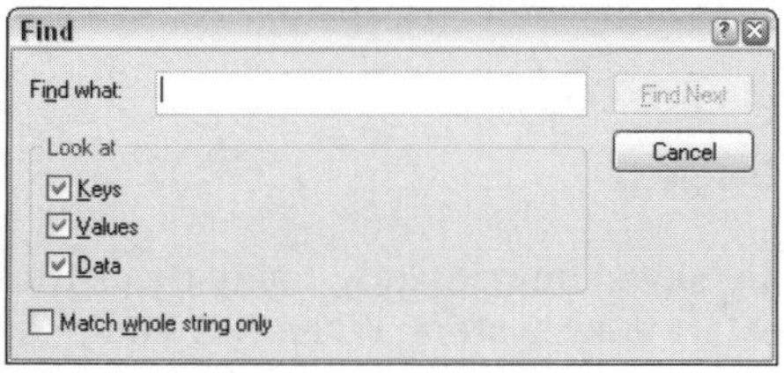

Figure 20-3:
Searching through the Registry.

2. **In the Find What field, enter what you want to find.**

3. **At the bottom of the dialog box, specify where the Registry Editor should look for the information: Keys, Values, or Data.**

4. **Click the Find Next button.**

   The Registry Editor attempts to find the string you entered. If a match is found, it's highlighted in one of the Registry Editor windows, depending on where the information was found.

   For instance, if the match was found in a key name, then the information is displayed in the left portion of the Registry Editor. Conversely, if the match was found in a value, the information is displayed in the right portion.

Editing values

Once you locate a value that you want to change (see the preceding set of steps), carefully examine it in the context of what you understand about the Registry structure; then make an educated guess regarding whether it's the value that you want. The problem, however, is that when you're poking about on your own, you're never really sure unless you try things out. Thus, in many respects, working with the Registry Editor is a trial-and-error proposition unless you're given a detailed reference or specific guidance.

To edit a value, follow these steps:

1. **Open the Registry Editor by choosing Start⇨Run, typing** regedit **in the Open field, and clicking OK.**

   Most editing tasks take place in the values shown in the right portion of the Registry Editor window. Refer to Figure 20-1.

2. **Either double-click the value name or highlight the value and press Enter.**

   A dialog box prompts you to change the value's contents. The exact dialog box depends on the value's data type. For instance, if you're changing a value that contains binary data, you see a dialog box similar to the one shown in Figure 20-4.

3. **Make your changes and click OK.**

   The Registry value is changed.

Even though your changes are saved immediately, many times those changes don't take effect until you restart your system. Whenever you're done editing the Registry, it's always a good idea to restart your system.

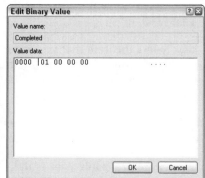

Figure 20-4:
Use the
Registry
Editor to
change
values.

Adding keys or values

The Registry Editor allows you to add new values or new keys to the Registry.
(You cannot add new hives; Windows sets those in stone.) Why would you
want to add keys or values? Quite honestly, it doesn't do you much good to
add either item unless you know that an application or Windows can use it.

To add a key, select the existing hive or key under which the new key should
appear. Select the hive or key on the left side of the Registry Editor window;
then choose Edit⇨New⇨Key. The new key is added and you can change its
name as desired.

If you want to add a value to an existing key (or to a key you just added), you
do so in much the same manner. To add a value, follow these steps:

1. **In the left pane of the Registry Editor (refer to Figure 20-1), navigate
   to the hive or key where you want the new value stored.**

   Click the plus signs at the left of the hive or keys that lead to the new
   value's desired location. The Registry tree expands to show the path to
   the key in which you want the value placed.

2. **Choose Edit⇨New.**

   You see a submenu of items you can create.

3. **Click the choice that represents the type of value you want to create.**

   The new value appears in the hive or key you selected. The value's name
   is selected, so you can change it as desired.

These steps create the value only; they don't store anything in the value. To
store something in the value, edit the newly created value, as described in the
previous section.

Deleting Registry items

Deleting keys or values is quite easy: Select the item that you want to remove and press the Delete key. Windows checks to make sure that you really want to delete the item. If you click the Yes button, the item is immediately — and *permanently* — deleted from the Registry.

The Registry Editor is very obedient about deleting items. You need to make very sure that you want to delete something before you do so. If you delete a critical key or value by mistake, you're simply out of luck. (If you delete the wrong thing, you can cripple your software or disable your entire system.) In such a circumstance, you have only a couple of options available:

- ✓ Manually recreate the deleted keys and values
- ✓ Reload the Registry keys, if you previously exported them to a text file for safekeeping
- ✓ Reinstall Windows XP

Using Registry Cleaning Software

Programs in addition to Windows use the Registry. Virtually every single program you install on your system uses it. (Some programs are small enough that they don't affect the Registry.) Some programs write only a few things into the Registry; others write lots.

As new information gets stuffed in, the Registry increases its size to accommodate the changes. Windows stores the Registry on disk (in the hives, discussed earlier in this chapter) and in memory, so both disk space and memory are required to manage the Registry.

If your Registry grows too large, your system performance can suffer. The larger the Registry, the more resources Windows requires just to manage the sheer file size and the entry numbers.

Unfortunately, removing software isn't the answer to a bloated Registry. When you uninstall a program, that program is supposed to remove its entries from the Registry. Some programs do this completely, but most leave some orphan entries. The result is unused "stuff" in the Registry, cluttering up the other, more important information there.

Even if the Registry entries are deleted, Windows doesn't shrink the size of the hives stored on disk — they remain large. Windows XP does a better job of managing the Registry than did previous versions, but large Registry files still place an unnecessary burden on Windows.

The solution to a cluttered Registry is to use software to go through and suggest things you may want to clean up. In general, three types of programs can be used on the Registry: analyzers, cleaners, and compactors.

Registry analyzers

A *Registry analyzer* does just what its name suggests: It analyzes the Registry, looking for and finding unused keys, invalid characters in keys, broken keys, and other common problems. Different programs analyze the Registry in different ways, but most of them do these things. Not all Registry analyzers fix the errors they find, but most provide information that explains how you can fix them. The focus in analyzers is on the analysis, not the repair.

Dozens of Registry analyzers are available. If you do an Internet search, you can find freeware, shareware, and commercial versions. Here are just two:

- ✔ **Registry Drill:** I particularly like this one. It has won many awards and does in-depth analyses that other programs seem to skip.

  ```
  http://www.easydesksoftware.com/regdrill.htm
  ```

- ✔ **Registry Analyst:** This analyzer is easy to use and very inexpensive.

  ```
  YavSoft at http://yavsoft.com/registry/
  ```

Registry cleaners

Software billed as a *Registry cleaner* includes analysis (as discussed in the preceding section) but also provides a more automatic approach to fixing errors in the Registry. While the analyzers are intended for folks who feel at home in the Registry, the cleaners do things without user intervention. Of the many Registry cleaners available, I recommend a couple:

- ✔ **The Registry cleaner included with System Mechanic:** This cleaner is my favorite. It runs easily and takes only a few clicks to fix most problems. The speed with which you can streamline a Registry is very impressive. Figure 20-5 shows an example of items that can be cleaned in a Registry.

  ```
  http://www.iolo.com
  ```

- ✔ **Registry Mechanic from WinGuides Software:** Another good option, this software is almost as easy to use as System Mechanic and even catches some Registry errors that other tools don't.

  ```
  http://www.winguides.com/regmech
  ```

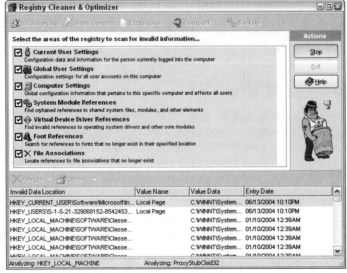

Registry compactors

The Registry doesn't shrink, even when Registry entries for uninstalled software are removed. To fix this situation, a class of software called *Registry compactors* was developed. This software essentially reads the Registry and rewrites a new, smaller version of all the hives.

A good choice for compacting is Registry Compactor, by Elrise Software (www.elrise.com). You can download a functional version and then pay the shareware fee ($19.95 as of this writing) if you continue using the software.

Because of the way the Registry is handled in Windows XP, compaction doesn't offer as much benefit as earlier versions did. You can find programs that compact the Registry in Windows XP, but don't feel that it's mandatory to get a Registry compacter for your system.

Restoring the Registry

By this point, you should be very aware that everything in Windows revolves around the Registry. The Registry is so powerful in its system control that I cannot stress strongly enough that you should not make Registry changes without being sure of exactly what you're changing. The Registry Editor provides no undo feature. Changes are essentially written to the Registry immediately.

If the Registry becomes corrupted for some reason, you have Trouble with a capital T. A couple of things can be done, however, to attempt recovery:

✔ **Import the backup copy:** The first thing you should try is importing the backup copy of the Registry that you should have made before making changes. During the import process, the saved version of the Registry overwrites the new, corrupted version, hopefully solving the problem.

✔ **Restart the system:** If you don't have a copy to import, restart your system. Whenever you restart your system, you can press F8 to display the Windows XP startup options. With the startup options displayed, you can press F8 a second time to display the Advanced Startup Options screen. (This is not a dialog box, since Windows has not yet started. It's a text menu displayed by the Windows startup functions.)

Last Known Good Configuration is one option. Every time Windows starts, it copies the last-used Registry to a backup copy of the Registry. If you choose Last Known Good Configuration — which you should do if you have corrupted the Registry — then the backup copy of the Registry is not made. Instead, the backup copy starts the system. You may lose all of the Registry changes that you made since your last startup, but that can be a good thing if your Registry is corrupted.

After you start Windows, you should do a few additional tasks:

✔ If you have a copy of the Registry that you recently exported to a text file, start the Registry Editor and import the copy. This overwrites the current Registry settings and restores your system to its latest condition.

✔ If you installed programs during your last Windows session, you must reinstall them. Even though the program files are on disk, the configuration information that was written to the Registry was lost when you tossed out the last version of the Registry.

✔ If you deleted programs during your last Windows session, you must delete them again. This may sound strange because the programs are no longer on your hard drive. Because you restored an earlier version of the Registry, however, Windows thinks that the programs are installed. Deleting them again updates the Registry.

✔ If you made changes in your desktop configuration during your last session, make the changes again.

Chapter 21

Wiping the Slate Clean

· ·

In This Chapter

▶ Repairing your Windows XP installation

▶ Running your system vendor's restore disc

▶ Starting fresh by wiping out your system

· ·

Cleaning you system is an ongoing task. Systems either get dirty on a daily basis or they get clean on a daily basis. If a system suffers from months or years of neglect, you need to balance the time required by a thorough cleaning with the time necessary to simply wipe the slate clean and start all over. In some cases, the clear choice is starting over.

This chapter presents the three main ways to start over with your current system: doing a reinstall, doing a system restore, and wiping everything out. None of these tasks should be undertaken lightly by anyone. Starting over destroys data (hopefully data you have backed up), disrupts work for a day or two, and generally is a huge pain.

Doing a Windows XP Reinstall

If clutter on your system has caused Windows to malfunction in any way, or if you deleted some system files when trying to clean up, then you may want to reinstall Windows XP. The Setup program for Windows includes the ability to reinstall operating system files without hurting any of the data on your hard drives.

Technically, when I say *reinstalling* Windows XP in this context, I mean *repairing* your system. This process is different (and much faster) from reinstalling Windows XP from scratch — a process I describe in the "Wiping Out Your System" section later in this chapter.

For Windows XP to fix itself, you need to get the original Window XP installation disc provided by Microsoft. Once you have the disc, you can proceed in either of two ways: from a fresh boot or from within Windows. I give you the steps for each method in the following sections.

Understanding the Recovery Console

When you're repairing Windows XP using the Setup program (see the steps in the "Fixing from a fresh boot" section), you see mention of a program called Recovery Console. Except in closely parallel universes, this tool is not for use by mere mortals. The Recovery Console allows a system administrator or ubergeek to perform low-level operations on the system, with the goal of repairing it.

For most people, using the regular repair function in Setup works just fine. You should use the Recovery Console only if you're online with a technician who guides you through exactly what needs to be done.

Both methods end up at the same place. I tend to find the fresh boot method easier and faster. However, if your system does not allow you to boot from CD-ROM, you should use the within-Windows method.

Fixing from a fresh boot

With your computer turned off and the Windows XP CD-ROM in the drive, follow these steps:

1. **Turn on the PC.**

   The computer should go through its normal startup machinations. A prompt saying Press Any Key to Boot from CD appears.

2. **Press a key — you want to boot from the CD.**

   Most PCs manufactured in the past three years allow you to boot from CD-ROM. If you never see a prompt about booting from the CD, you may need to modify your system BIOS so that it tries to boot from the CD before booting from other sources, such as the hard drive.

   For information on how to access your system BIOS, refer to the manual that came with your computer. The process is different on different systems. It normally involves pressing some key combination when first booting, such as F1, Esc, or Delete.

   During the boot process, information is loaded from the CD and your system is inspected. Eventually you see a Welcome to Setup screen offering three choices: setting up Windows XP, repairing a Windows XP installation with Recovery Console, and quitting Setup.

3. **Press Enter (to choose setting up Windows XP) and then press F8 to accept the license agreement for Windows.**

   Does anyone ever read these things?

Don't choose the R function. You don't want to use the Recovery Console, even though you want to repair your copy of Windows XP. If you press R by mistake, you'll need to turn the system off and start all over again.

Next you see a screen that includes the following text: If one of the following Windows XP installations is damaged, Setup can try to repair it.

At the bottom of the screen, you should see the drive on which Windows XP is installed.

4. With the drive selected, press R to indicate you want to repair that copy of Windows XP.

The Setup program looks at your system, determines what to copy from the CD, and then copies it. Eventually your system reboots.

5. When your system reboots, boot from the hard drive — not the CD-ROM.

What happens next depends on how extensive the repairs were. If they weren't too bad, then you can start using Windows right away. If they are more extensive, then the repair process continues after the reboot.

In many respects, what you see during the repair process is very similar to what you see when Windows XP is being installed anew.

6. XP informs you of the progress and prompts you for information to move through the steps.

When the setup is complete, your copy of Windows XP should be repaired.

Repairing Windows XP involves copying operating system files from the CD to your system. This means you need to visit Microsoft's update site for Windows so you can download the latest service packs and critical updates for your system.

Starting from within Windows

You need your product key (which should be on the jewel case that contains the Windows XP CD-ROM or somewhere else on the packaging) to perform the steps in this section. Searching for the key can be a real pain if it's been a year or so since you last saw it, but you can't get around it — you need the product key to continue, so get it before starting.

With Windows running, follow these steps:

1. Insert the Windows XP CD-ROM disc in the drive.

The disc should run automatically and bring up a screen asking what you want to do. See Figure 21-1.

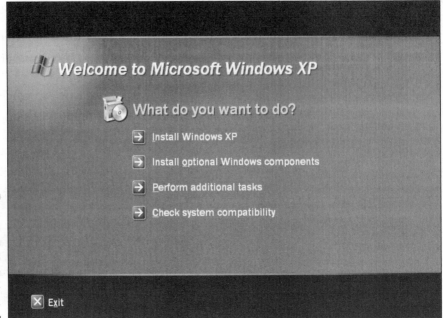

Figure 21-1:
The
Windows
Setup
program
automati-
cally runs.

If you don't see the screen shown in Figure 21-1, your system may not be set to automatically run CDs. In that case, browse to the CD's contents and run the Setup program on the disc. You should then see the screen.

2. **Click the arrow next to Install Windows XP.**

   Setup gathers information about your system. Shortly you're asked whether you want to do an upgrade or a new installation of Windows XP.

3. **Choose to perform a new installation and click Next.**

   Setup displays the Windows license agreement.

4. **Accept by choosing I Accept This Agreement and then click Next.**

   You're prompted for your product key, as shown in Figure 21-2.

5. **Enter your product key and click Next.**

   You see a few more screens that offer different setup options. On each screen you can click Next until you see Get Updated Setup Files screen in Figure 21-3. You can perform the check, but it isn't necessary because the Setup on your CD works just fine.

6. **Select No and click Next.**

   At this point, Setup has all the information it needs. It starts copying some files to your hard drive; eventually your system reboots.

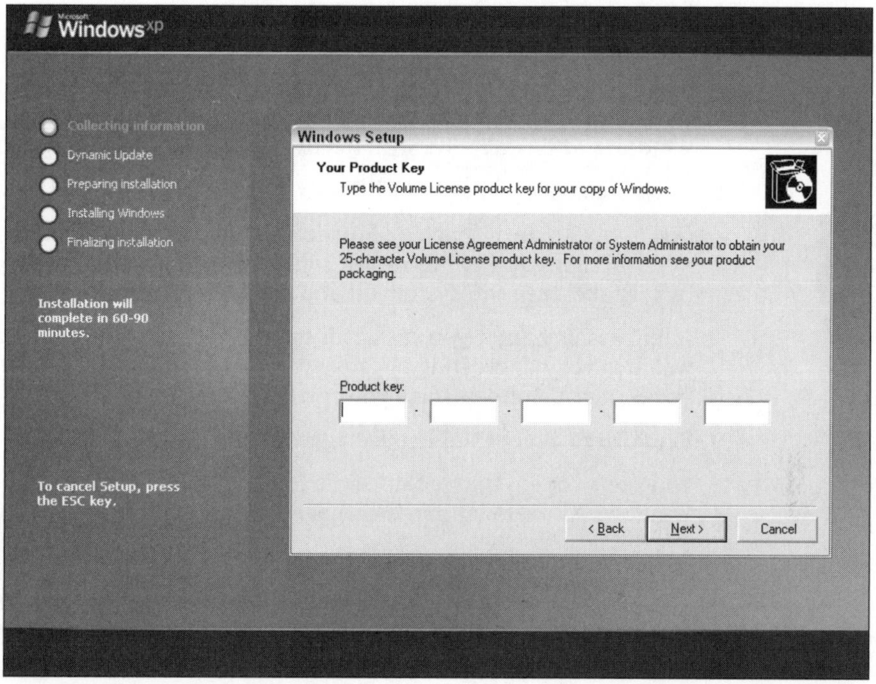

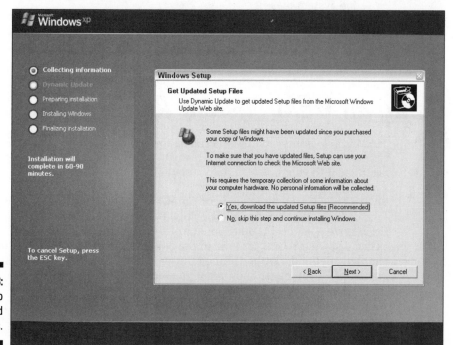

Figure 21-2:
Enter your product key.

Figure 21-3:
Choose to get updated Setup files.

7. **When it's time to reboot, do so from the hard drive — not the CD-ROM.**

   From here on, the setup procedure is very similar to the fresh boot procedure discussed in the preceding section. Shortly you see a Welcome to Setup screen offering three choices: setting up Windows XP, repairing a Windows XP installation with Recovery Console, and quitting Setup.

8. **Choose to set up Windows XP now (the first option) and press Enter.**

   Don't choose the R function. You don't want to use the Recovery Console, even though you want to repair your copy of Windows XP. If you press R by mistake, turn the system off and start all over again.

   After pressing Enter you see again see the license agreement for Windows, which is very interesting because you just saw it in the Windows dialog boxes, just before entering your product key.

9. **Press F8 to accept the license agreement**

   You see a screen that includes the following text: If one of the following Windows XP installations is damaged, Setup can try to repair it.

   At the bottom of the screen, you should see the drive on which Windows XP is installed.

10. **With the drive selected, press R to indicate you want to repair that copy of Windows XP.**

   Setup copies more files to your system, overwriting your existing operating system files.

After the system reboots, you may see more setup information. Eventually the reinstall is completed and you have a functioning copy of Windows XP.

Using an OEM System Restore Disc

OEM is a computer-industry acronym for *original equipment manufacturer*. Just think of the OEM as the company that put your computer together and shipped it to you.

When I purchased a system from Gateway, I eagerly awaited its arrival. When the delivery guy dropped it off, I ripped open the box, took out the gleaming new system, and set it up in a place of honor in my office. It was so cool! Then, I started rooting around in the box and the wrappings to see if I had missed anything. (We go through the same process after opening Christmas presents — you never know what you may be throwing away.)

One of the things I missed was a little packet of CDs, all in a handy, petite binder. One of the CDs had the title System Restore Disc. It wasn't until about a year later that I would fully understand how helpful this disc could be.

You see, my system got seriously messed up due to an unfortunate set of events, compounded by too much caffeine and not enough sleep. At the end of the mess, it became obvious that I would need to start over with the system.

The really cool thing is that all I needed to do was plop the System Restore Disc into the CD-ROM drive and reboot the computer. Windows didn't boot, but the CD did. In no time, I saw a menu that provided me with a set of options ranging from a partial reinstall to a full-bore remake of my entire system.

After a few simple choices, the programs on the CD went to work and I went to lunch. When I got back, the system was completely restored to the pristine condition it existed in on the day I unpacked it from the shipping box — it couldn't have been much simpler!

Gateway is not alone in providing System Restore Disc; I use it as an example only because I have firsthand experience with its version of system recovery. Other vendors, such as Dell, include such discs.

Hopefully you kept the discs that came with your system. If you decide to restore your system, make sure to use the disc that came with your system. If you try to use a disc from a different system (even one from the same manufacturer), the results may not be pretty because of hardware and the drivers that work with that hardware. System restoration discs install drivers based on the hardware that was with the system when it shipped to you. That means that the disc is tied closely to the system it's for. If you use a different disc, you run the risk of installing drivers intended for a system different from yours.

If it's been a while since you received your computer, the system restore discs won't include Windows XP SP2. Before doing a system restore, you may want to check with your system's manufacturer to see whether you can get an updated system restore disc that includes this important upgrade to Windows XP. (Either call your system manufacturer or visit its Web site for more information.)

When you're done doing a system restore, you still aren't done. Remember that your system now looks exactly like it did when you first unboxed it. To make the system better reflect the way you work, you need to do a few more things:

- ✔ **Configure the system.** Change your system configuration, as necessary, to match your preferences and requirements. Pay special attention to things like display settings and Internet configuration.

- ✔ **Update Windows.** Connect to the Windows update site to download updates to Windows. Remember — your system is fresh-from-the-box, without the critical updates and service packs released since the CD was created.

✔ **Remove the chaff.** Many systems come with preinstalled software that's helpful only when trying to make a buying decision. Get rid of these programs; uninstall them as discussed in Chapter 5.

✔ **Reinstall programs.** Install the programs you really need and configure them for your working style.

Wiping Out Your System

It used to be that I kept a bootable diskette lying around that contained everything I needed to wipe out a system and start over from scratch. Of course, that was back in the days when the operating system files could fit on a single diskette.

Those days are long gone, but wiping out your system and starting all over again in this day and age is easier than you may think. All you need is your original Windows XP CD-ROM and a system that can boot from the CD.

Reinstalling the Windows XP operating system from scratch takes a lot of time. It's not unusual to spend a full day installing the operating system and all the programs you need. It can take even longer, depending on the type of data you need to use. Allow enough time to wipe and reinstall the system correctly.

Preparing for the wipeout

Do a few things before wiping out your current Windows system. Hopefully, your Windows XP system is usable enough that you can still perform these tasks:

✔ **Find your product key.** You need the Windows XP product key to install the operating system. It's 25 characters long and should be somewhere on the CD packaging.

✔ **Create a program inventory.** As discussed in Chapter 3, a program inventory is invaluable when it comes to figuring out what you really want on your system. It's much easier to create the program inventory based on your current system than it will be after wiping out that system.

✔ **Archive your data.** If you have old data on your system, transfer it to archive media. Chapter 7 covers how to archive your data.

✔ **Back up your remaining data.** Figure out what data you want to keep from your old system. Transfer it to CDs or other easily accessible media. Remember that you're wiping everything out and need the data in a format you can later access.

✔ **Print screen shots of configuration dialog boxes.** If you're like most people, you spend a fair amount of time setting up Windows and other programs just the way you want them. Display the dialog boxes where you do configuration changes and print screen shots of them. (Don't forget a screen shot of your Internet configuration settings.) The screen shots are very helpful when you need to configure your newly installed system.

I think the easiest way to print a screen shot is to display the dialog box, and then hold down the Alt key as you press the Print Screen Key. The screen shot of the dialog box is now in the Clipboard, and you can paste it into your favorite word processor, such as Microsoft Word. Print the page with the dialog box, and you have your record.

Doing the deed

After performing that preparatory tasks that I outline in the preceding list, follow these steps to wipe out your system:

1. **Shut down your computer and put the Windows XP CD-ROM in the drive.**

2. **Boot to the CD-ROM.**

   You should see the Setup program running. One of the first screens you see is the Welcome to Setup screen offering three choices: set up Windows XP, use Repair Console to fix Windows XP, and quitting Setup.

3. **Press the Enter key to signify that you want to set up Windows XP.**

4. **Accept the license agreement that appears by pressing F8.**

   You see a screen that includes the following text: If one of the following Windows XP installations is damaged, Setup can try to repair it.

   At the bottom of the screen you should see the drive on which Windows XP is installed. You don't want to repair Windows XP; you want to start over completely.

5. **Press Esc to continue installing Windows XP.**

   Setup displays a screen that shows the existing hard drive partitions. Your system may have a single partition or it may have multiple partitions. The idea here is to wipe out the partitions, recreate them, and then install Windows XP.

6. **Select the first partition on the hard drive and press D.**

7. **When Setup asks you to confirm that you really want to delete the partition, do so.**

   You again see the screen that shows existing partitions.

8. **If other partitions remain, select them and press D for each one, in turn.**

   When the partitions are all deleted, the entire hard drive should show as unpartitioned space. Everything on the hard drive has been wiped out, and you're ready to start clean.

9. **Select the unpartitioned space and press C.**

   Setup asks you to specify the size you want for the partition. If you accept the default, then Setup uses all the space for a single drive.

   In Chapter 7 I mention that partitioning your system into multiple drives can be beneficial. You can use one for the system, one for programs, and one for your data. Now is the time you could implement such a plan, if desired.

   When you're done partitioning your hard drive, you must select a partition as the destination for Windows XP.

10. **Select the first partition and press Enter.**

    Setup informs you that you need to format the partition so it can be used.

11. **Choose NTFS and press Enter.**

    In most instances, choosing to format using NTFS will work. (See Chapter 14 for a discussion of file systems.)

    Once the formatting is complete, Setup starts copying files to the hard drive and then reboots the system. The setup process continues.

12. **Answer additional questions about how you want Windows configured.**

    You can refer to your screen shots of dialog boxes to determine how to answer some questions.

    When you're done answering questions, Windows reboots one more time. You are almost ready to start using the system.

Picking up the pieces

After installing Windows, you still have quite a bit to do before your system is usable:

- ✔ **Configuring your Internet connection:** If you didn't configure your Internet connection during Setup, now is a great time to do it. Grab the screen shot you made of your connection settings and refer to it while entering the settings.

- ✔ **Installing Windows updates:** With the Internet connection active, visit the Windows update site to download the latest XP service packs and patches. Perform these updates before you start installing programs on the system.

✔ **Formatting partitioned drives:** If you partitioned your hard drive into multiple drives, now's a great time to format those other drives. (You need to format each of them except the one where Windows XP was installed.) To format the other drives, follow these steps:

1. **Choose Start⇨My Computer, right-click the drive you want to format, and choose Format.**

   Windows displays the Format dialog box shown in Figure 21-4.

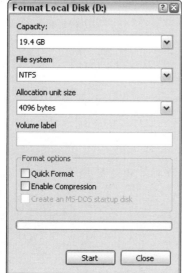

Figure 21-4:
Format a
fresh hard
drive.

2. **Choose the file system you want to use from the File System drop-down list.**

   In most instances, you should choose the NTFS file system. In some instances you may want to use a different file system, as discussed in Chapter 14. Leave the Capacity and Allocation Unit Size options set at the default settings.

3. **In the Volume Label text box, enter a name for the drive.**

4. **Click Start.**

You can do other work while the hard drive is formatting.

✔ **Installing other programs:** Gather your program installation discs and any program keys necessary to install the software. When all of your hard drives are formatted, install your software programs one at a time. Make sure you start each program and configure it using the information you gathered before starting to wipe your system.

✔ **Transferring the data from the temporary storage media back to the hard drive:** Do this last. You may need to modify where the data is stored, based on how you partitioned your hard drive and installed software. Once copied, make sure you can load the data into your system.

Voila! You have a brand new system, fresh from the mill.

Part VI
The Part of Tens

"So far he's called up a cobra, 2 pythons, and a bunch of skinks, but still not the file we're looking for."

In this part . . .

If you're looking for extra tidbits of information, you've come to the right place. In these chapters you find troubleshooting ideas, software tools for cleaning, a multitude of online resources, and a list of Service Pack 2's features.

Chapter 22

Ten Troubleshooting Ideas

· ·

*W*hen trouble strikes, everyone needs ideas. The ideas in this chapter are designed to provide a starting point for pinpointing the cause of your troubles.

Check Your Startup Files

Loading too many programs at startup can cause system problems. Make sure you load only the programs you really need.

To find out what's running at startup, check the Startup folders by right-clicking the Start button and choosing either Open or Open All Users. After choosing one, double-click Programs, Startup. Then choose the other and do the same.

For a more in-depth analysis of what's going on when you start Windows, use either msconfig (see Chapter 13) or the AutoRuns utility, available free from

```
www.sysinternals.com
```

Install Windows Updates

Keeping your system updated can help head off and remedy problems. To get your system up to date, visit the following site and click Scan for Updates:

```
http://windowsupdate.microsoft.com
```

To keep your system updated, click the Start menu, right-click My Computer, and choose Properties. Use the controls on the Automatic Updates tab to control how updates should occur. Head to Chapter 15 for more information on updates.

Run a Spyware Removal Program

Spyware is the bane of many a system and most people don't even know it. For instance, most people who use a pop-up blocker don't realize they're only treating the symptom, not the problem. The cause of most pop-ups is spyware.

Use a good spyware removal program, such as

Spybot Search & Destroy at `www.safer-networking.org`

Ad-aware at `www.lavasoftusa.com`

I cover removing spyware and other noxious Internet programs in Chapter 10.

Remove Unused Programs

Like dust bunnies behind the refrigerator, programs seem to collect and multiply on our systems. If you fail to keep them cleaned out, they eventually clutter your system and you could run out of disk space or other resources.

As a general rule, you should remove programs that you don't use on a regular basis. If you don't use it once in six months, for instance, you can probably get rid of it. For more about removing old programs, see Chapter 5.

See What Processes Are Running

If you feel your system is becoming sluggish, a lot of programs may be running on your system that you don't know about. The easiest way to see what's running is to use the Task Manager.

Right-click an empty area of the taskbar and choose Task Manager. Use the Applications tab to see what full programs are running and the Processes tab to see what is running behind the scenes.

If you don't know what a process does, search Google for the process name — you can find a ton of information.

Run the Disk Cleanup Utility

Windows XP includes a free utility that helps clear much of the easy clutter on your system. It doesn't do a deep-cleaning job, but provides a great starting point. It can get rid of temporary Windows, Internet, and program files, download controls and applets, set up log files, and empty your Recycle Bin.

To run Disk Cleanup, choose Start⇨All Programs⇨Accessories⇨System Tools⇨Disk Cleanup. Chapter 6 contains more detail about this tool.

Defragment Your Disk Drives

The daily grind of adding programs and creating data can, over time, clutter up your hard drive. As files are added, resized, deleted, and overwritten, they become fragmented on the drive. This fragmentation can slow down your overall system performance.

To defragment your disk drive, choose Start⇨My Computer, right-click a drive, and choose Properties. On the Tools tab, click Defragment Now. You can find out more information about defragmenting your disk drives in Chapter 14.

Check File Sizes

If you use database or spreadsheet programs, developing monster database files is easy. (I have some almost 10MB data files.)

Big files can lead to big problems for some programs. If you suspect needing smaller data files, look for ways to archive older data and move it off your system. For more about archiving data, check out Chapter 7.

Check the Size of Your Registry

Checking your Registry's size isn't easy, but its size can affect your entire system's performance. If it gets quite large, then running Registry-cleaning software can help alleviate some types of problems.

To check the size, display the folder containing the Registry hives and add the different hive files. If the total seems inordinately high, run a cleaner. Chapter 20 contains information about the Registry and its cleaning software.

Start Your System in Safe Mode

Safe Mode — the idyllic haven of anyone having trouble running Windows. *Safe Mode* is established by starting Windows without loading drivers and other startup programs. In essence, Safe Mode presents a bare-bones Windows system.

While in Safe Mode you can do what the geeks do: tinker to find out what's causing problems. Change configuration settings, remove drivers, modify the Registry, and so on, until you nail down exactly what the problem is.

Start Safe Mode by pressing F8 early in the boot sequence, before any Windows screens appear. To find more information on Safe Mode, check out *Troubleshooting Your PC For Dummies*, by Dan Gookin (published by Wiley).

Chapter 23

Ten Software Cleaning Tools

●●●

*T*he marketplace is crammed with software programs designed to help you free up resources and declutter and protect your system. With so many choices available, knowing which products to use can be confusing. I've put together ten products I've found interesting and helpful. You can't go wrong with them.

System Mechanic: `http://www.iolo.com/sm/index.cfm`

Iolo Technologies publishes System Mechanic, an award-winning collection of tools that help clean your system. Some of its tools fix shortcuts, clean and optimize the Registry, defragment disks, optimize memory, remove duplicate files, block pop-ups, and remove some spyware. This is one great set of tools!

Window Washer: `http://www.webroot.com/wb/products/windowwasher/index.php`

Window Washer is a system cleaner that helps maintain your privacy. It removes information collected with browsing, such as your cache, cookies, history, deleted e-mails, and so on. It also cleans your Recycle Bin, program run histories, recent documents lists, and the like.

Spring Cleaning: `http://www.aladdinsys.com/win/springcleaning/index.html`

Spring Cleaning, from Aladdin Systems, is a comprehensive system cleaner. It uninstalls and removes unwanted programs, cleans the Registry, finds and cleans duplicate files, removes plug-ins, and eliminates cookies. It also includes complete undo capability to protect against accidental file erasure.

McAfee VirusScan Professional: `http://us.mcafee.com/root/package.asp?pkgid=145`

VirusScan is one of the largest selling anti-virus programs. It automatically scans e-mail, attachments, and downloads, then immediately starts cleaning infections. The Professional version of the software comes with a two-user license (to protect two systems), system cleanup functions, and a security file eraser.

Norton Antivirus Professional: http://www.symantec.com/nav/nav_pro/

Norton Antivirus protects e-mail, instant messages, and other files by recognizing and removing viruses automatically. The software also recognizes and alerts you to the presence of spyware and other hacking programs. It includes advanced tools for data recovery and secure file deletion, plus a license for two computers.

Spybot Search & Destroy: http://www.safer-networking.org

Without a doubt, Spybot S&D is the best spyware detection and removal software available. To top it off, it's free. Constantly updated, the software recognizes and removes a huge number of spyware programs from throughout your system. With the recent addition of the TeaTimer, it can even provide real-time continuous protection against surreptitious spyware activities.

Popup Ad Filter: http://www.meaya.com

Popup Ad Filter, from Meaya Software, works with Internet Explorer to block ads while you're browsing the Web. It can be configured to allow pop-ups from specific sites and logs all the sites from which pop-ups were blocked. The filter's easy to install and easy to use.

Super Ad Blocker: http://www.superadblocker.com

Super Ad Blocker prevents not only pop-up, but also spyware, pop-under, messenger, Flash, and floating ads. Includes capabilities to clean your cookies, cache, and browser history. Includes the ability to generate graphic reports on the quantity and type of ads blocked. Designed to work with Windows XP Service Pack 2.

Cookie Pal: http://www.kburra.com

Cookie Pal, from Kookaburra Software, allows you to decide what types of cookies you want to accept and what type you don't. It works with a wide number of browsers and e-mail programs to give complete protection against unknown sites.

ZoneAlarm: http://www.zonelabs.com

Zone Labs created ZoneAlarm as personal firewall for Windows systems. It stops intruders from accessing your PC, essentially making your system invisible to hackers. The Pro version includes a pop-up blocker and rudimentary cookie management capabilities. It also analyzes incoming and outgoing e-mail to identify and quarantine potential viruses.

Chapter 24

Ten Online Resources

*W*hen it comes to cleaning your system, the Internet is full of much more useful information than I could possibly distill to a single chapter. That leaves me with a huge problem: coming up with the ten best online resources for everyone. Part of the problem is that no two people's systems and cleanup needs are the same. Because of this, I tried to make this list of sites as broad as possible. I provide many of the sites I use on a regular basis to help keep my own systems clean.

Windows Update: http://windowsupdate.microsoft.com

Perhaps the best online resource out there is the Windows update site. Here's where you check your system to make sure it is up to date with the latest service packs and critical patches. Why avoid updates when getting and applying them is so easy?

Sysinternals: http://www.sysinternals.com

Sysinternals is operated by Mark Russinovich and Bryce Cogswell, two consummate system geeks. Their free tools and utilities are unique and uniquely powerful. I particularly like the Autoruns utility, which shows every program scheduled to run when your system starts — even those listed only in the Registry.

Google: http://www.google.com

It may seem odd to include a search engine as a cleaning aid, but I find Google very helpful. If I have a question about a file on my hard drive or a process running on my system, all I need to do is type in the file or process name and I can find information about it. This makes Google a great research tool for tracking down potential problems.

Gibson Research Corporation: http://grc.com

This site includes a number of helpful resources. Perhaps the most helpful online resource is the ShieldsUP! Analysis tool, which is a free security check that analyzes your system's weaknesses (as viewed from the Internet) and tells you how to make your system more secure.

HouseCall: `http://housecall.trendmicro.com/`

This online virus scanner allows you to check your system for infestations, without the need to install actual anti-virus software on your system. Trend Micro maintains the site, which also offers various standalone anti-virus products.

Symantec Security Response: `http://securityresponse.symantec.com/`

If you want to find out about the latest virus and security issues for PCs, Symantec Security Response is the place to do it. You can search its extensive database or you can browse through information about various viruses and threats.

SpywareGuide: `http://www.spywareguide.com`

A great resource for figuring out the latest spyware scams and how they can affect your system. Includes an online spyware scanning tool to help check your system. Also features information on different privacy and systems tools that can help you protect your system.

SpywareInfo: `http://www.spywareinfo.com`

This site is dedicated not just to education, but to getting spyware removed from your system. It publishes a weekly newsletter that has updates on the latest spyware threats. I find the online forums particularly helpful because you can post questions and get answers from others willing to help you clean your system.

Spam Arrest: `http://www.spamarrest.com`

This challenge/response tool helps block unwanted e-mail from your inbox. Challenge/response works because most spam is generated by computer and sent from unresponsive or fake addresses. All incoming e-mail is challenged and requires unique human response before the mail actually makes it to you.

Urban Legends Reference Pages: `http://www.snopes.com`

Did you get the e-mail about the dying child who wanted postcards, the one that told you to delete a file on your computer, or that camel hunting is illegal in Arizona? These and thousands of other urban legends are cataloged at the Urban Legends Reference Pages. If you receive lots of e-mails containing stories that you consider passing on to others, visit this site first to see if the story's true.

Chapter 25

Ten Cool Things in XP Service Pack 2

• •

*H*ave you felt the urge? The urge to get Windows XP Service Pack 2? Service Pack 2 (SP2) has been attended by the biggest Microsoft publicity campaign in years. There's good reason for the hubbub — SP2 includes a number of changes to the operating system, Internet Explorer, and Outlook Express. All of the changes work together to provide greater stability and greater protection from viruses and worms. In other words, SP2 makes it easier to keep your system from getting cluttered by bad guys intent on messing things up.

Many of the changes in Windows XP SP2 are behind-the-scenes; you will never know they're there. Some changes, however, are quite visible — if you know where to look for them. To assist you in making sense of the changes, I put together this list of ten changes in SP2. The items in the list are in no particular order, but all of them increase the security of your system.

Windows Firewall

Windows XP includes the Internet Connection Firewall (ICF), which has been renamed as Windows Firewall in SP2. The biggest change is that Windows Firewall is now turned on by default (you need to go out of your way to turn it off), and it provides better protection. Most of the changes in the firewall are in the underlying code that controls what's blocked by the firewall and how its work is done. For more about firewalls and ICF, see Chapter 18.

Memory Protection

Memory, of course, is where programs and data reside in your system. Some newer hardware systems allow memory to be protected by the operating system. Windows XP SP2 offers this protection — it can mark different blocks of memory so that the computer itself knows whether they contain data or executable code.

This is a big deal because it prevents certain types of malicious intrusions into your system. Before, a Trojan program was potentially able to place itself into a data area of memory and then execute itself by modifying some code in your program. Now, if the Trojan program is placed in a memory area marked as "data only," it cannot be executed, and your system is protected.

Network Administration

If you're a network administrator, SP2 offers all sorts of improvements in how you work with computers on your network. Administrative tools are improved to reflect the increased security options, and a number of new tools are introduced to help you administer the computers you are responsible for.

Network administration is obviously beyond the scope of this book, but if you are a network administrator, you should dig through the SP2 information provided by Microsoft to ferret out the ways in which you can better perform your responsibilities.

Windows Media Player

The Windows Media Player has been around for years, playing tunes for untold millions of people. SP2 automatically installs Windows Media Player 9, which includes better security and the ability to play some types of media that weren't playable before.

Automatic Updates

The Windows XP automatic update feature has been improved. It now provides ways to download not only Windows updates but also updates for other Microsoft applications. In addition, updates are better categorized according to their importance, and you can choose to be prompted about any remaining updates before shutting down Windows.

Additional information on automatic updates is covered in Chapter 15.

Outlook Express

Many people use Outlook Express as their e-mail client, simply because it is included with Windows XP for free. If you're one of these people, you'll be happy to know that with the release of SP2, Outlook Express received a long-needed update for security purposes. In particular, the program now provides the ability to receive incoming mail in plain text so that malicious programs cannot be executed automatically. It also turns off the downloading of external HTML content, which protects the user against spammers who use HTML to automatically verify e-mail addresses.

Add or Remove Programs Filter

When you open the Add or Remove Programs applet in the Control Panel, you see a list of the programs installed on your system. You also see a list of updates installed by Windows XP. Over time, the sheer number of updates makes it harder and harder to see the real programs installed on the system.

SP2 provides a filter that hides all the updates that have been done. This makes it easier for you to find the program you want to work on. (This change in SP2 is certainly not security related, but it does make using Add or Remove Programs much easier.)

Security Center

SP2 adds a new applet to the Control Panel — the Security Center. This is a one-stop utility that allows you to check several different security features on your system. For more details about the Security Center, check out Chapter 18.

Pop-Up Blocker

Internet Explorer now includes an integrated pop-up blocker, designed to make visiting many Web sites less "intrusive" (for lack of a better word). When a pop-up is blocked, Internet Explorer notifies you in the Information Bar area. Chapter 10 has the lowdown on pop-up blockers.

Internet Explorer Improvements

Besides the pop-up blocker, SP2 adds quite a few improvements to Internet Explorer. Most of the improvements are *transparent*, meaning that you won't notice them at all. They are still there, however, doing their work unobserved.

These changes include better handling and monitoring of attachments, better management of browser add-ons, improved crash handling, better notification of what's happening (via the new Information Bar), and improved object caching. Internet Explorer also increases the role that security zones play and how they're administered.

Index

• G •

• H •

FOR DUMMIES®

The easy way to get more done and have more fun

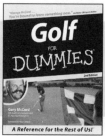

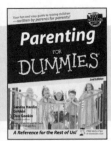

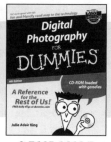

FOR DUMMIES®

Helping you expand your horizons and realize your potential

GRAPHICS & WEB SITE DEVELOPMENT

0-7645-1651-5

0-7645-1643-4

0-7645-0895-4

Also available:

Adobe Acrobat 5 PDF
For Dummies
(0-7645-1652-3)
ASP.NET For Dummies
(0-7645-0866-0)
ColdFusion MX For Dummies
(0-7645-1672-8)
Dreamweaver MX For
Dummies
(0-7645-1630-2)
FrontPage 2002 For Dummies
(0-7645-0821-0)

HTML 4 For Dummies
(0-7645-0723-0)
Illustrator 10 For Dummies
(0-7645-3636-2)
PowerPoint 2002 For
Dummies
(0-7645-0817-2)
Web Design For Dummies
(0-7645-0823-7)

PROGRAMMING & DATABASES

0-7645-0746-X

0-7645-1626-4

0-7645-1657-4

Also available:

Access 2002 For Dummies
(0-7645-0818-0)
Beginning Programming
For Dummies
(0-7645-0835-0)
Crystal Reports 9 For
Dummies
(0-7645-1641-8)
Java & XML For Dummies
(0-7645-1658-2)
Java 2 For Dummies
(0-7645-0765-6)

JavaScript For Dummies
(0-7645-0633-1)
Oracle9i For Dummies
(0-7645-0880-6)
Perl For Dummies
(0-7645-0776-1)
PHP and MySQL For
Dummies
(0-7645-1650-7)
SQL For Dummies
(0-7645-0737-0)
Visual Basic .NET For
Dummies
(0-7645-0867-9)

LINUX, NETWORKING & CERTIFICATION

0-7645-1545-4

0-7645-1760-0

0-7645-0772-9

Also available:

A+ Certification For Dummies
(0-7645-0812-1)
CCNP All-in-One Certification
For Dummies
(0-7645-1648-5)
Cisco Networking For
Dummies
(0-7645-1668-X)
CISSP For Dummies
(0-7645-1670-1)
CIW Foundations For
Dummies
(0-7645-1635-3)

Firewalls For Dummies
(0-7645-0884-9)
Home Networking For
Dummies
(0-7645-0857-1)
Red Hat Linux All-in-One
Desk Reference For Dummies
(0-7645-2442-9)
UNIX For Dummies
(0-7645-0419-3)

Available wherever books are sold.
Go to www.dummies.com or call 1-877-762-2974 to order direct